EBURY PRESS

CRIME, GRIME AND GUMPTION

Former IPS officer O.P. Singh has the unique distinction of having commanded three premier police organizations for close to six years. He was chief of India's largest police force (Uttar Pradesh Police) and also the world's stand-alone and multi-skilled response force (the National Disaster Response Force). He was also chief of the Central Industrial Security Force mandated to secure critical infrastructure and vital installations of the country. A recipient of the President's Police Medal for Distinguished Service and Police Medal for Gallantry, Singh is recognized for his role in introducing the police commissionerate system in UP.

Known for his innovative approach to law enforcement, he also led rescue operations during the 2015 Nepal earthquake. After retirement, he has been on advisory assignments to various institutions and served as an independent external monitor for Oil India Ltd, Cochin Shipyard Ltd and the Department of Post, Government of India. He is a security and risk adviser for NatWest Group Services and CEO of the India Child Protection Fund, an organization involved in protecting children from exploitation and abuse.

Besides reading, he enjoys listening to music, travelling and mentoring young aspirants for the civil services.

T0124147

ADVANCE PRAISE FOR THE BOOK

'It is difficult to exist so firmly and transparently in the public space and yet have the passion to share the good, the bad and the ugly with the world at large. For OP, retirement is another word for a tongue-in-cheek reflection by the most powerfully effective man in the state of Uttar Pradesh as he turns a new page in his life—a dialogue with himself on what he did, couldn't do and would now like to do'—Muzaffar Ali, film-maker

'Shri O.P. Singh's distinguished career as an Indian Police Service officer, culminating in his role as the director general of police, Uttar Pradesh, reflects a lifetime of dedicated service to the nation. *Crime, Grime and Gumption*, his memoir, promises to provide invaluable insights into the challenges and triumphs that shaped his journey. Singh's commitment to upholding law and order, coupled with his leadership in managing complex security scenarios, has left an indelible mark on the policing landscape. This book not only chronicles his professional exploits but also offers a glimpse of the man behind the uniform, providing inspiration for aspiring officers and the public alike. It stands as a testament to a life devoted to the relentless pursuit of justice and the tireless safeguarding of society. I'm sure readers will find this book quite riveting'—Justice Ritu Raj Awasthi, chairperson, Law Commission of India

'The memoir is a testament to a life dedicated to upholding law and order, safeguarding communities and navigating the intricate landscapes of justice and human experience'—Kiran Bedi, India's first woman IPS officer and former lieutenant governor, Puducherry

'A gripping tale of resilience and determination. *Crime, Grime and Gumption* is an authentic journey through a life lived on its own terms. Expertly written, this memoir is a compelling and highly recommended read'—Amitabh Kant, former CEO, NITI Aayog, and G20 Sherpa

'O.P. Singh's innovative leadership, perseverance and visionary approach paved the way for the establishment of the police commissioner system in UP. This significant shift in the state's law enforcement structure marked a turning point, leading to improved crime management and a more efficient police force'—Prof. Himanshu Rai, director, Indian Institute of Management Indore

CRIME, GRIME & GUMPTION

Case Files *of* an IPS Officer

O. P. SINGH

EBURY
PRESS

An imprint of Penguin Random House

EBURY PRESS

USA | Canada | UK | Ireland | Australia
New Zealand | India | South Africa | China | Singapore

Ebury Press is part of the Penguin Random House group of companies
whose addresses can be found at global.penguinrandomhouse.com

Published by Penguin Random House India Pvt. Ltd
4th Floor, Capital Tower 1, MG Road,
Gurugram 122 002, Haryana, India

First published in Ebury Press by Penguin Random House India 2024

This book is a work of non-fiction. The views and opinions expressed in the book are
those of the author only and do not reflect or represent the views and opinions held by
the Government of India and/or the Government of Uttar Pradesh.

This book is based on actual events that took place in the author's life and is drawn
from a variety of sources including published materials. It reflects the author's present
recollections of experiences over time as truthfully as recollection permits and/or can be
verified by research. All persons named in the book are actual individuals and the names
and characteristics of some individuals have been changed to respect their privacy.

The objective of this book is not to hurt any sentiments or be biased in favour of or
against any particular person, political party, society, gender, creed, nation or religion.

ISBN 9780143464167

Typeset in Adobe Garamond Pro by MAP Systems, Bengaluru, India

www.penguin.co.in

Contents

Prologue

A Life on the Move . . .

I have come a long way.

No, I'm not tired.

The hands that wielded the gun and the frame that donned many uniforms have taken a pause. A genial pause.

'Never look back at the time gone by,' said my father. I was barely nine years old then. 'Do your work. Do it diligently. And then, move on.' Those words have stayed with me. I have lived and celebrated that thought. Done my job. Done it diligently. And yes, moved on.

I have lived a fairly public life. The service commission or omission would always find a mention in the media, print or otherwise. It's a natural outcome of a system construct, and in all fairness, it ensures the transparency factors are kept intact. However, there's a minuscule catch. While the reins of the actions were in my hands, I had no control over their representation. To top it, stories get omitted, images get blurred and details get dissolved, influenced by the pressures of time, or simply not touched upon. It's not without a deep purpose that the expression the 'horse's mouth' finds literary favour.

Well, the time has come to wield the pen.

It's time to tell my story.

I promise to do justice to it and move on.

1

It All Began Here

The day is etched in my mind. Martyrs' Day, 30 January 2020. I was due to hang up my boots the following day. It would be curtains for thirty-seven years of committed service as an Indian Police Service (IPS) officer. I sat in my mahogany-rich office of the director general of police (DGP), Uttar Pradesh (UP), as a stream of visitors and media persons made a beeline to offer their courtesy and wishes. It was overwhelming and humbling at the same time. The hands of my desk clock stood perfectly at the 4 p.m. indication. In precisely thirty-two hours, my life would change. The fact played on in my mind.

My last day in office was lined up with ceremonial events. The day would begin with the traditional farewell parade at the Reserve Police Lines and culminate in a tea party on the lawns of my official residence attached to the sprawling DGP camp office. I needed a break but knew none was coming. The state police machinery and the policing system were at it. The digital chatter of the Control Room continued to churn out information and action by the second. The capital and the state were at peace and no major mishap had been reported. The stack of files needing my final input refused to recede. Thankfully, there was no social engagement for the evening in my official calendar. It was good news, for I wanted the rest of the day to be with myself.

By six in the evening the rush had ebbed away, but the official files still needed to be hustled. Desperate for a soothing cup of lemon tea, I retired to the lounge area of the office. The 'no visitors' intent was clear for the office staff. A quick supine position and the first sip of the tea and my mind was transported several years back. To a distant land. My village, Mira Bigha.

A cluster of a few hundred families, muddy roads and farmlands made up the hamlet of Mira Bigha. It was about 8 km shy of the mofussil tehsil. For my reader's convenience, Mira Bigha lies in the district of Gaya, Bihar. Life here was easy paced. Our house stood strong in its bricks-and-mortar avatar. A nondescript pathway with a fair sprinkling of small concrete pebbles made for the road that led to the door of our house. There was no marking on the door, but everyone knew the house as *'Barrister Saab ki Kothi'*. The gate opened to a small compound. Semicircular steps with mosaic imprints led to a covered veranda. Four round pillars added aesthetics, served as a natural gateway and, of course, provided support to the design. Pathways on either side led to a huge open space behind the house. It was lined with two guava trees and one mango tree on the eastern side. The mango tree had established a dominant position and threatened to encroach on our neighbour's air space. Pomegranate, mulberry, custard apple and tamarind trees formed the periphery towards the western side, where a sizeable patch was occupied by vegetable beds. *Mircha* (green chillies), *louki* (bottle gourd), *kaddu* (pumpkin), *nenua* (snake gourd), *saim* (broad beans), *tamatar* (tomato), *bhindi* (lady's fingers/okra), *baigan* (brinjal/eggplant)—you name it and the vegetable had its earthy presence. Gayatri, the cow, and her month-old calf, Bacchua, occupied the shed next to the vegetable beds. Moti, the desi dog, was the boss around the compound area and the garden in the backyard. He was not permitted inside the house, the limit being the outer courtyard. This was my mother's law, so to speak, and it was strictly adhered to. Moti would often position himself in the front veranda and await any movement or command from my mother. He would spend the day around the lady of the house when she ventured out. My mother had not taken a liking for Moti initially but, with time, a strange bond developed between the two.

My room was the first one on the left flank of the house. A narrow passage connected the outer veranda with the inner one. A small, identical flight of steps opened to the inner courtyard, which was squarish and high-walled on all three sides. A set of straight stairs, inclined at 140 degrees, provided access to the first floor, which boasted identical accommodation. The only difference was that the verandas below served as open terraces for the first floor.

My mother occupied the right flank. The first room on the left side of the inner veranda was my father's study. The room had not been locked after my father passed away, although I had feared my mother would do so. But that was not to be. It was bolted but never locked. I had free access to the treasure trove of books it possessed.

My mother's carefree self underwent a dramatic change after my father's death. I was just fourteen then. That day, both of us suffered a loss—my mother her companion, and me, my babuji. That small frame of a body took upon herself the responsibility of managing not just the household but also ensuring their mainstay, farming, was not hampered. It was one task around the house, and the lady was not found wanting. Of course, we had house help in the form of Ramadeen and Kanak, who had been with us for a long time. I cannot recall since when, for I had always found them around in my living memory. Ramadeen lived in the outhouse adjacent to the cattle shed.

One day, barely a month after my father had passed away, I came upon my mother sitting on the steps of the veranda. 'Babu, come, sit here,' she said, patting the floor by her side. She placed an arm around me, and I melted in her lap. She gently stroked my hair and hummed her favourite *bhajan*, it made me hug her even tighter. It was a natural gesture then, but today I realize the immense importance and the need for it. We both missed my father. Neither of us said anything, but we exchanged a life in that moment.

'Go, wash yourself. I have prepared your favourite baigan ka bharta.'

'Why don't we live in Dadi's old house?' I asked abruptly. I was referring to the ancestral house where I had spent wondrous days. That house of mud and wood had so much: Dadi's warmth and her stories, my three sisters, my brother, and my uncle and aunty, whom we affectionately called Bade babuji and Badi maa, respectively, and their children. That house was so much fun. I already knew the answer to my question, and my mother understood that. She simply continued stroking my hair, saying nothing. My dadi was no more. She had quietly walked away to a different world seven years back, a world from where no one returned. Now my father had joined her too. Following my father's demise, the property was divided amongst the family and our share included the house where I lived with my mother. The concrete structure in our house was constructed as a *doori*, *baithaki*, a kind of male bastion. It was built by my uncle in 1950 and still stood as an imposing structure in the entire village. My elder sisters—Suma, Prabha and Urmila—welcomed their husbands in our ancestral house, and my elder brother, Shree Prakash, had his forehead gleaming with a *tilak* when he was going away to the Institute of Medical Sciences (IMS) in Banaras Hindu University to study medicine. But all of that was behind us. Now we had mostly silence to share with each other. The baigan ka bharta was forgotten. Mother continued to caress my hair.

The next day, I woke up to loud hammering at my door. 'Oma. Oma. Open the door. Are you alright, Oma?' It was Mother.

She sounded desperate. When I opened the door, she embraced me with all her strength. I could feel her palpitations.

'We have been robbed. They broke in and took away a trunk,' she managed to say. Her desperation was a mix of fear. The reference to 'they' sounded ominous. I could feel the pounding of my heart, and it had risen to an alarming level in a flash. Ramadeen stood behind my mother, his ashen face a reflection of the grave situation. Kanak, too, was there.

'What about Moti?' My mind raced. Before my eyes could begin the search, Ramadeen spoke, '*Maaji, kutta ko behoshi-wala daway khilayein hai. Woh khet mein soya pada hain* [Mother, they've drugged Moti. He is asleep in the fields].'

Mother released me from her embrace and my eyes darted towards the room in question. In one quick stride, I reached the entrance to the room. The doors were wide open. Nothing seemed amiss. The well-made-up bed with its T-shaped wooden stand for the mosquito net stood mute and undisturbed. The steel almirah! My mind was racing. *Don't touch the handle.* A voice in me called out. I carefully pressed the handle with my folded elbow. It was locked. One black trunk was gone. The only thing disturbed from its position was my mother's footwear—the soft, black leather shoes fondly bought by her elder son from some store in Gaya.

'Babu,' my mother framed the door.

'Ma, don't touch anything. This room is evidence. I must report this to the police,' I said matter-of-factly.

'Babu, Ramadeen is going to inform your uncle. He will tell us what needs to be done.'

'Ma! We simply need to inform the police. I will go to the police *chowki* and do that. I am a big guy now. Plus, we shouldn't be dependent on anyone for every little thing.' I spoke with an authority that surprised me as well. My father's voice rang in my mind as he had sat in his study with someone I didn't recognize: 'You should have informed the police. Always do that.

Never delay.' A much smaller me stood by the imposing desk, barely reaching its edge.

'Babu, no. You should not go alone.'

I put my arm around my mother and led her out of the room.

'It will hardly take any time. The police chowki is not far off. Father would have done the same,' I assured her.

My mother had tears in her eyes. She insisted Ramadeen accompany me to the chowki, but I wanted him to stay home with her.

I was strangely possessed.

The village had come alive, but no one noticed the fourteen-year-old boy taking the grubby pathway, crossing a *bigha* of farmland awaiting paddy plantation and reaching the police chowki set amidst a mango grove.

No khaki colour was visible but two men were, in their undershorts and bare chests. Neem *datuan*[1] was in liberal use around the hand pump, in the corner of the chowki compound.

'*Itni subah* [This early in the morning]?' the datuan-muffled voice questioned me.

'*Report likhwani hain* [I have to lodge a report],' my voice nearly choked.

'*Kya hua* [What happened]?' the man asked.

'*Chori hui hain* [There has been a theft].' I somehow found my voice.

'*Kagaz laye ho, report likhne kay liye* [Have you brought a piece of paper to lodge the report]?'

I shook my head in a clear sign that meant a 'no'.

'*Kagaz le kay aao aur likho* [Bring the paper and start writing].' The man wrote me off.

'*Kagaz toh aapke paas hoga?* [You must have the paper?]' I refused to budge. Going back the entire distance just for a piece of paper was beyond me.

'*Nahee hain kagaz* [Don't you have paper]? Then go.' The man returned to his vigorous brushing of his teeth. I stood my ground.

'*Mere paas kagaz nahee hain* [I don't have paper]. I want to report a theft that possibly happened in the wee hours. Our dog was drugged. The thieves scaled the boundary wall. Our black trunk is gone,' I said with faulting authority.

My subconscious mind registered everything. The khaki men acknowledged an insistent young boy, the sub-inspector recognizing my lineage with 'Barrister saab' and then the clichéd excuse about the lack of funds to even manage a few sheets of paper at the police station.

The trunk was never found nor were the thieves caught, but that young boy grew many years that summer morning.

Barrister saab

I heaved a sigh. I had by then completely downed my tea, sheer nostalgia gripping my senses. My chain of thoughts was suddenly interrupted by Rajnish Verma, my personal security officer, entering the room.

'Sir,' he said. 'Sir, the Chief Minister's Office called to confirm the presence of the Hon'ble CM at the tea party,' he announced.

'That's good. That's good,' I repeated to no one in particular, my mind already racing back to Mira Bigha and to Barrister saab, my babuji.

My father, Sheo Dhari Singh, was a man of great stature. A qualification in law from the prestigious Middle Temple, London, one of the four Inns of Court, contributed to his stature and gave him the title 'Barrister saab'.[2] The remainder, and major chunk, of his stature came from his diligence and righteousness.

My father was a reasonably tall man at five feet and ten inches. Though his stocky build made him look shorter, he exuded an air of confidence. A photo of him in a double-breasted coat with gleaming buttons, atop matching flannel trousers, the man pose-ready on one of the balconies of the Middle Temple buildings, remains my treasured possession. The visual memory I have of my father is that of him adorned in a crisp and sharp attire. He always had well-groomed hair, with a lock strategically dropping over the right side of his forehead, immaculately polished shoes and measured ways and expressions. He had an aura of discipline and strictness. He was known to his peers as a man of great erudition. His value system was unmatched, and he ensured his children had their values and principles in place. Meals were to be had at the dining table. One must wear shoes when they step out of the house. Save water and electricity. Value time and hygiene. I could go on and on. Father's presence often made the air in the room that he stepped foot in tense and taut. Alcohol and tobacco were looked down on as inessentials. He spent on good food, books and school fees but not on clothes, expensive furniture or any vulgar display of opulence. The greatest virtue he inculcated in us children was integrity. It ranked above love for one's wife and children, one's family. Sheo Dhari Singh always spoke of probity, parental duties and resignation to the will of God as the highest virtues men should aim at and strive for. Born in Mira Bigha, with an innate curiosity and a thirst for knowledge, my father pursued his legal education at Patna Law College where he honed his skills and developed a deep understanding of the law. His journey eventually led him to the prosecution wing of the Bihar Police where he took on the role of Senior District Prosecutor, serving in various districts of the state. His tireless efforts in this capacity played a vital role in representing the interests of the state and ensuring that justice prevailed in all matters. His ability to analyse complex legal issues, coupled with his compassion for those seeking justice, made him a beacon of hope for many. Beyond his professional achievements, he was a beloved family member and a pillar of strength for his loved ones. As a son, I always entertained the greatest regard for his austere and upright conduct in all things.

A note in my father's personal diary relates to the precise moment when I was born. I was born in the rented accommodation of the district prosecuting officer to the Government of Bihar. The entry was: 'The time was five minutes past midnight, when Suma, the firstborn came to the kitchen for hot water. Maa was in labor, she informed me. I quickly relieved myself and then stood on the veranda and intently listened to the night sounds and the sound of the happenings inside. At precisely twenty-five minutes past midnight, Suma gave the news of a new brother being born to her mother. I retired to the study room. Sleep eluded me. I took to reading and continued with it till 3 a.m. Finally, I slept.'

I never became the brat that was expected out of the youngest child, nor did my father's social status make me shirk my responsibilities. I was naturally disciplined and rather timid and shy. Father's professional commitment as a counsel of law took him to different towns and cities of Bihar. Like his travelling gear, one thing remained common in all his postings—me. I went wherever he went. From Danapur Cantt to the undivided Bihar, Hazaribagh, then to Ranchi, the summer capital, Chapra, at the confluence of Ghaghra and Ganges, and finally to our home district, Gaya.

My brother, my closest sibling by age, was about four years my senior. Shree Prakash, as he was named by Barrister saab himself, was sent away to Netarhat, then a hill station of Bihar (now in Jharkhand). With him away from home and our sisters tying the nuptial knot one after the other, I was the lone warrior left to be with my parents.

The year 1969 saw a distinct happening in the family—a division. I was barely ten when the grand old lady, our grandmother, passed away and the strong adhesive bond of the family weakened. The two brothers—my father and his elder brother, Raj Dhari Singh—signed the agreement of division in the family. Six years and two inches separated the two brothers. It was a trying time for the family. The doora, the baithaki came in my father's possession. This effectively meant that my mother had to shift to Mira Bigha the same year. Farming was the primary profession of the family, and the farmlands needed a close watch. From a joint family we became a nuclear family.

A separate innings between Barrister saab and a fifth grader began.

* * *

Being the youngest in the family, I was the darling of my mother. I was the most loved member of the family, the recipient of everyone's care and attention. Contrary to a popular belief that the youngest sibling does not follow the rules, I was a rather disciplined and well-behaved child, never one to throw tantrums. As a matter of fact, the 'all-hat-and-no-cattle' attitude was never possible as both my parents were very grounded and reasonable. But I will not deny the slightly bigger dose of motherly affection I enjoyed. She forgave me for my transgressions, and she was the one I turned to for everything. My father, though very simple and straightforward, appeared too big and distant because of his persona. I could say anything to my mother, ask anything of her. There was a constant dialogue between us. My separation from her, after she started living in the village, created a vacuum that my father could not fill. I became more sentimental and somewhat withdrawn. My father could not fathom what was going on in my mind.

Father sometimes talked about my performance in the class among family members, making me feel I was different. I distinctly remember, it was in Ranchi that my academic awakening happened. My early years at school were a somewhat pleasant but nondescript period of my childhood. I made no lasting friendships and have only a dim recollection of my classmates. Barrister saab had either given up on my mediocrity at school or possibly made friends with it. My classmate Jagmohan Narsaria, a short, fair-complexioned, good-looking boy, smaller and leaner than myself, became a reason for my academic emancipation. Jagmohan was from an affluent background and justified the extra attention he got by procuring grades that matched none—yes, he would be the first rank holder in the class, year after year, examination after examination. I remember taking a liking for him at once. I found him frank, with an open disposition, and ready to laugh at the most insignificant of jokes. In all fairness, I was in awe of his prowess. Then, in one academic fluke, I claimed the first rank in the class. The unbelievable had happened and Jagmohan was relegated to the second position. This was nothing short of an academic coup. All hell broke loose, literally. I do not, to date, know how the news travelled home to Barrister saab, even prior to my return from school. He immediately sent a written note to the headmaster: 'Mr Prasad, kindly confirm the grades of my son, Om Prakash.' It was only after receiving a confirmation from the headmaster that my father believed the result. Barrister saab's mediocre and impassioned boy was slowly but surely coming to terms with himself and the environment around him. Finally, the rookie came home to roost.

I was writing the pre-boards of my tenth standard. It was October 1973. Barrister saab had retired from his government position and started a private practice in law. He never refused counsel to anyone, and he maintained that habit right till the end. An innocuous fever at around three in the morning and a visit to the washroom at six. He collapsed in the washroom. Never to rise again. A cardiac arrest consumed Sheo Dhari Singh, my babuji. At that moment, I was in my room, awake at the early hour, preparing for the social science examination the same day.

I was fatherless when I wrote the examination a few hours later.

The passing away of my father shook me to the core. In retrospect, Barrister saab's death became one of the biggest learnings for me.

Raj Dhari Singh and the Tikari Estate

In sharp contrast to the personality of my father was my uncle Raj Dhari Singh, whom we affectionately called 'Badke babujee'.

He was my grandfather, Kishun Singh's eldest son. Raj Dhari Singh and studies were like chalk and cheese. While he remained aloof from academics, my uncle was the proverbial 'networking-guy' with perfect social networking skills. No wonder educational degrees or the lack of them made no difference to him in his professional quest. In fact, he landed an interesting breakthrough when he got the offer from Tikari Raja Gopal Sharan Singh to serve as the estate manager. My uncle was more than willing to take over the responsibility. Badke babujee did not just sustain his job right till his end but even made them, the children, feel like royalty. In my childhood, my uncle was my role model and we spent a lot of time engaged in activities we both enjoyed which helped build a stronger bond between us. After the death of my father, it was he who helped me come to terms with my emotions. A tall, handsome man, who stood confident. He was a charming man with a commanding presence. He always carried himself with much grace and poise. Stories and anecdotes about the estate and royalty abounded.

Raj Dhari Singh told us that the Tikari state originated, as legend goes, with an ancestor of Raja Gopal Sharan Singh, who enjoyed plundering the Mughal caravans that used to ply between Delhi and Patna. The emperor realized the only way to stop the attacks was to hand over charge of the revenue collection of the area to the most successful dacoit. The dacoit was then gifted lands by the emperor, and he became the maharajah of Tikari.

Furthermore, Rajie (Raja Gopal Sharan Singh) ascended the throne through his maternal grandfather, the ruler of Tikari. The title was passed on to Rajie's mother, who became the maharani of Tikari. In 1889, when Rajie was seven, his mother died and he became maharajah. His father was to be the guardian until Rajie attained his majority. Rajie was educated by two English tutors. The female rulers of Tikari who preceded Rajie had been very frugal, so when he became the maharajah, there was a great deal of money in the treasury. Nevertheless, he managed to spend it all in six or seven years.

Raja Gopal Sharan Singh, the last Maharajah of Tikari, was a multifaceted personality. He was a politician, playboy, soldier, big-time hunter, Grand Prix racer and an incorrigible spendthrift, all rolled in one. He was probably better known in the European capitals than amongst the Indian rulers. He saw active trenches in France during World War I. When the war was declared, he insisted on signing up and went as a lieutenant dispatch rider to Field Marshal Haig. He took a loan from Darbhanga and presented the British government with a squadron of tanks. He was the first Indian prince to race in the European Grand Prix. He also hobnobbed with white hunters in Africa while hunting big games. The maharajah was quite popular with women too. He also travelled the world and was a popular member of the princely order.

In 1909, Elsie Thompson, an Australian actress, became Rajie's wife number two. They were married according to Arya Samaj rites. Elsie converted to Hinduism and took the name Sita Devi. Theatrical from head to toe, Elsie loved dressing up. She wore her hair parted in the middle and tied it in a knot. She was especially fond of the Indian custom of wearing armlets. Rajie gave her a pair that was studded with precious jewels.

In the town of Tikari, the original land that was given to the Tikaris by the Mughals was Killa Fort. The fort was massive and sprawling, spreading out far beyond the boundaries of Tikari town. The fort was given to Maharani Vijayawada on her marriage to Rajie and its caretakers would remain faithful to her even after her death.

Rajie was a consummate womanizer and, in the course of time, he and Elsie began to find their amusement separately. While Elsie did not approve of Rajie's action, she was in no position to complain given that she herself had been guilty of similar behaviour. They managed to retain the form of their marriage by agreeing on some ground rules.

Raj Dhari Singh also told an interesting fact from history when the maharajah paid a special visit during the marriage ceremony of one of his cousins in their village Mira Bigha.

Tikari Raj was a zamindari estate and belonged to the Tikari family of the Bhumihar community. Established in the medieval times, the Tikari estate governed more than 2000 villages and was in charge of the revenue system. Through allegiance, alliances or pure annexations, the Tikari estate spread its influence over various parganas, first during the Mughal rule and later survived under the benevolence of the East India Company. The estate and the maharajah played a crucial role in the sociopolitical arena of Bihar. The abolition of the zamindari system reduced its influence drastically. Regardless, since the epicentre of the entire governance happened from the neighbouring Tikari Raj, Badke babujee grabbed the opportunity with both hands.

Raja Gopal Sharan Singh, the royal descendant of the clan and the head of the Tikari estate, was impressed by the dedicated service of my uncle. The carefree attitude of Badke babujee would rub on to them. An interesting fact about our family history got revealed because of Badke babujee's association with the Tikari estate. Records revealed that our late grandfather, Kishun Singh, was entrusted with two dozen villages by the Tikari estate for influence and revenue collection. Cut to the year 2017, when my elder brother, Dr Shree Prakash, an orthopaedic surgeon, during his tour to discover the roots of our family, stumbled upon an amazing page from history. About 50 km north of Gaya lies the village of Jaipur, where there is a Shiva temple established by our grandfather more than 100 years ago. There, Shiva takes the form of Sandeshwar Nath Baba. My brother could not hold his emotions as he entered the precincts of the temple.

30 January 2020

I got up from my supine position and stretched myself. The break had done me good. The emotional kitsch had taken me to a different age. Reality beckoned me, my pending work looming.

I hurried back to my desk and to the waiting files. The next half hour had me completely embroiled in paperwork.

When breaking news flashes on the television screen, the rapid change of graphics catches your eye, even though the volume might be muted. That is exactly what transpired. A news channel was reporting a hostage situation in UP's (Uttar Pradesh) Farrukhabad district. In a reflex action, I reached for the remote to turn up the volume. 'More than twenty children have been taken hostage by a man in UP's Farrukhabad district. The incident has been reported from village Kasaria, which is about 200 km from UP's capital, Lucknow. The local police have reached the incident site. Sources say—'

'Sir, Dr Anil Mishra, SP [Superintendent of Police], Farrukhabad, on the line.' Rajnish stood with his hand extended, holding out the phone.

'Jai Hind, Sir. It's a hostage situation. Subhash Batham, a murder convict, is holding about twenty-two children hostage in his house,' the SP said.

'This is serious. Whose children are these?'

'It sure is serious, Sir. The children are from the same neighbourhood. Batham had invited them for his child's birthday party. When the parents and family went to collect their children, Batham opened fired on them.'

'An armed murder convict with twenty-two children! Is he out on bail? Any accomplice?'

'Yes, Sir, he is out on bail. Apparently, Batham's wife is also there, but her involvement is not clear yet. We have cordoned off the house and our men are trying to negotiate with him.'

'Any demand?' I quipped.

'None so far, Sir.'

'Okay. Keep me posted. I'll speak to the National Security Guard [NSG]. No one should be harmed.'

'Yes, Sir. I'm on my way to Kaisara.'

'Good. Anil, ask your team to send me the coordinates immediately. Jai Hind.'

I checked the time, it was 7.09 p.m. Popularly known as the Black Cats for the Nomex coveralls, balaclavas and assault helmets they wear, the NSG is part of the Central Armed Police Forces. A central government-administered force, it comes under the Ministry of Home Affairs (MHA). Communication with the DG NSG was instantly established, and the situation was explained to him.

'Our commandos are on alert mode, but there's no landing strip in the region. It could take seven to eight hours to deploy our men there,' he said. The response was crisp, but it offered zilch by way of a solution.

I had SP Anil back on line again.

'The NSG is out of the scene at the moment. How much time for you to reach there?'

'Sir, I'll be at the site in twenty minutes.'

'Good. Meanwhile, ask your men to keep things calm. Get the local MLA [Member of the Legislative Assembly] to talk to this fellow Batham. I'm sure he'll hold sway.'

'Sir, I have already done that. Not only the MLA, but the seniors of the village have also been summoned.'

'Hmm. Keep it tight, Anil.'

I turned to the screen again, where the same information was being repeated. 'Rajnish, send out message to the media cell to ensure the TV channels do not provide live coverage of the situation. We don't want this turning into a circus. And no news should go out about the NSG commandos either.'

The ringing phones and shuffle of the feet multiplied around the office in those intervening minutes.

'Sir, the MHA is on the line,' Rajnish handed me another phone.

It was the Union home secretary of the Government of India.

'Any help required from our side?' The home secretary came to the point without any fuss.

'The NSG has been put on stand-by, but we'll have to take the assistance of the UP Anti-Terror Squad [ATS] or the Quick Reaction Team [QRT] to ensure prompt action,' I assured. I had just mentioned the ATS and the QRT in one breath. The former is a formidable unit of the police force specially trained to combat modern-day terror attacks. Existing as a state unit in different states of India, it has been modelled on the lines of Special Weapons and Tactics (SWAT) of the Los Angeles Police Department.

'Sounds good. Let us know if anything else is required. Good luck.' The line went dead.

'Inform the CM's office if they're not already aware. I am shifting my base to the CM's residence. I move in two minutes.'

It was a five-minute drive to the CM's residence-cum-war room. CM Yogi Adityanath's hands-on approach to any situation is an open secret. I had found an ally in his style of functioning— to be a step ahead of the developing situation.

'Rajnish, get me Mohit Agarwal, Inspector General of Police [IG] Kanpur Range. Put him on the job with the ATS. It's going to be a long night.' The car door opened. I was already on the steps leading to the imposing CM residence.

'Sir, IG Agrawal is holding the line,' Rajnish interrupted as he maintained the pace of the dash inside.

Mohit Agrawal's throaty voice came on the line next. 'Jai Hind, Sir.'

'Mohit, look, get in touch with the ATS. I have already alerted them. You must lead the ATS operation if need be. Gear up. I'll be with the CM till we get the children out safely.'

'Yes, Sir,' Mohit responded.

My mobile came alive the moment I disconnected the other. It was SP Anil again.

'Sir, the situation is tense here. The parents and relatives of the children have gathered in large numbers. We are trying to keep them calm. But their anger has been growing, and understandably so. This is about their children. Most of them are under ten years old, Sir. A crying mother has a six-month-old baby along with her daughter inside. Some elderly people of the village have come too,' SP said.

'Buy time, Anil. Stall him. And exercise complete restraint as of now.'

'Sir, we are doing just that, although Batham has been constantly provoking and threatening anybody who tries to approach his door. He shot at his own friend who tried to reason out with him. The friend got a bullet in his leg.'

'Any demands yet?' It was an elementary question.

'The villagers claim to have heard the culprit shouting from the door that he's innocent and has been wrongly implicated in the murder case.'

'Keep at it. Wear him down.'

'Yes, Sir.'

'You must have shared the coordinates with the headquarters by now?'

'Yes, Sir, I'm in touch with the team. Photos and live images too are going to them. The District Magistrate [DM] is also here,' Anil was efficient with his response. I cut the phone.

Rajnish had instantly gelled into the changed working space. Now he made himself heard. 'Sir, it's the same news on all the channels. No further addition to the news,' The room was spacious, and the air was tense.

'Yes, so it seems. That is good. They haven't put the cameras on the ground. But it's time we put our feet on the ground.'

The door that led to the inner chambers of the building opened and the familiar face of the additional director general [ADG], law and order, P.V. Ramashastry, appeared on the scene.

We were quick with our greetings. Every passing minute was a ticking time bomb.

'The CM has interrupted his meeting with a delegation. He's greatly concerned,' he said as we both moved out of the room, crossed a gallery and entered the atrium, and turned left. The CM's office door was already held open. He was grim. I was quick to fill him in on all the details, including the news about ATS and QRT. The CM insisted we ensure the full and complete safety of the children. I assured him about the same.

'You have faced so many trying circumstances in your career. Keep in mind the young girl you and your National Disaster Response Force [NDRF] team pulled out alive from an impossible debris in Nepal. I believe in you. I'm in the middle of a meeting. Let me wind it. Then I'm with you till this matter is resolved,' he assured me.

His unwavering faith in me gave me the operational clout and independence I needed to tackle this hostage situation. I checked the time; it was just a minute past eight.

A memory flash

The CM had triggered a memory that was best left untouched, but the visuals came to me in perfect clarity. On 25 April 2015, an earthquake of demonic magnitude struck the Himalayan kingdom of Nepal. I was heading the NDRF, as its director general then. It was around midnight when one of my teams reached Bhaktapur. The NDRF was the first to reach Nepal as part of the global aid. The destruction had to be seen to be believed. The CM was not wrong when he used the word 'impossible' to describe the debris. Not one building had escaped destruction on that street. A four-storey structure had collapsed. Imagine four floors flattened in an awkward and deadly state, and tremors returning again and again as aftershocks. It was a precarious situation. The Nepal Army and

Police detected a sixteen-year-old girl trapped underneath the pile of rubble, logs, iron structures and whatnot. They were successful in creating a vent opening to reach the girl, but the pathway was obstructed by two wooden logs. It would have been fatal to cut the logs as that would have led to further collapse of the heavy mess. The girl herself was trapped in an awkward manner. Both her legs were stuck and faced opposite directions as if she had been in the middle of a leap when disaster struck. To make matters worse, her body was dangling upside down. It was Assistant Commandant Kuleesh Anand of the NDRF who led a team of highly trained, brave men who achieved the impossible. It was only in the third attempt that they were able to reach the girl, from the rear side of the collapsed building, without the structure coming down any further. The girl was extracted after hours of hard work and extreme precautions. Alisha survived with minor cuts and bruises.

A disaster averted

The phones had not stopped ringing for a long time. Even their rings seemed imbued with a higher intensity of purpose that night. Many a call added to the grimness of the situation. Others aided the process of preparation and hope. The soldier and the officer in me were oriented and matured to respect the waiting game. The man was a lone wolf and his only accomplice was his wife, Ruby. In our assessment, she had the benefit of doubt. Possibly, she too was the victim of Subhash Batham's coercive intent, although the villagers were convinced that Ruby and Batham were operating as a team, for she too had gone around the neighbourhood with the birthday invitation. The parents were convinced and trusted the invitation because of the presence of a lady in the house. The parents had discounted the fact that the wife possibly had no prior knowledge about her husband's nefarious designs.

The ATS and the QRT were on the spot, weighing and strategizing the options. The district magistrate, the SP standing next to IG Mohit Agarwal were all parked at the site, playing the waiting game. The culprit was armed. Nerves played an important role in such tense situations. While constraint was a normal and conditioned aspect of the men of law, the same could not be expected from an outlaw. With young lives under his direct control, it made Batham all the more dangerous.

I returned to my war room. The pending files had followed me. I glanced at Rajnish, acknowledging his smart management. He was unmoved in his expression; it was part of his job. I settled at the new station, but not for long. I received a call from Ajit Doval, national security advisor. The news had made international waves.

'All eyes and expectations are on us, OP. I have my faith in your men and you,' Doval was quick and crisp. This effectively meant that the prime minister was also in the loop. I had seen many difficult and challenging situations but here, my last few hours in office, and I was in the middle of another one. I was blessed differently.

'Sir, IG Agrawal is on the line.' Rajnish had taken no break the entire day.

'Sir, we have exhausted all our options. Batham is refusing to talk to anyone. The DM and SP have also tried talking to him, but he ends up using his gun each time. He has fired at least six rounds till now. He agreed upon meeting the MLA of the region but when the latter arrived, the guy suddenly changed his stance and mind. The mother of the six-month-old baby has been wailing for the release of her child on the Public Address System. There's a possibility that Batham might release the infant soon.' IG Agarwal gave a complete report from the ground.

'Our moment will come, Mohit. You have my go-ahead for the ATS to take over the operations from hereon. Then they'll flush out the man soon. Keep him engaged. The news agencies have not been kept in the loop to ensure the focus of our operation. We don't want a scenario where the culprit gets a whiff of our action and our guys end up sitting ducks.'

'That's good, Sir. This operating procedure has been giving us dividends.'

'I know, Mohit. Keep vigil. It must be tough on the children. Their safety is paramount. If this guy is not negotiating, he's either dumb or too smart for his shoes. The psychologists consider him to be emotionally unstable. We need to finish this drama soon,' I rounded up.

I must admit, it was an uneasy waiting game. Completing the pending paperwork was excruciating. The interruptions continued. Defence Minister Rajnath Singh also connected briefly to inquire. The scenario hadn't changed at ground zero. Batham continued to throw his weight around, refusing to cooperate and giving threats of gun and harm. At one point, he hurled a crude bomb at the DM, SP and a constable as they tried to engage with him.

The end to the entire hostage episode came sooner than expected. The ATS commandos forced their entry from the back door of the house, post-midnight. Caught unawares, Batham tried to flee the scene but was shot. The twenty-one children cooped up in the basement of the house were rescued, with no bodily harm. In those critical moments, a few villagers also entered the house and caught hold of Batham's wife, Ruby, and thrashed her. She succumbed to her injuries.

By the time the forensic team scanned the premises and the media exchange of this hostage drama at Lucknow concluded, it was close to 1.30 a.m. I was drained, but the satisfaction of a fruitful closure of the case was immense. I checked my watch again. The new day had broken. I had just enough time to catch a few hours of sleep.

My farewell was just a few hours away, I desperately needed to hit the bed.

Once again, the UP Police had proved its mettle. The children were united with their families.

Morning of the farewell

The morning newspapers were agog with news about my last day in the office. The apex position in the police department of one of the largest states of India was on the verge of being vacated. The successor had not been picked yet. I had scotched all rumours and talks about getting a three-month extension by clearly indicating my resolution to the CM. There was a precedent where an outgoing DGP attended the ceremonial farewell parade at the Reserve Police Lines on the morning of his last working day, but by the evening, just prior to the traditional tea party at DGP's residence, was handed the letter of extension.

I had denied any hope to such speculators. For me, the moment to hang the boots had truly arrived. The newspapers also speculated about my role as Chief Information Commissioner of UP post-retirement. Bemused, I let the news pass.

My morning tea was served, and my mind was already on the beverage. Post some satisfying hot sips, I took to my official Twitter handle. In quick time, I had sent the following characters float out into digital space: 'Today is my last day in uniform. (Trust me, the first line threatened to open sluice gates of delicate emotions.) For thirty-seven years it was a privilege to serve this country and the state. I thank each and every one of you with whom I had the honor to work with. Gratitude to my fellow citizens who offered their selfless help.'

'Papa!' That was my princess, a budding legal eagle on the verge of starting her independent law practice as a counsel. The warm hug came at the perfect time and was followed by the young-mind's youthful inquisitiveness.

'You have so many firsts to your name, Papa. You gave the Commissionerate system of policing the state, innovated some of the features in UP-112 emergency response mechanism, besides managing the state so well . . . I could go on. Come on, Papa, you should get an extension! I'm so proud of you. Everyone has such good things to say about you. And you handled last night's Farrukhabad hostage situation so smoothly. You truly are my hero.'

'I love you, princess. Your world is small, but the state is a huge ocean. It's easy for me to ask for an extension, and I'm sure my request will be considered with respect. But your father has served his time—served with pride, diligence and respect. Now is the time to go.'

More hugs followed.

It was time to put on the khaki uniform one last time.

2

The Academic Route to Khaki

I stood and stared at the khaki shirt positioned dramatically on my bed. It had been delivered the evening before. It was precisely forty-five days post the commencement of our training regimen at the Sardar Vallabhbhai Patel National Police Academy, (SVPNPA), Hyderabad. My dream of making it to the Indian Administrative Services (IAS) was formally quashed by my score rank. I wasn't complaining. After all, how many get the opportunity to serve the nation, upfront?

And now here I was. I had earned my single star along with the IPS insignia. It sure was a proud moment. The moment to don the colours was at hand—a formal ceremony for my induction into the folds of the police, which would be followed by indoor training sessions. I reached for the uniform, gently caressing the crisp texture of the fabric all the way up the sleeves until my hands finally rested on the shoulder blades. My fingers instinctively reached for the buttons, and I touched the IPS insignia. There were no camera phones back then, yet the image and feelings are firmly ensconced in my living memory.

My first indoor session was to start soon. I met Rishi Shukla, a batchmate, in the corridor of the main building. We pumped each other's hand with renewed vigour. 'Om, buddy!' Rishi's greeting was marked with excitement. I tried to match his exuberance.

His soft-spoken demeanour was obvious, but the excitement of the new beginning overwhelmed him. Apparently, we were the last to leave our rooms. 'Others are already downstairs, at the reception area, waiting for us. We'll march together to the auditorium today.' Although we were more than a month old in the Academy, not to forget the fifteen days of exposure to the Civil Defence training programme at Nagpur, the feel of wearing the colours and its sight on our buddies added to the excitement. Our collective dreams, trials and tribulations had crossed the frontiers. The best and chosen few were here together. A new beginning, a new future was being carved. The squeak of our new shoes in unison provided the perfect musical score as we descended the stairs from the second floor of the hostel building. A sea of khaki brimmed in front, greeting us with a grin. Sixty-three first-year probationers indulgently holding the rank of IPS of the 1983 batch then marched towards the administrative block. I knew for sure that Ma and Babuji too walked with me that day.

* * *

I completed my tenth from Gaya Zila School, with my academic score a healthy 80 per cent. The day I got my report I waited eagerly to place it on my father's study table. When I reached home, I stood by his desk as he sat in his semicircular chair, reading a file. When he finished reading, I handed him my report card, waiting for him to look up and embrace his mediocre, impassioned son. He smiled warmly. I was immensely assured.

It was the summer of 1974. The hot and dusty plains of the northern part of the country had taken upon themselves the arduous task of absorbing the sun's fury. The political scene was on the boil. College and university students had started a movement which popularly came to be known as the Bihar Movement. Jayaprakash Narayan, popularly referred to by his initials JP, a Gandhian socialist, led the movement against the existing corruption in public life in his state.

Teachers at primary and secondary schools kept a tight leash on any conversation among students related to the movement. It was no different at my school.

'You know, this movement draws inspiration from the Navnirman Andolan of Gujarat, which happened almost a year ago,' Raghu said with an excitement that had more pride and less purpose. Raghu, elder to me by four years, was my friend in the village.

'Really! How do you know so much?' I was overwhelmed by his knowledge. Although I could not make out much about its relevance.

'It's my relative. He's a politician, you see. I overheard him discussing it with my baba.' His pride had not died.

I simply let the conversation pass over me.

A distinct feature of the structure of state education in Bihar was that while the tenth-standard examination was conducted by the state board, the twelfth-standard intermediate examination was governed by the affiliated university. St Xavier College at Ranchi was the next milestone in my journey towards establishing a strong foothold in the education front. Physics, chemistry and mathematics were my companions in this journey. The college campus was a different world altogether. It was humongous but immaculately kept. The facade, the corridors, the gardens, the fields, the assembly hall, you name it, everything had a stamp of order. It was a lesson for me in management. Take real good care of the infrastructure under your command. The head of the institution, the principal, Father Proust, was an imposing man with a booming voice that echoed in the corridors and other closed space. He had an amazing command over about 1600 of us boys. Six feet tall and well-built but quick on his feet, with not even the slightest hint of a smile but a sparkle in his eyes, that's

Father Proust for you. He was fond of his cigar and the smell of tobacco always lingered in his office. Every week or so, Father Proust lectured students on ethics. With a voice that reverberated through the entire lecture hall, we were treated to an orderly intellectual feast. We listened to him spellbound, sometimes making notes. I have fond memories of another teacher from the time, Father De Brouwer. He used to teach physics but was very popular among all students, cutting across departments. He had a sharp memory and would remember students by their first names, long after they had passed out of the college. He looked very busy all the time, yet approachable. With long, silken-white hair, Father De Brouwer was a familiar figure to generations of Xavierites at Ranchi.

Shared hostel rooms, tasteless and boring mess food, Sunday movies and Sudipto Ghosh, Pradeep Ambastha, Deepak Kumar, Mani Kant, Dilip Thakur, Harun Rasheed, P.N. Shukla and many others became a routine for the next two years of my life. The ragging of juniors was a culture then and Sudipto, my roommate, and I were battered by our seniors on quite a few occasions. Sudipto Ghosh exuded more genuine charm than most of my friends. Another close friend, Pradeep Ambastha, originally from Netarhat, where my elder brother also studied, came from Tikari of Gaya, my home district, where Ambastha's father was a doctor. I found Pradeep to be clear-headed and decisive, voicing his approval or disapproval instantly. We remained good friends throughout and shared a hostel room at Delhi University while pursuing our postgraduation. Later, he joined the Indian Revenue Service (IRS) and retired as principal chief commissioner of income tax.

* * *

During the last two years of my schooling, the JP movement, spearheaded by Jayaprakash Narayan, gained much momentum. An ailing JP had exhorted the people of Bihar in pouring rain at Gandhi Maidan in Patna to fight the corruption and venality of the government. And when the state took up the chant, *'Bhrashtrachar mitana hai Naya Bihar banana hai'* [We have to eradicate corruption and build a new Bihar], there was hope all around. A student body called the Bihar Chhattra Sangharsh Samiti was formed in Bihar which provided muscle power in this fight against corruption in public life. Agitations, protests and bandhs became the norm. Lalu Prasad Yadav, Sushil Kumar Modi, Bashistha Narain Singh, Mohammad Shahabuddin and Ram Vilas Paswan emerged as the new faces of student politics. We were elated when the pathetic conditions of hostel rooms and the mess food also became a strong rallying point. My home district of Gaya also felt the ripples of the agitation.

In hindsight, the JP Movement initially began as a student movement. Bureaucrats had been appointed as vice chancellors of universities and the students rose in agitation. The charter of demands included bus fare concessions, hike in scholarship stipends, campus amenities, hostel upkeep and better-quality mess food. The demands were genuine, but the moment politicians stepped in, the scale of the theatre was altered and the force of the agitation was directed towards Indira Gandhi, the then Prime Minister of India and her nominee in Bihar, Chief Minister Abdul Ghafoor. Public anger had built up against the Ghafoor ministry. JP saw the ouster of the Congress government in the state as only a means to an end. He saw the Bihar movement as a revolutionary movement and the change of the party in power as only a small part of it. A move to paralyse the government turned ugly and resulted in police firing and deaths. The objectives were partially achieved but at a heavy price. An embattled Mrs Gandhi declared Emergency in 1975, sending shock waves through the whole country.

Prayagraj: Oxford of the East

I sustained my performance and the grades in my final examinations at St Xavier. My mother was a happy woman.

My mind, however, was made up. It was bye-bye science and hello to humanities. The Sampoorna Kranti (Total Revolution) agitation delayed the end of the academic calendar and my hopes of entering the portals of Delhi University were quashed. My brother, Shree Prakash, came to my rescue and strongly proposed Allahabad University as an apt replacement. 'It's the Oxford of the East. It would do you great,' he assured me. Allahabad University, renowned for its rich legacy, stood as a venerable hub of knowledge, nurturing countless bureaucrats, writers, jurists, politicians and esteemed scholars. During the 1960s and 1970s, a multitude of civil servants emerged from the hallowed halls of this institution. Notable figures such as Madan Mohan Malaviya, Meghnad Saha, Firaq Gorakhpuri, Harivansh Rai Bachchan and many others graced the university with their association in the past. As the fourth-oldest university in India, it had soared to remarkable heights as a bastion of higher learning at the time when my elder brother contemplated sending me to Allahabad (now Prayagraj) to pursue my undergraduate studies.

I took the train to Sangam city for the admission formalities. Political science, English literature and ancient history became my new companions. This was a popular combination choice for most civil service aspirants well into the 1970s and 1980s. I was no exception. Sir Sunder Lal Hostel's Room Number 15 became my refuge and Kapil Jain my roommate.

'You should take to farming; the road to civil services is thorny,' Kapil said, smiling to all.

I looked at him squarely and gave an answer that summarized everything and surprised me as well: 'I come from a state where bureaucracy rules and misgovernance and corruption are rampant. The simple task of transferring the registration of my father's gun to my brother's name took me more than a year. I don't have the patience to be a farmer but possess all the patience to see myself in the civil services zone.'

We became good friends, Kapil and I. Pawan Singh and Sanjeev Tiwari formed the other two of our circle. The four of us were bound together by destiny, to be on the same boat. Kapil belonged to Moradabad, UP, where his father was a practising lawyer of taxation. Pawan's background had a civil services imprint. His father was then serving the district of Etah, UP, as the DM. A summer break in the precincts of the *DM ki kothi* in Etah still stands out in my memory.

We lost Kapil to time and a second cardiac arrest a few years ago. Sanjeev, a dogged fighter and achiever, has gone on to rule the corporate world. Based in Dubai, he has made us proud by winning the NRI Achievers Awards and Pravasi Bharatiya Samman Award. Pawan, like me, has hung his boots post his stint as state prosecutor to the UP government. The three of us still carry warmth and the torch of friendship—four friends who came together like the waters of the divine rivers at Prayagraj.

I also developed a good friendship with Deepak Deo, who was my classmate in English and political science and lived in the Holland Hall Hostel of the university. His father was a very senior IPS officer of the Bihar cadre. Deepak was very fond of photography and would often participate in photography and collage contests in university hostels. With a great love for English literature, he cultivated a flair for writing and always maintained a diary.

One of the many interesting anecdotes I came to hear from Deepak was the unique yet popular ragging technique in Holland Hall back in the 1930s. It would involve the female students residing at the Sarojini Naidu Hostel coming out on their hostel terrace and being an audience to the parading of the Holland Hall freshers as they marched up to the girls' hostel. The girls would laugh at the hilarity of the military-style march by the freshers and indulge their bows and salutes with reciprocating waves and applause. The boys would then march back to Holland Hall in the same manner, and the whole event overall made for a much-anticipated annual entertainment. In all the university hostels ragging was very common, and I had my fair share of 'affectionate attention' from seniors like Arvind Srivastav, Rajeev Sharma, Deepak Singhal, Sanjeev Sahai, Arun Gaur, Indu Prakash Mishra (of current India TV fame) and many others. Persistent attempts to escape to Civil Lines, late nights spent at Alfred Park, mandatory *farshis*[3] to seniors of the hostel and fragments of earthen pots in the corridors were frequent occurrences at Sir Sundar Lal Hostel.

The Mahakumbh of 1977 stands firm on the pedestal of my memory. A sea of humanity had descended on to the holy city. Even the hostel rooms were choked with the surge. You lifted your eyes and found people and faith moving towards the Sangam ghats. Most of my friends were drawn towards it. Flags, sadhus and slogans of 'Har Har Gange' reverberated through the town. Stalls with an array of items, and vendors with their eatables, marigold and *kumkum* in multiple colours stood out. Unmindful of the crowds and the jostle, everyone just moved in the direction of the Sangam. Nothing else mattered. It was humbling, this open theatre, the biggest human congregation. And to top it, no advertisement, no calls to march-on, but a simple belief and faith guided all the people. With the imposing fort of the sixteenth century against the backdrop, the believers converged at the turquoise blue waters of the Yamuna as it merged with the muddy brown of the Ganges. They were drenched in divinity. Who else but the stars would have known that some years from then, I would be given the charge of the Kumbh and would oversee the Mela's police bandobast, not just once but twice in my professional life.

Another memory from this time remains etched vividly— the unprecedented floods of September 1978. The flood was massive and watching its severity became a sort of sightseeing expedition for me as a youngster. As the swirling waters of the Yamuna threatened to breach the bund, the students at Allahabad

University heeded the administration's call to action. United by a shared purpose, we responded with *shramdaan*, offering our efforts to rescue the inundated city. Together we toiled, filling sandbags to fortify the embankments of the Yamuna. It was an invaluable lesson in the power of collaboration, a testament to what can be achieved through collective effort. Moreover, it taught us the intrinsic value of physical labour, a vital aspect woven into the fabric of our lives.

An array of learned professors at Allahabad University became our source of learning and engagement. Their distinct styles of teaching and nuances found minute dissection on the campus. Professor Bhattacharya, a very erudite individual, was so popular that students from other departments would come to listen to his lectures. The Department of Ancient History, Culture and Archaeology was known for scholars such as G.R. Sharma, G.C. Pandey, J.S. Negi and B.N.S. Yadav. Our English professor, Rajamani, had a crazy sense of humour along with a great command over prose and poetry. A colleague of ours joined his course late and he got a welcome that I will never forget: 'Gentleman, why don't you take two more weeks to join? You can easily miss the works of Hopkins and Hardy in that case.' Professor Rajamani's instincts were so sharp he could smell a proxy attendance. Each of us was wary of him. Lectures in political science by professors A.D. Pant and Alok Pant were incredibly immersive and edifying. The political science department had, in the past, iconic professors such as Beni Prasad, Tara Chand and Ishwari Prasad, each one of them regarded as a legend in their own right.

It cannot be denied that there has been a subtle decline in the university from the eminence of its yesteryears, but its illustrious roster proudly includes the names of our most renowned administrators, jurists, journalists and academics. Allahabad University, once a vibrant hub of intellectual vitality, remains a place of animated scholarly discourse, focused and gratifying.

I bow in grace to all my mentors for touching me with their sunshine. I'm forever blessed.

Delhi University

(August 1979)

For my higher studies, I was accepted into postgraduate courses at Delhi University (DU) and Jawaharlal Nehru University (JNU). I continued my love affair with political science, choosing DU over JNU as the former offered my preferred choice in humanities. The course in international relations offered by JNU excited me, but a delay in the academic session at Allahabad University changed my course of action. Eventually, I found the DU campus compact and much to my liking. I was anointed into the proverbial Dilli Darbar, and Jubilee Hall, one of the university hostels, became my next pit stop in my academic journey. Close to Khyber Pass, the accommodation sported a refurbished facade with more than 150 dwelling units. Near-swanky interiors, along with a massive dining area and a canteen added to its utility. A comfortable lounge area with a mandatory television set, newspapers and magazines talked of a thoughtful administration. Incidentally, Jubilee Hall was the first hostel with in-house living for the administration and support staff. A table-tennis table, carom board and a chess board graced the common area and fanned our recreational thirst.

The famed Delhi Transport Corporation (DTC) bus became my *saarthi,* my companion that daily helped me reach my destination—the DU Arts Faculty. It was a set routine—wake up, freshen up, exercise, shower, breakfast and then, out of the hostel. A short walk took me to the Mall Road intersection, where I would wait for my bus to arrive. The scene on the road was far from just busy; it was chaotic. The traffic scene on the Delhi roads epitomized a unique philosophy, me-before-you. There was some undefined rule that encouraged or provoked everyone to 'move ahead'. And moving ahead meant doing just that, with impunity. It was your birthright to blare your way ahead, or stare your way ahead, or the most convenient one, simply push people away and move ahead. Very soon, I realized that survival in Delhi required a different set of rules, and they certainly were not hampered by any niceties. Spotting a vacant seat on the DTC bus was no guarantee of getting the seat. Elbowing fellow passengers with a practised skill to respond swiftly and in an impassioned manner was the key. Elbowed out on the first few occasions, the experience offered me a new perspective. Soon I, too, was sucked into the stream.

On certain days, when the metallic contraption (DTC bus) and its aggressive competitiveness would weigh too heavy on my system, I would simply walk to the campus. During the Allahabad University days, we would refer to the act of walking as the ever-dependable *gyarah-number-wali bus*. The chaotic cacophony would reach my room number one at Jubilee. Time is kind. It helps one overcome everything. And it did. Sundays offered a different perspective to the day. Roads and the traffic exhibited controlled sanity. Both studies and recreation got a different meaning on Sundays.

The academic scene at the DU campus was competitive. I mean, you could really feel it, the sense and the urge to learn, to grow big. I found my years at DU intellectually most satisfying. I cannot escape the mention of some of my professors with whom I had the privilege to cover a distance. Randhir Singh, the master of political theory and thought, was an exceptional professor. His oratory skills had the audience eating out of his hands and he was quite popular among the students too. Prof. Manoranjan Mohanty, another exceptional mind, handled comparative politics. International relations was the domain of Prof. Mahendra Kumar, while Prof. Susheela Kaushik talked about Indian politics. Last but not the least, Prof. M.P. Singh and Prof. R.B. Jain professed political theory and public administration, respectively. It was one august line-up and I immersed myself in the holy waters of Delhi academics.

Besides looking forward to the edifying lectures of eminent faculty members, I used to have after-dinner talks with Shekhar Singh, my senior in academics and also a lecturer at Kirori Mal College, till midnight. We would often discuss threadbare Western political thought, Indian political thought of leaders such as B.R. Ambedkar and M.N. Roy, and politics of representation and participation along with discussions on changing international political order. Shekhar Singh joined the IAS and retired as chief secretary of Telangana. The Central Library offered a refuge of a different kind. Innumerable boys and girls, research scholars and professors from different departments would converge and recreate a *sangam*, a confluence of varied interests. I, too, became part of the furniture in the library, and I could smell the aspiration for the civil services around me. I was convinced I had come to the right place. My preparation for the exam of my lifetime began in earnest.

I visited my mother and Gaya during the long breaks, especially during the summers. The train journey across the Gangetic plain held an unparalleled charm. In the company of friends and friends of friends, we travelled in a spirit of camaraderie. Second-class journey, reservation or no reservation, crowded platforms— nothing dissuaded our spirits of adventure. I still remember Gaya Station and its crazy, cacophonous milieu of coolies in red shirts, with their golden brassards in place, the shouting brigade of vendors and the lone shout of 'chai-chai' resounding even after one had left the premises of the rail station.

After my master's with distinguished honours, I rested my eyes and hope on my MPhil programme in political science. My dream of clearing the civil services exam was still on. Deshbandhu College of Delhi University offered me a lectureship and I grabbed the opportunity. Thus began a small yet significant start to my career. Though my heart lay elsewhere, I was lucky to keep myself and my mind on course. The year was 1982. The urge and the thirst to do something big was alive and I knew it was just a matter of time.

Dates hold a strange fascination for me, and 19 May 1983 became another such landmark. No, it wasn't the day of the results of the UPSC examination but the day I appeared for the selection interview. As I stepped out of the cool confines of the imposing UPSC building and on to Shahjahan Road, I exuded a certain confidence, the confidence of having arrived. The forty-five-minute interview had been a breeze. I was grilled by the chairperson of the interview board, R.O. Dhan. She was possibly the vice chancellor of some university and had real pointed questions in her armoury. Former IPS officer John Lobo, another board member, carried the legacy of having investigated the famous homicide case of Admiral K.M. Nanavati. From the United Nations to the Chauri Chaura incident, the interviewers were thorough in their approach.

The UPSC interview was held in the month of May. The news of my selection came through in June. Life has its own way of springing surprises. At times I think back on my journey to academic success, a candidate who cracked one of the toughest examinations in the country, in fact in the world. There is always a trigger that catapults one from a modest follower to a fiery leader. Fifth standard had been mine. I had started believing in myself and taking myself more seriously when I stood first then. This precisely was a moment when I reinvented myself afresh and a sense of competition was instilled in my young mind.

My training and induction were fixed to commence in the first week of December. For me, the ultimate had happened. God had blessed me with his indulgent embrace. My mother was with me in the momentous occasion, so were my sisters and brother Shree Prakash. Babuji was missing in the picture and that stung me.

And then, out of nowhere, the love of my life tiptoed into the family and straight to my heart.

My forever partner

Neelam entered my life like a breeze. I wasn't ready for my nuptial journey.

'Men are never ready; they have to be made ready.' My mother laughed away my concerns. 'Omi, a marriage not only brings two people together, but it's also a union of two families. It's time now, give me that pleasure,' she continued calmly with her benign wisdom.

'Maa, my training begins in December. I'm not even a police officer yet,' I put forth my defence.

'Don't worry, we'll have you married before you leave for your training. They are a good family with a lovely daughter.'

I can say with reasonable surety that neither Neelam nor I would have such a straightjacketed conversation on the M-word with our children.

So, exactly eighteen days prior to my departure for the first leg of my probationary training, I tied the nuptial knot.

Neelam came from a family with big judicial 'luminaries'. Her great-grandfather, Babu Saligram Singh, had a towering presence and influence as a member of the Calcutta High Court Bar in 1877. A degree in law from Law College, Calcutta (now Kolkata) as well as a sound understanding of the subject, a cheery disposition and a persuasive eloquence made him one of the leading members of the Bar Council. His passing away was considered a major loss in the judicial circles, and while unveiling his portrait under the roof of the Bar Council, Sir Lawrence H. Jenkins, the then chief justice of the Calcutta High Court, paid a glowing tribute to his memory. In the course of his remarks, on that occasion, he said,

Mr Saligram Singh was a fine type of Bihar manhood, of commanding presence, of kindly temperament, gifted with a rich fund of strong common sense, and above all guided by an integrity of purpose that assured to him the confidence of those before whom it was his duty to plead, and the respect of those to whom he was opposed. He was one of those happy persons in whom the carping spirit of envy could strike no root and his generous outlook endeared him to all with whom he came into contact.[4]

For those who would consider the above as cosying up to the imperial Raj, Babu Salingram had much more to contribute. He, along with his brother Bisheshwar Singh, decided to set up an educational institute in Bihar for the sole purpose of shoring up indigenous and nationalist feelings amongst the youth. When the proposal reached the commissioner's office for approval, the use of the word 'national' in the college's name was objected to. The brothers were pressured by the ruling dispensation to change the name of the college from Bihar National College to Raja Saligram College. Babu Saligram Singh was not just offered the title of 'Raja' but also the *jagir* (feudal land estate) of many villages. But he refused to succumb to the immense pressure. Thus, Bihar National College was born in Patna in 1889.

Saligram Babu's youngest son, Shashi Shekhar Prasad Singh, was Neelam's grandfather. He too was a counsel and practised at the Patna High Court. Besides being a legal eagle, Shekhar Prasad was a proponent of Persian poetry and was closely involved in the translation of the great epic the Ramayana into Persian. His son K.B.N. Singh carried forward the family legacy. He joined the bar in 1944 and soon became a leading lawyer at the Patna High Court. At the young age of forty-four, he was made a high court judge and rose to occupy the seat of chief justice of the Patna High Court. He was also the acting Governor of Bihar on two occasions.

He later became chief justice of the Madras High Court, from where he retired in 1984.

Neelam is the progeny of Chief Justice K.B.N Singh and continues to hold the family flag high as a lawyer practising at the Supreme Court of India. A product of St Joseph's Convent, Patna, she was a sports representative for badminton in inter-school tournaments. A graduate of Patna Women's College and postgraduate in economics from Patna University, she eventually went on to obtain a law degree. She initially practised at the Lucknow Bench of the Allahabad High Court, but subsequently, on account of my transfer to Delhi on deputation, started her practice at the Supreme Court of India. Her elder brother Samrendra Pratap Singh was a judge at the Patna High Court until recently while the younger one, Jitendra Singh, is a senior advocate practising at the Patna High Court. She has always stood by me through thick and thin and has given me two beautiful children. While our daughter Avni has followed in her footsteps, our son Apoorv has an engineering and management background and works in a multinational company. Like any loving parent's assessment, both are brilliant in their own respective fields.

3

Early Foundation

The campus of the Sardar Vallabhbhai Patel National Police Academy (SVPNPA), Hyderabad, is a sprawling affair and the aesthetic setting of the structure, in tandem with the greens, warms the heart. Like a perfectly matched couple doing a tango, it mesmerizes the beholder. Simply put, it's a beautiful place.

Before reporting at the NPA, my probationer training journey commenced at National Civil Defence College (NCDC), Nagpur, on 15 December 1983. The Nagpur Academy was formally christened Central Emergency Relief Training Institute (CERTI) in 1957. Founded in 1957, CERTI was, in a way, the first disaster management training institute of India. The wars that were forced upon India in 1962 and 1965 compelled the Government of India to restructure its emergency training activities. Consequently, the orientation of the academy shifted from training in national disaster management to those related to protection of life and property. The year 1968 marked the changeover and thus NCDC was born, replacing the previous entity. Another momentous occurrence awaited India when, more than two decades later, a specialized disaster response force—the NDRF—was constituted and the NCDC training facility came under its wings. Not even in my wildest dreams did I imagine then that I would get the supreme privilege of reshaping the disaster response management in the country, as the head of the NDRF.

We were a batch of about sixty-three probationers when we entered the portals of NCDC. The leadership at the academy was with one retired army general, who was a designated commandant of the college. The Civil Defence Act 1968 became our bible, the objectives and our roles. For us, it was *the* commandment to follow. The training was a constructive exercise in orienting ourselves with nation-building activities, which included providing assistance to the district administration in relief and rescue work in dire times, such as floods, earthquake, cyclones and droughts.

The stopover at the NPA was a much longer one. We shifted to Hyderabad on the seventh of the new year. It was to be our home for the entire year. Our accommodation was clubbed at the Central IPS Mess and each one of us had a well-appointed room, with an attached washroom. When you come straight from your student ecosystem, such additional facilities seem luxurious. The expansive dining hall of the Central IPS Mess exuded an air of grandeur and magnificence. Radiant chandeliers, resplendent in their brilliance, dangled gracefully from the high ceiling, casting a shimmering glow upon the surroundings. Adorned with mementos and trophies, the hall bore witness to a history of remarkable achievements, each displayed with pride. The walls of the dining hall were a canvas of vivid tales, showcasing colossal forts encircled by imposing cannons and dignified officers, their countenance the epitome of gravitas. These officers, whether astride powerful steeds or standing resolute on the battlefield, conveyed a profound sense of duty and honour. In the midst of such splendour and historical reverence, I found myself utterly overwhelmed, my senses enraptured by the sheer awe-inspiring ambience of the place.

Our curriculum consisted of drill sessions, conducted either with or without arms. Lathi, sword and cane were the arms used.

Riot control drill was another prominent activity we trained in. Then came weapons training. We were oriented with all the weapons used by the state police forces. The use of a pistol, revolver, Sten gun, carbine, light machine gun and hand-grenades, including their proper maintenance, was a mandatory test. Horse riding held its distinct grace and charm. The equestrian drills, one must add, created much positivity and self-worth amongst the probationers. Some of us took to horse riding like a fish to water. Stable management became part of the exercise. Mounted Police, as a part of the UP Police, is used extensively for crowd management in events such as the Kumbh Mela and any unlawful assemblies, besides ceremonial occasions. I carried the equestrian skill to different districts of UP as part of my work regimen.

Our instructors for physical training (PT), weapon training and the drill squad were amazing. They truly were a class apart, with each being an expert in their field, and made our experience one great affair. We were split into squads and then each squad would have dedicated trainers for drill, PT, weapons training, field craft, tactics, map reading and equestrian training. The PT exercises make one a complete athlete. With disciplines such as obstacles, apparatus works, through vault, front roll, back roll and many others, one's mind and body become aligned. Strong and aligned.

The head of the academy was G.C. Singhvi, who belonged to the Rajasthan cadre of the IPS. His just and fair demeanour and intellectual capital made all of us realize quickly that we were still a work in progress, uncut diamonds awaiting polish and shine. Singhvi made it a point to visit us at least once every week during our PT to get a first-hand review of our outdoor training progress. After all, we were his babies, and he wanted each one of us to excel. Singhvi's indoor sessions were a class apart. His anecdotes about his field postings in Rajasthan only made all us probationers admire him more. He was fond of quoting professional boxer and activist Muhammad Ali's famous lines: 'I hated every minute of training but said to myself, don't quit, suffer now and live the rest of the life as a champion,' and it became my personal anthem too. As director, Singhvi impressed one and all with his sincerity and integrity.

P.D. Malviya, S. Subramaniam and T. Madiyal were other big names from the forces who guided the batch in the training phase. Malviya, a Madhya Pradesh (MP) cadre IPS officer with a redoubtable reputation, had an impressive personality. He was tall and dapper, with a slender face and intelligent eyes. I don't remember him taking regular classes, but he taught us the basic nuances of administration in general and police administration in particular. Subramaniam was exceedingly warm and friendly. He went on to become the founding director of the Special Protection Group (SPG) in the year to follow. The SPG, we all know, was raised to provide proximate security cover to the prime minister post the assassination of Indira Gandhi. Madiyal, of the Karnataka cadre, was our assistant director (outdoor training). He had fought in the 1965 Indo-Pak War as a commissioned officer. He joined the IPS in 1971 and rose to the rank of DGP Karnataka, from where he hung his boots in 2004. This illustrious officer was a stickler for rules, fastidious about dress code and meticulous with regards to etiquette. 'Don't just look like an officer, behave like one too,' was his golden rule. Madiyal's deft handling of his responsibilities directly impacted on our outdoor training regimen. We had a serving faculty member of the rank of additional district judge to teach us legal subjects, as well as language instructors to teach probationers the basics of the spoken language of the state they were assigned to.

Life as a trainee-probationer was no doubt tough. Ungodly hours. Unrelenting drills. Crazy outdoor activities that would leave us stone dead, and a time schedule that ensured we were sleep deprived. As our bodies and mind bore the weight of exhaustion, a profound weariness settled upon us, rendering the majority of our cohort lethargic during indoor classes. Occasionally our lethargy betrayed us, leading to reprimands, yet the age-old tradition of succumbing to slumber within the classroom persisted, undeterred by occasional interruptions. But we were a work-in-progress, and our mind and body needed to be perfectly aligned. Camaraderie and shenanigans ruled. Despite our position as probationers, this seemed like an extension of our student days, and we behaved as such. The great respect and awe we had for our mentors and trainers definitely stood its ground, but during breaks, banter and humour flew thick and fast. The fabulous sense of humour of my batchmates kept us in splits despite the mental and physical toll. During the breaks in between lectures, one could see a variety of activities taking place: probationers recounting the previous night's experiences, money exchanging hands as short-term loans, jokes being cracked and some of us facing the brunt of those practical jokes. The scenes in the mess had to be seen to be believed. A quick snooze after lunch acquired momentous value. It made up for the deprived sleep and late nights. Weekends found us planning for outings and visits to relatives or friends.

Bharat Darshan, an exercise to get to know our country and its people better, was an integral part of the entire training programme. When our group reached Bombay (now Mumbai), one of the lady officers from Bhutan Police, Kesang Choedan, shared a strange desire. The Royal Government of Bhutan, under a special agreement with the Government of India, deputed selected trainee officers to be trained for Bhutan Police at the NPA. Kesang had nurtured a pen pal since her school days, who was in Bombay in the Worli area. Kesang expressed a desire to meet her. I offered to help, and post a few telephone calls and logistic management, was able to fructify the union of two friends. Kesang was touched by the gesture and thanked me profusely. Although we could not remain connected, I bumped into her at the Delhi airport many years later. I was heading the CISF as DG, then. I promptly invited her over for dinner at my official residence in New Moti Bagh. Kesang sportingly accepted the offer. Without her knowledge I also invited Sudhir, Rina, Ashok Patnaik and Sunil Sinha from our NPA days. The dinner that evening became an impromptu get-together for the batchmates of NPA.

My NPA days, although far removed from the ugly happenings of November 1984, strangely got me close to the scenes. Harjit Sandhu, my friend and batchmate, had his nuptial date fixed for 1 November 1984. Harjit took a week off from the academy to partake in the marriage ceremony. He promised a grand celebration on his return. As fate would have it, Indira Gandhi was assassinated by her own security guards on the fateful day of 31 October, leading to uncontrolled mob reaction on hapless Sikhs in many parts of north India, especially Delhi. Harjit not only had his home in Delhi, but his bride-to-be also belonged to the same city.

Ugly and heartbreaking news about rioting and killings began pouring in from the capital city and other parts of the country as well. There was no news about Harjit. A week turned into two, then three. Neither did Harjit come back nor there was any news about him. We weren't even sure if he was still alive. It was disturbing and troubling. Then, out of nowhere, as we lounged in the Common Room, the pasty but smiling face of my friend appeared as he stood before us in flesh and blood. Shouts of surprise and hugs erupted all around.

Harjit's story was not just a potboiler, it had heart-wrenching trappings. Harjit's marriage day on 1 November was the day when Delhi burnt. The entire *baraat*, comprising six cars, moving from Lawrence Road to Paharganj Gurudwara, got stuck amidst burning vehicles and marauding mobs. Harjit, all decked up, as the groom, sat in the lead vehicle along with his mother and sister. Sensing extreme trouble, Harjit responded with the alacrity of a soldier and directed the driver to break through the mess and speed towards the Paharganj Gurudwara without stopping. His directions and presence of mind helped, but the other five vehicles and their occupants were not so lucky. None of the other five vehicles made it to the gurudwara. In dramatic scenes to follow, the Paharganj Gurudwara was attacked and set aflame by a frenzied mob. Harjit's in-laws managed to whisk away Harjit and his family to the safety of their home. It was a narrow escape from certain death.

For three days, Harjit had to remain cooped before he could take the help of the army officer and the battalion that was given the responsibility of restoring peace and order. Luckily, each family member was located and found over the next few days. They too were given refuge by good people around the area. They all survived with minor cuts and bruises. It was the mental scar that was going to trouble Harjit and his family the most.

I found some friends for life at the academy. Rishi Shukla was one of them. He would rise to become the director of the Central Bureau of Investigation (CBI), post his serving the MP cadre as DGP. Sudhir Pratap, easy-going and fun during the academy days, but totally committed to the social cause in his police career, would go on to hold the rank of DG NSG. Rajiv Rai Bhatnagar and his studious and meticulous ways would take him to the rank of DG Central Reserve Police Force (CRPF). Yash Pal Singhal, the legal eagle, would hold the confidence as chief information commissioner with the Government of Haryana, after serving the state as DGP. Neelmani, the down-to-earth girl with a quiet disposition and analytical mind, would make us proud as DGP Karnataka. Ranjit Pachnanda, the handsome Stephanian, would rise to be DG, Indo-Tibetan Border Police and then serve as chairman of the Haryana Public Service Commission. Radhakrishnan, a recipient of the Queen's Award for Innovation in police training and development, came to be known as an encyclopaedic source of knowledge about the police force. Two of my batchmates, Abraham Mathai and Harjit Sandhu, joined the United Nation's (UN) assignments after doing very well in their police careers in India. Sanjiv Nandan Sahai, Dr Lalit Verma, Dr Prabhat Kumar, Jalaj Srivastav, Alok Kumar, Rajnikant Verma, UP Singh and Chandramouli would later join the Indian Administrative Services (IAS).

Ultimately, the sun did set for the last time at the academy, as we wound up eleven months of togetherness and companionship. It was a strange culmination; despite the toughness of the programme, we had begun to enjoy the dynamics of it. But it was time to move ahead. Our jobs beckoned us, our responsibilities needed doing and, above all, the nation looked up to us for deliverance. The passing-out parade was a proud and poignant moment and we all basked in its glory.

Well, the change was upon each one of us. Despite the horrors of Indira Gandhi's' assassination and the gory Sikh riots, India was looking up under the leadership of Rajiv Gandhi. Our entire batch of IPS officers of 1983 had arrived in all states of the country. I was allotted Moradabad district for my six-month practical police training which I really enjoyed professionally, especially because of my two senior police officers. T.N. Mishra, a 1965 batch IPS officer, was posted there as DIG Range. He impressed me enormously as a man of great equanimity, cultivated manners and scholastic understanding of a wide range of subjects. As a towering personality in the police fraternity, he was clearly a cut above the others, and by today's standard, a class apart. His meetings with the district field officers were very enriching. Once he tasked me with filing a mock first information report (FIR) in a rural police station. It was an exercise to test if the police were fulfilling the responsibilities assigned to them. Before tasking me, T.N. Mishra explained to me all the procedures and formalities. The concerned police station failed to accept the mock FIR. The station officer, on the basis of my report, was placed under suspension. The experience reinforced in me the need for continuous review and checks. I adopted that as part of the work culture.

Mishra had a tough exterior that hid a soft heart. He expected officers to perform professionally and helped them raise the bar and achieve their goals. I was privileged, in my later years, to work with him in SPG and CRPF from where he superannuated as DG. My senior superintendent of police (SSP), S.K. Chandra, was another police officer who taught me the correct way of doing police work. He was an honest and sincere officer who advised me to be with him in his office every morning, observe the handling of the complainants and take note of everything in a register. He would often take me to visit scenes of crime, especially in rural police stations, and insist on going through various registers kept at the police stations. During the period under probation, I would go through crime registers, village crime notebooks, case diaries and other important documents. My SSP's thrust in the skills of supervision over crime investigation as well as prevention were essential for an assistant superintendent of police (ASP) working as a circle officer. Chandra also gave me the independent charge of police lines to have closer supervision over police personnel. Thus, I regularly began attending the parade and interacted with constables and subordinate officers in police messes, playgrounds, offices and welfare centres. I received a great deal of appreciation from my seniors and other fellow officers which strengthened my morale and determination. Moradabad was and continues to be a communally sensitive district and officers stationed there had to be invariably deployed for various duties for maintaining law and order. There were many occasions during festivals when I was camping at places where there were chances of communal disturbances. Eid, Bakra Eid, Moharram, Holi, etc. were always considered as occasions of serious concern and priority. Undertaking a tour of all police stations and sensitive places falling under their jurisdiction well before the start of festivals was a normal drill and police officers posted in Moradabad were expected to perform these duties with perfection. In those difficult times, in Moradabad, as in many other sensitive districts, communal passions often flared and gone unchecked. Learning policing methods to deal with them created a new enthusiasm in me and boosted my energy.

After the practical district training at Moradabad got over, I took charge as ASP at Varanasi, which is the epicentre of Hindu religion. It has been depicted as the abode of Shiva, a city perched on Shiva's trident. Varanasi is considered the world's oldest living city. Its blend of spirituality, culture and history makes it a unique and vibrant city of India. The one-and-a-half years that I spent there as ASP was a great learning experience for me not only in terms of police work but also in terms of the discovery of the city's identity. When I reached Varanasi, certain parts of the city was under curfew because of some communal clashes. Having spent some valuable time in the communally sensitive district of Moradabad, I could see the law-and-order machinery tackling the crisis professionally. B.K. Pandey, a very competent police officer who rose from the ranks, taught me certain crucial aspects of basic policing like managing crime records, supervising the work of the SHO, collecting intelligence through community engagement and so on. Similarly, Ranjan Dwivedi, another outstanding IPS officer posted as SP (City), impressed me greatly with his hard work, integrity and professional acumen. This education proved to be handy when I held charge of the districts as Police Chief later in my career. The circle of Mughalsarai, which was entrusted to me to look after, was so big that almost the entire district of Chandauli was later carved out of Varanasi.

4

Almora

'Whoa! That's fantastic,' my wife exclaimed. I was still in the office that day and had just communicated the news of my transfer to her over the phone.

The hills beckoned me after my stint with the plains of UP. Uttarakhand had still not been carved out of UP. The stress and grind of Aligarh and Prayagraj were behind me. I had served there for a good three years as the city superintendent of police. This was a welcome posting, and I was already looking forward to the change.

I joined in June 1990 and the Kumaon hills and its people welcomed me. The salubrious weather and expansive sights of the Himalayas added to the charm. Almora city and its district were to be my command area. The law-and-order scenario of the hills was dramatically different from that of the plains. Land disputes, traffic disorders and petty cases dominated the crime scene. The approach to policing was laid back and lacked professional drive. Police investigation using scientific intent and tools was non-existent. I was keen to change that.

In the late 1980s, a fervent call for a separate homeland, the state of Uttarakhand, echoed among nearly 5 million people residing in the eight hilly districts.[5] The year 1987 witnessed a remarkable response to the demonstrations organized by the

Uttarakhand Kranti Dal (UKD), serving as a clear reflection of the prevailing sentiment. Over a thousand individuals, including women—a substantial gathering by local standards—converged in the district town of Pithoragarh, alongside the neighbouring district of Almora, to lend their voices to the UKD rally, passionately demanding the formation of the Uttarakhand state. Previous rallies held in Pauri Garhwal and Dehradun and advocating the same cause had garnered thousands of fervent UKD supporters. The agitation stemmed from the sluggish pace of development in the hill districts, with the exception of the tourist destinations of Nainital and Dehradun, leaving the remaining districts of the hills in a state of utter neglect. As per the words of Jaswant Singh Bisht, a Member of the Legislative Assembly (MLA) from Ranikhet, with whom I crossed paths on several occasions during my tenure in Almora: 'The development in Nainital and Dehradun was a façade to hide the ugly truth.'

Almost five months prior to my joining Almora, on 14 January, a house theft had been reported. The house in question was a colonial cottage set amongst the higher ridges of Binsar, about 40 km from Almora. Binsar is an ecologically protected area, with its flora and fauna attracting visitors from far and wide. The Victorian cottage in question had an idyllic setting with envious views of the mountain range. There was no motorable road to the cottage, and one had to trek for 3 km to reach it. Dense pine woods lined the area.

The owners of the cottage had been away in Delhi and coincidentally, the security guard, Basant Ram, had to take an undeclared leave as his ailing son who was living in the nearby village needed immediate attention. The theft occurred under these circumstances on the intervening night of 14 and 15 January. The break-in was reported by one of the house helps, Jagat Singh, who informed the owners in Delhi, who then reported the matter to the police.

The crime scene was promptly visited by the local police officer along with the field unit team and a thorough inspection was made. Preliminary investigation revealed that the break-in happened via the kitchen door at the back of the cottage. Adjoining the kitchen was a big hall from where an old model tape recorder which was kept on the dressing table was reported stolen. Another tape recorder, kept at the fireplace rack on the hall's western side, was also reported missing. A sum of approximately Rs 200 was reportedly stolen from the drawer of a small wooden table kept in the hall. The kitchen presented a messy sight. A wooden almirah meant for stacking raw materials in the kitchen had been rummaged. Eggs and packets of butter were missing. A few plastic containers kept in the almirah filled with pulses, edible snacks, biscuits, etc. were found scattered all over the kitchen floor. The act seemed to be a deliberate move by the criminal(s). To add to the deception, the criminal had sprinkled kerosene and mustard oil on the floor. In room after room, none of the expensive items had been touched or tampered with. Warm clothing, trunks, suitcases, carpets, binoculars—absolutely nothing had been stolen. Even a Double Barrel Breech Loading (DBBL) gun was left untouched.

The selection of the kitchen to effect entry indicated intimate knowledge of the cottage and the surroundings. Some fingerprints were found on the outer surface of the abandoned empty plastic containers in one corner of the kitchen room. They were carefully lifted by the investigating officer with the help of a crime kit box. A thermos flask kept on the kitchen table and an envelope inside the drawer of the table also had visible fingerprints on them which were also lifted. Besides these fingerprints, there was absolutely nothing to suggest the identity of the criminal(s). However, it seemed apparent that the criminal(s) was a petty one and not at all interested in expensive articles. All the trappings of the crime suggested it was an insider job, that the person had complete knowledge of the house and the environment.

The fingerprints were dispatched to a lab in Lucknow for forensic analysis. The results took a couple of months to arrive then, and the investigation came to a halt. One crucial piece of information I have not revealed to you yet is the identity of the cottage owners. The cottage belonged to MP Arun Singh. Till a few weeks prior to the burglary, Singh had been the Union minister of state for defence, but he had to resign from his position after the Bofors case surfaced. The procurement of Bofors, the Swedish artillery guns procured by the army, had come under scrutiny. It was against this backdrop that I entered the scene, and the case file was brought before me.

'Sir, both Jagat and Basant have been questioned twice and their antecedents vetted. They seem clean,' the investigating officer reiterated.

'Hmm. What about the neighbourhood?' I wished to know.

'That's the thing, Sir. There's nothing around the house for miles, except for a lone cottage belonging to a retired couple, the Duttas, and their environmentalist daughter. Nothing else.'

'What about their staff?'

'Yes, they have one. Their domestic help, Teeka Singh. He too has been questioned. He has vehemently denied any association with the crime, let alone committing it. In fact, the Duttas raised objections against the questioning. It was only when I assured them that it was a routine investigation that they relented—'

'But still, the crime was committed,' I interrupted and added, only to accentuate my point.

'There are at least two hands, two eyes and a mind behind it. You know what? The environmental chronology talks about the geometry of crime. Don't be surprised about the inference. My mind had raced away to the criminology lectures of my training days. The understanding of this science and its principles can be a great benefit for us.'

'What does it say, Sir?' I had the officer's attention.

'Crimes occur not in the immediate vicinity of a culprit but in slightly faraway areas. In its immediate vicinity, the criminal runs the risk of being recognized and apprehended. A diametrically different psyche rules the twisted mind when it comes to slightly faraway areas. The confidence grows.'

'Got your point, Sir.'

'So, when you say you've ruled out Jagat and Basant, you're more likely to be right. We still need to investigate further. Good old sleuthing helps. Plus don't forget that this is a high-profile case. There's a rumour floating about some mystery Bofors documents the criminals were after.'

'Sir, there's another, that the Duttas have conspired to harass the Singh family. The Duttas want Singhs out from that land.'

'Let's try for more evidence,' I concluded.

As if in solidarity, fresh information came faster than expected. Singh called to inform me that Dutta's domestic help, Teeka, had shared some expensive biscuits with Jagat. 'There's no way he could have purchased them locally. In fact, I'm sure the said brands of biscuits would be not available here. And I have a growing uneasiness that he shared the same biscuits that were stored in the kitchen.'

This was huge. Teeka was questioned again. There was no change in his stance. He denied any involvement. For the biscuits, he mentioned a shop from where they had been bought. The shopkeeper, on his part, refused to have ever stocked the biscuits or sold any to Teeka. The needle of suspicion turned a full circle. Teeka was immediately put under surveillance and his fingerprints were taken. The Duttas were furious, but the investigation was on course. The waiting game for the forensic report began again.

Meanwhile, the press had gone berserk. *India Today* reported that 'the mud-and-wood cottage perched high on a hill in Binsar in remote Almora was hardly a tempting target for burglars. . . . What added to the intrigue was the occupant of the cottage – Arun Singh, former Minister of State for Defence who resigned over the controversial Bofors issue. . . . That Singh was suspected to possess confidential papers immediately raised suspicion of the involvement of intelligence sleuths'.[6]

The results of the forensic science expert were on the expected lines. The fingerprints found on the empty plastic containers at the scene of the crime matched those of Teeka. He was immediately arrested and interrogated. Though completely dazed, he maintained his stance, denying any involvement in the crime. However, on the basis of the fingerprint report, he was sent to jail after being produced before the judicial magistrate. The arrest of the criminal involved in Singh's house-breaking incident was extensively reported in all local dailies and the efforts of the local police to nab the culprit was widely appreciated by all as a fine work of investigative skill.

The coverage by the media, however, proved advantageous to the police in another way. On reading the news item, a local shopkeeper came to the police station and informed us that the arrested person had come to him sometime in January and had mortgaged a tape recorder to him saying that he needed money because of his daughter's illness. Believing his words, the shopkeeper loaned him an amount of Rs 450. However, he had never turned up again and the tape recorder was still with him. Subsequently, the shopkeeper handed over the tape recorder to the police. It was the same one stolen from Singh's cottage. The recovery of the stolen property confirmed beyond doubt the involvement of Teeka, who at once admitted his guilt and promised the investigating officer that he would return the other tape recorder if taken out from jail. He did the same thing before the chief judicial magistrate when produced in connection with a police remand moved by the investigating officer. Remanded in police custody, the accused led the police team for the recovery of another stolen tape recorder which he had sold to a local shop at a price of Rs 150 with the same plea.

'Yes, Officer, that's our tape recorder, a gift from a dear friend. This seems in good order. I have no words . . .' Singh had driven to my office to identify the recovered tape recorder.

'You don't have to feel obliged. This is our job,' I assured Singh.

'I'm really impressed, and I'm here as an ordinary citizen, not as an MP. Your persistent investigation has saved me much embarrassment. The press has hounded me in recent weeks.' Singh was honest and direct.

For myself, I was gloating because the good old investigative effort had us on the winning side.

We shook hands.

In a letter dated 10 December 1990, addressed to the SP, Singh wrote the following:

I would like to place on record my sincere thanks and appreciation for the very fine work done by the Almora police authorities in solving the robbery at my residence in Binsar.

The combination of sound forensic work and a solid investigative approach has led to the recovery of the stolen goods and the identification of a suspect. As a citizen, I am most impressed by the handling of this case.

My posting in Almora lasted exactly thirteen months. 1 July 1991 saw me bidding farewell to the hills.

5

The Siege of Kheri

I was far removed from sleep. The radium dial of my wristwatch showed twenty minutes past midnight. It was an ungodly hour and even the shrill of the crickets had subsided. The wooing game of the males had been halted or possibly culminated. But our game of hide-and-seek was still on. It was the second night of waiting.

We were in the middle of a field operation, hidden in anticipation of some wanted terrorists showing up. I was leading the charge. The turf was new to me. It was the Terai region, and I was merely a week old in my new responsibility as district police chief. I was chief of a region that had recently acquired a new claim to fame. Khalistani terrorism had raised its deadly head. This time in the Terai belt.

'Sir, chai,' said R.K. Chaturvedi, Deputy SP. He had been handpicked by me for the crack team for he had evoked that confidence in me. Chaturvedi had served the region for a good amount of time in his career. A budding young officer of the State Police Services, Chaturvedi's knowledge of the geography, as well as the nuances of the Terai demography were a major asset.

'*Bass*, no more. Enough for the day. Only a militant's head will satiate me now,' I quipped. My eyes continued to strain at the night scene. The near-180-degree canvas, an expanse of paddy fields interspersed with a handful of *machan*s was absolutely still not only that night but the night before as well. An informant, a Sikh himself, had appeared from nowhere in the very first week of my joining as the district police chief. 'Militant activity expected in Palia' was the crisp message of the man. The place was almost 70 km from the district headquarters. Apparently, the informer's family was threatened—the militants were eyeing his daughter. It was a tricky situation; this was information which could have been easily ignored or brushed away. But the man was risking his life in the face of honour for his family. I had let instinct dominate and immediately initiated a crack team of six. The distance was covered in no time, and we had laid siege around the man's *jhala*[7]. Eight hours of back-breaking vigil and the team drew a blank. No one turned up at the jhala and the waiting game simply got prolonged. Our spirits were down but the informer was hopeful, and he insisted on his knowledge of another militant movement scheduled for the following night.

'We have no reason to distrust him. He seems to be telling the truth,' Chaturvedi backed the man. The action had shifted about 19 km further towards the Nepalese border. This was where we were holed up that night. Four of us were atop the open terrace of the only jhala, covering the area in a complete 360-degree swoop. The remaining two had been positioned 200 m away across the cobbled pathway, in the tractor shed of the neighbouring farm. Waiting is a tricky game; it is also an art. My thoughts fled to the sessions on surveillance at the NPA. 'Think of yourself as a tigress on the hunt. Please remember, your stealth, your alertness and your ability to stay unheard and hidden will determine your next move. You mess up any of these and your game goes for a toss. The game belongs to the man of patience.' That was seven years behind me, yet it seemed ingrained in my conscience.

The radium hands were now in a near-straight line, 12.30 a.m. A gift from my mother. I had travelled home to be with her and changed into my uniform before I had de-trained.

My mother had indulgently felt the silver twin stars on my shoulders. I could see the pride in her eyes. I held her in a warm embrace for a long time. Time had stopped.

Time seemed to have stopped here too, moving interminably slow. By 1 a.m., I became grimly aware of my stiff legs. A soft 'hey' and I had R.K.'s attention. I signalled to him that I was going to take a break. I needed to stretch my legs. We were positioned against the balustrades of the terrace, on wooden beds, face down, our guns rested on the top brick layer of the balustrade and the beds raised a few fractions above the brick wall to give us a clear view of the fields. Nothing had moved in the last four hours, but for a few twig alarms of a jackal on his night prowl. About 500 m on the north beyond the farms stood the deciduous woods that extended right up to the Nepal border. I rolled over from my flat position, and in a quick shift rested my feet on the ground, stooped low and took the stairs. I descended on to the inner courtyard of the jhala. The family of the informer had retired for the night. The jhala was absolutely still. A solitary oil lamp had been deliberately left lit. My mind raced to the day I got the posting of the Terai region.

A week back

It was the summer of 1992 and post my arrival from the deputation to SPG, Government of India, I was officer-in-waiting. The protocol required that I report to my boss, the DGP UP Police. As a lower-rung officer in the command-chain, I was nervous, but I braved the moment and the travel to meet my commander, Prakash Singh, in Lucknow. At the academy, all of us probationers had been in awe of Singh and his exploits. It was an honour to present before him in the colours of khaki.

Prakash Singh's reputation preceded him. He was an epitome of integrity, courage and decision-making. A broad smile and warm handshake greeted me when I met him, and I felt calmer. My father's wise counsel to my elder brother, many years ago, rang in my ear: 'Son, when you meet iconic seniors early in your career, make the most of the blessing.' I had barely settled in the chair when Singh came straight to the point: 'We have decided to post you as SP of a Terai district, either Lakhimpur Kheri or Pilibhit.' I sat unmoved in expression, but deep inside a little unsettled at the enormity of the assignment. Any district of the Terai region was no child's play. A low-lying area in the northern part of UP, the Terai is to the south of the outer foothills of the Himalayas, Shivalik. It lies above the Indo-Gangetic Plains, and is characterized by tall grasslands, Sal woods, Savannah shrubs and clay-rich swamps. The Terai region also extends into Nepal and covers its southern part. Lakhimpur Kheri is but a small part of the region; Rampur, Bareilly, Pilibhit, Shahjahanpur, Bijnor and Nainital, all make up the Terai. Apart for its geographical reach, the entire region was then living under the grim shadow of Sikh terrorism that emanated from Punjab.

My field postings in the first seven years as a police officer had decent coverage and included districts of Moradabad, Aligarh, Prayagraj and Almora. But every district of the Terai region was a different ball game. 'Trust me, a good stint in this region will propel your reputation and career.' The DGP seemed to have sensed my dilemma. A handshake, a salute and the meeting was concluded.

I came out of the office, burdened in the face of raised expectations. Though I had been away from UP on account of my deputation with SPG, I sensed how the political climate was turning out. Considerable communal violence and polarization had occurred in the late 1980s. The Bharatiya Janata Party (BJP) made large gains in the parliamentary and legislative elections that followed in 1991 and was able to form a government in UP, with Kalyan Singh becoming the chief minister (CM) for the first time in June 1991. As CM, Singh attempted to run an efficient administration. A tough administrator, he ran a statewide campaign to curb mass copying in educational institutions which was rampant in UP. Besides, his focus on law and order, especially the anti-mafia drive, created an excellent image of state government. It elated me to hear from others that the CM and the DGP were on the same page in choosing officers to run the districts. A free hand to run and operate a district is a blessing in UP.

'The UP cadre is a baptism by fire,' I had been warned at the start of my career. My job was cut out for me. Still, challenges are tough till the time they are met. I dispensed my hesitation and proceeded to take charge of the Lakhimpur Kheri district. I knew that counterterrorism was going to be a new addition to my resume. Here, I realized how the multifarious training modules and diversities of All India Services came to your help when needed. The anti-terrorism policing required different strategies based on intelligence inputs from central agencies and the sources created, nurtured and sustained by you. My previous posting as SP of SPG was going to come handy because in VVIP security duties, I interacted with various agencies, state governments and different police organizations. That experience, I was confident, would give me an edge. I landed in Kheri with a fresh sense of accomplishment, forgetting that I was just nine years old in the service.

We draw a blank

The squeeze on my shoulder broke my stupor. It was Chaturvedi. He pointed left and said: '10 o'clock.' I instantly followed the pointer of his hand. The rustle in the sugar cane field was distinct. There was a steady build-up that clearly sounded like the movement of feet, and it was coming straight towards the jhala.

Dawn had broken. Would we be rewarded with the sight of the terrorists? It was nearly five by the watch. I wondered if the two men at the tractor shed also had their eyes on the same scene. There was a sudden shift and the noise decibel rose quite a few points. The feet were on the run. *Why?*

A loud squeak broke out in the stillness of that morning as a wild foal appeared right at the edge of the sugar cane field where it met the dirt road. On its heel were two jackals. The finishing pounce was deadly and precise. The yell was muted. The still catch fully secure in the jaws of death soon disappeared inside the tall growth. I shook my head. The anxiety was released.

'We give this another sixty minutes, then we move.' Chaturvedi nodded.

It was a disappointing start to our campaign. There was no show of any terrorist movement. We drove away from the Nepal border and proceeded straight to the headquarters, about 120 km away. There was desk work that needed immediate attention.

The right perspective

Sikh terrorist activities hit the Terai region around the 1980s. Operation Blue Star of 1984 proved to be a catalyst for terrorism to grow in momentous proportions. The malaise had infested the entire Terai region and frequent encounters between the police and terrorists began to be reported. The alarming aspect of the situation was that it was mostly the men in khaki who were at the receiving end of the terrorist's gun. In encounter after encounter, the number of policemen killed in action was far more in comparison to that of terrorists. The police force was a demoralized lot and there was a sense of insecurity and fear amongst the populace. The huge jhalas, a common sight in the Terai belt, had become shelter homes for terrorists. The situation in Lakhimpur Kheri was no different. The previous year had been distressing for the district, with killings and robbery by the militants becoming a norm. The morale of the police was so down that they were reluctant to patrol the area with their blue beacon lights. The year had reported thirty-two lives lost to unmindful killings in the areas of Gola, Mailani, Palia Kalan, Sampurna Nagar and Phool Behar.

My research of the region prior to joining had been thorough. The beautiful Terai area at the foothills of Garhwal and Kumaon was bleeding. The populace was in fear and the administration was on tenterhooks. Something had to be done and done fast. The area was getting branded as 'mini-Punjab', the negative connotation distinct. The militants literally had a free run, as they would escape to the shelter of the forests or the jhalas post their crime. The porous Indo-Nepal border further accentuated the scenario.

The Terai region had seen a revolution of sorts after Independence. Prior to 1947, the region was inhabited by tribal settlers (mostly Tharus) and the hill people of UP.[8] Tharus is an indigenous tribe of Lakhimpur Kheri. Legend goes that they came to the region as escorts and servants of Rajput ladies, who fled Rajasthan in the wake of Muslim invasion in the fourteenth century. Tharu women dominate the clan and are extremely independent and hard-working, unlike the men in the community.

The influx of Sikh and Punjabi peasants after Partition was welcomed, and the tough and industrious farmers transformed the jungle into cultivable land. The economy of the region transformed into a thriving and prosperous one. Terai soon became one of the highest paddy and sugar cane-producing areas in the country.

Post-Independence, the chain of subsequent Punjabi migrants continued. Bengali refugees from East Pakistan (now Bangladesh) added to the influx. This was followed by more batches of Bengali refugees during 1963–64, and again in 1971. Ex-servicemen, agricultural graduates, political refugees, freedom fighters and repatriates from Burma (now Myanmar) added to the demographic melting pot. In subsequent years, the demand for land increased and the man–land ratio, which was favourable earlier, was threatened. The result was that the same Sikh and Punjabi farmer who was well received earlier became a reason for social jealousy and tension. The original inhabitants of the area felt threatened by the economic prosperity and land holdings of the new settlers.[9] The economic prosperity of the Punjabi migrants stood out with their spacious farmhouses.

Terrorism found a greater foothold in the Terai region when the Khalistan movement began its armed campaign against the Government of India in the early 1980s. Operation Blue Star altered the pattern of terrorist activity in the region. Prior to it, terrorism activity was confined to bank robbery and arms snatching. The massacre of Sikh pilgrims in the Terai further aggravated the situation. The incident took place on 12 July 1991. A group of Sikh pilgrims from Gurdaspur in Punjab was returning by bus after visiting Nanakmatta, Patna Sahib, Huzur Sahib and other holy places. The police intercepted the bus near a bridge at Kachla Ghat in Pilibhit at around 11 a.m. Eleven Sikhs were forced to step down from the bus. Later, they were killed in an alleged staged encounter. (The Hon'ble High Court of Allahabad convicted in 2022).[10]

The 1990s saw the emergence of at least three major terrorist groups which became active in Terai. The first group was the Bhindranwale Tiger Force of Khalistan, which was led by Satnam Singh Cheena. Then there were the Bhindranwale Saffron Tigers of Khalistan led by Swaran Singh Jawanda and Khalistan Commando Force (KCF)-Panjwar, which was headed by Mehtab Singh at the local level. Besides these, there were quite a few splinter groups active in many parts of the region.

While some groups were clearly defined by a code of conduct for their members, there were others who had thrown norms and limits to the winds. KCF-Panjwad was very active in the main areas of Kheri: Gola, Mailani, Bheera and Tikonia along with Chandan Chowki.

Having done my homework, I drew a three-pronged strategy to deal with the prevalent situation. The primary objective was, of course, to wipe out militancy. I simultaneously aimed to not only restore the morale of the police force but to take it to a constant high. Instilling a sense of security amongst the 3-lakh populace of Lakhimpur Kheri was a natural expectation from the police chief's job profile.

The date of 2 July 1992 brought me to the district of Lakhimpur Kheri. I combined my joining with a hurriedly called staff meeting. I advised my personnel to open communication channels with the public and never lose an opportunity to meet a cross-section of society. People's trust had to be regained and a direct outreach plan had to be readied. 'Effective communication and undiluted transparency have been a constant in my career graph, and I have used them as an evergreen companion,' I told my officers in our first meeting.

It was against this backdrop that the recent informer had appeared from nowhere and the current operation was quickly put together. It was almost three in the afternoon by the time I was rounding up the last of my paperwork post that failed operation. I was bone tired and desperate for a break. Mobile phones had not yet broken into the scene, so the switchboard officer reported a call—it was the same informant.

'Sir, he wants to talk to you directly. Says it's urgent.'

'Put him through,' I responded instantly.

'Sir, *pakki khabar hain* [We have accurate information].' There are four of them, and they have been sighted in the jungles near Motia Ghat. This is the time to strike, Sir.'

I looked up to find the expectant face of Chaturvedi, who had been drawn by the buzz around the call. We were on the road in the next fifteen minutes. The variation was that this time the crack team comprised fifteen personnel and the tactical intent was to undertake a combing operation of the jungles.

A mega surprise!

I directed the entire team to spread out in a near straight-line formation and comb the area. Except for the two at the furthest ends, every individual was in the line of sight of the persons on either side. In a purposeful and quiet manner, our party entered the forest area from the southern end of Motia Ghat. By the time the operation began, the day was fast losing light. The operation took place very close to the Nepal border and there was always the chance of the terrorists sneaking to the other side of the porous front. There was no time to lose. We had a job to complete.

It was a measured walk. Measured and stealth-like. The oft-repeated phrase—trying to find a needle in a haystack, held true, but differently for us. We had to find a handful of men hiding in the thick of the deciduous forest and, to top it off, in the dead of the night. Our progress was slow but thorough. We pressed on, one step at a time. Vigilant was the word. The walkie-talkie would crackle every thirty minutes to touch base with the control room. It was a one-way connection; they had been specifically forbidden to reach out to us. We had to do away with all the unwanted noise. The forest has its own sounds and anything alien would have alerted the probable terrorists. We continued to move forward through the night. The team was equipped to handle and survive the terrain. It was around 3 a.m., with a new day knocking at the door, when we suddenly spotted some suspicious movement. The alarm calls of animals rose in the air. Everyone froze in their position.

One of our personnel was spotted by the suspicious men, and they opened fire. There were four of them and armed to the teeth.

The gun battle that ensued was ruthless from both sides. We had to keep up the pressure and not let anyone of them slip away in the dark. The suspected terrorists were outnumbered but relentless in their return fire. It was around 3.30 a.m. when the guns went silent. The bodies of four terrorists were recovered, and one of them, much to our disbelief, was Sukhwinder Singh, alias Pola.[11]

Sukhwinder Singh alias Pola led the Azad Babbar Khalsa. Pola had broken away from the terrorist group Babbar Khalsa International (BKI). He hailed from the Sangrur district of Punjab and frequented the Terai region to purchase weapon. The police records pointed towards nineteen cases against him in Punjab, with more than half a dozen registered against his name in Kheri district.[12] The standard operating procedure required us to run through a verification process and the team immediately contacted its counterpart in Punjab. The response came fast. The man who had a Rs 40,000 reward on his head had been brought down along with three of his accomplices. His bullet-riddled body was sent to the morgue.

I dialled the DGP's number.

Ganga-Jamuna to Katrua

The operation (code-named Ganga-Jamuna) turned out to be the biggest achievement of the Kheri police. Two AK-56 assault rifles, two .30 Springfield rifles, one SLR, one .315 bore rifle, one revolver, dozens of cartridges and Rs 32,000 in cash were recovered.[13] As the news rolled out, a big media contingent swarmed the district headquarters, and the Kheri police was all over the print and media. To cap it, CM Kalyan Singh announced a cash reward of Rs 15,000 for the police party involved in the operation.[14] All of this became a shot in the arm for the Kheri police specifically and the UP Police in general. It was a major morale booster, more so because the state had lost many precious lives, both citizens and police personnel, to mindless killings.

Post the success of Operation Ganga-Jamuna, in a staff meeting, I stressed the need to neither lower the guard nor let go of control of the situation. My colleagues, in unison, agreed to keep the morale of the police force high and not let it fizzle out. Because of our sustained policing, we were able to reign in the situation in Lakhimpur Kheri. During the same period, other districts of Terai too saw a dramatic surge in militant activities and confrontations with police. In Kheri, the district police had upped the antennae and were reaping rich dividends. The recitation of *Akhand Paath* was restored in the Gola Gurudwara. There seemed complete trust within the communities, indeed the Sikh community at large. It was the end of July 1992, less than a month since I joined. Ecstasy, they all say, is invariably short-lived. It was no different for us. As a major blow to peace in the area, a gory massacre took place. Although the incident happened in the neighbouring district of Pilibhit, its intensity was such that it shook the entire Terai.

Katrua is a wild vegetable found in the jungles of Terai. July–August is the period when this vegetable is ripe and ready to be plucked. It is quite popular amongst the local populace. Katrua grows on river banks and villagers venture to such places to harvest it. That year, the banks of the Khannaut River in the adjoining district of Pilibhit witnessed a harvest of a different kind. A total of twenty-nine people had entered the forest area to gather katrua. Death awaited them. All twenty-nine of them were herded and killed mercilessly right there on the riverbank. After many hours, when not even a single person had returned, the anxious villagers informed the police station. In an operation of a different kind, the search party comprising villagers and the police stumbled upon twenty-nine lives snuffed out brutally in cold blood. Terror won that day. Its ripples were felt across the state and in the adjoining areas. It was a sad day for humanity.[15]

None of the terror groups claimed responsibility for the heinous crime. It appeared as if the terrorists wanted to make the Pilibhit region their stronghold. The terrorists had deliberately targeted the villagers settled on the periphery of the forest. They wanted to send the villagers the message not to act as informers for the police.

To make matters worse, another major incident unfolded in Lucknow. Four terrorists escaped from the Lucknow Jail. To rub salt into the wound, the daring incident happened while the UP DGP Prakash Singh was on a visit to Pilibhit on the heels of the massacre, and its objective was a debrief of all the police actions taken to apprehend the terrorists. It was a major embarrassment for the UP Police. One of the escapee terrorists was Sukhvinder Singh and he was a resident of Lakhimpur Kheri. An inside job? Complicity? Questions were thick in the air. After all, how could four dreaded terrorists ease through three security gates and then scale, not one but two 18-feet walls undetected? The officiating jailer and two guards were later arrested and booked under Terrorist and Disruptive Activities (Prevention) Act, commonly known as TADA, for conspiring with the convicts.[16]

I make it to the hit list

It was a worst-case scenario for me and my district. Post my return from the meeting with the DGP, news filtered in about a hijacking of a truck by terrorists. One Lakhvir Singh's truck was forcibly taken away from his house in a village near the Sundarbal outpost. The terrorists, however, panicked when they reached the Sundarbal police outpost. They noticed a contingent of Police Armed Constabulary (PAC) personnel at the post and mistook the sight as the police being alerted to their movements. Their suspicious and abrupt behaviour was challenged by the PAC personnel posted at the outpost. In the gun battle that ensued, the terrorists abandoned the truck and made good their escape under the cover of darkness. It was a serious incident and I rushed to the spot with a contingent. Luckily, no one was injured. The truck was recovered. The descriptions matched that of the escapees from Lucknow Jail. They had intended to use the truck as their vehicle to freedom. Chaturvedi and I were on top of the target list of terrorists. Less than three months into my new position and I was getting more attention than I deserved! For me, it was nothing more than an extravagant extension of my job. It was an assurance that I was on the right track. My security cover was increased.

In the days that followed, sporadic news about the movement of the terrorists floated in the air. Amidst the terror conundrum, another incident took place, this time at a place near Bazpur, in Nainital district. A home guard was shot in the leg by three terrorists. This was followed by an even more alarming happening, a remote detonation of a police Gypsy. Four police personnel, including the deputy superintendent of police (DSP), were martyred in the attack. The detonation blast resulted in a pit being created that was a near-square and measured around 7 feet. A battery and a 100-m-long wire found at the site confirmed the fear that the terrorists had undertaken to scale up their operations with altered means. It wasn't good news. It was a clear indication that the terror groups were emboldened and wanted to strike at the root of the police morale.

Analytics and combing success

In October 1992, roughly ninety days into my role as district police chief, I decided to further up the ante. While maintaining public outreach to strike a proper balance between a crackdown on terrorism on one hand and diplomacy on the other, I initiated combing operations.

For the first time, we began to collate the data by analysing the frequent crossfires between the police forces and terrorists.

Skirmishes in Palia Kalan, Bareilly Farm, Mansuri Farm, Gola, Bichaila, Patihan, Dhaka and Anjikas became data points to decipher the trends, moods and the terror psychology at play. The idea was to pre-empt the attacks and get deeper psychological inferences of the terrorist mind. The water in the Sharda River was receding and the sugar cane plantations had grown tall, thick and dense. There was heightened concern about a rise in the terror activities.

In a counter-offensive strategy, I, along with my police team, launched combing operations by foot in and around the forest areas of Dudhwa National Park. The pride of the area and a major tourist attraction centre lay desolate and deserted. It was a morose sight. The game reserve where wildlife enthusiasts should have been, was teeming with police personnel and terrorists. But I kept my faith alive, and my faith reminded me of the silver lining that every thick cloud cover possessed. Our sustained efforts finally bore fruit and the police team caught Sardar Singh (name changed) during its combing operation. Singh had links with the Dheera Gang members. He was a big catch, and he sang like a canary during his interrogation. Apparently, he had links with Jammu and Kashmir terror groups, from whom he tried to procure weapons.

The Kheri police community outreach efforts were beginning to yield desired results. It was coming to the fore that the majority of the population wanted an end to the volatile environment. A cry for peace was a compelling desire. The favourable outcome further strengthened the police resolve, as the credibility of the police, which was on the wane earlier, began to rise. The populace was positive and expressed their gratitude, big and small. More importantly, information about the terrorists, again big or small, began to be shared with the police department. The community was specifically happy that none of the local Sikhs had been harassed under the garb of procuring information.

A perfect example of the new-found faith between the citizens and the police department was highlighted when a railway employee stationed at the Gauri Fanta railway crossing was beaten up by terrorists. The earlier norm of suppression of information, even non-cooperation, was binned, and the incident was promptly reported. Social policing is and can become a major tool for denting and deterring crime. I have always believed in an alert and active public and always advocated its importance right through my police career. Similarly, a friendly and tactful approach by the police with the public does wonders for harmony and crime. Affection theory is a two-way street, and our officers were committed to maintaining the status quo. Social tranquility is the best answer to either communal or terrorist disorder.

The month of October brought forth more reasons to be elated when the police nabbed another terrorist, Hazara Singh, from the Sampurna Nagar area of the district. A cache of arms was also recovered from his possession. The success story continued, and our police also arrested Gurnam Singh and Lakhvir Singh, a dreaded terrorist duo, from areas bordering Nepal.

The landscape of the region had transformed due to the rains. The Sharda river was a poor sister in comparison to its more robust monsoon form. The cane in the farmlands stood proud and tall. It was the last quarter of 1992 and heightened terror activities were speculated, but our countermeasures had sent a strong message to the terror groups. Based on information gathered from captured criminals, the terror gangs were on the lookout for new sources of arms and ammunition. Their stocks were depleted, and they were stressed for replenishment. The terror activities in the last quarter declined dramatically, although a few stray incidents continued to happen. And like in the recent past, each incident was reported by the populace. It was a great victory for consistency and transparency. It was music to the ears, but there was still much to be done and achieved.

* * *

In a major tactical move, the police of Kheri also stepped up patrolling at the Nepal border. We had received reports of terrorists taking advantage of the porous border. This has increased since their safe havens were ambushed by police mass reach. A disturbing news of a sergeant serving the Nepal Army and supplying bullets clandestinely to the terror gangs came to light. The police laid a net and lured Sohan Singh (name changed) to it. He turned out to be an important link in ammunition smuggling from across the borders. Sohan was a carrier, and he would procure bullets from one Dr Mehar Dixit (name changed) in Nepal. Dixit was a major conduit for the same sergeant of the Royal Army of Nepal. It was one convenient nexus. Dixit would get the bullets for Rs 20 per piece and would pass it on to Sohan for Rs 100 per piece. Sohan revealed he had channelized more than 5000 bullets from the same source to terror groups. This confirmed the fact that the Nepal connection was being used by terror groups not just for the to-and-fro movement but also to procure arms and ammunition directly or through conduits.

Soon a prominent member of the Dheera Gang became the Kheri police's next prize catch.[17] This member had acquired another identity and was living with his relative. In the operation that followed, the area was cordoned off and the house was searched. He was sitting ducks. It was a huge victory, and along with him, a stockpile of illegal weapons was also discovered: three AK-47 assault rifles, one SLR, one carbine and one revolver. The catch was immense, and it hit the gang where it hurts the most.

The arrest of this prominent gang member had a domino effect on the fate of the Dheera Gang. The air was thick with the news that the gang members were on the run and were desperate for a safe haven. The sugar cane farms along the Nepal border were believed to be their shelter homes. Similar was the fate of another militant, Kashmir Singh (name changed), who was holed up in the Patheda jungle. The Kheri police maintained the heat. Lack of arms and falling morale had the terrorist on the defensive. Not even a single case of loot or robbery was reported during the remaining last quarter of 1992. It was just the right moment to turn the tap dry.

Quiet returns, but just . . .

The year 1993 saw a dramatic turn in the fortunes of terrorists. It was a golden period in the war against terror. The siege of Lakhimpur Kheri by the terrorists had been breached, the terror agents were decimated, and the entire Terai region felt its impact. Right up to May 1993, the terror activities fell near silent. A few sporadic incidents did occur, but the changed scenario was a clear indication of the successful campaign that the Kheri police had run.

As terror activities were on the wane, we directed the energy of district police towards a more fine-tuned public grievance redressal system. It was found that complainants usually never received any information about the outcomes of the inquiries conducted by the field officers. On many occasions, enquiries were completed without any visit to the scene and reports were formalized based on general information available. The reports were then forwarded to the seniors. As a result there were countless complaints, leaving the general public with uncertainty about whether enquiries were genuinely and diligently pursued.

To fill the gap and to establish a better system of complaint redressal, I started to dispatch postcards to the complainants to inform them about the results of the enquiries conducted by the police. The system was started in October 1992 on a small scale. Based on positive feedback, the scope of the operations was gradually enlarged. The procedure adopted was simple and it was expected to instil a sense of credibility in the public about the Kheri police. I directed that on receipt of a complaint, it was sent to either the circle officer or the station officer for inquiry. The enquiring officer was further directed to complete the inquiry within a reasonable stipulated time. Furthermore, the enquiring officer had to ensure this report carries the statement of the complainant. This was to ensure the complainant was approached by the enquiring officer. It was also mentioned on the application of the complainant that he/she would be called by the SP after the inquiry report was received. Post the submission of the report, a postcard was sent to the postal address of the complainant informing them about the inquiry. The postcard mentioned that if the complainant didn't agree with the findings, they could approach the office of the SP in person. On the agreed date, the enquiring officer would also be present. In the discussion that ensued, any dereliction of duty by the enquiring officer resulted in instant action against the erring officer. A new inquiry officer would then be assigned to the case for fresh action. This small yet innovative system was well received by people from all walks of life, including those who resided in far-flung areas of the Kheri region. The media carried news after news lauding the efforts to reach out to people through the innovative idea.

The Police Chief of Kheri has initiated a noteworthy and favourable tradition.

The police in our society are entrusted with an important role. A role to ensure the law of the land is honoured, a sense of safety and security for the people and their property and to hold a strict check over the criminals and their activities. Their role is far removed from the Law of Fish, where the big fish gobbles the small fish or where 'might is right'. Instead, the weakest of the weak should feel secure and at ease. For this reason, the for-the-people aspect of the police force should come to the fore. Unfortunately, despite 45 years of independent India the police department has not been able to etch a clean and humane image for itself. However, the young Police Chief of Kheri, Om Prakash Singh's new initiative of dispatching a written review of the complaint directly to the complainant is appreciable and this innovation has the capacity to become a new norm.[18]

DGP Prakash Singh heard about our efforts and asked me to share my views on the initiative with an assembly of police officers at a conference held during Police Week in Lucknow. I ended the presentation by elaborating on the need to deliver despite a scenario of constraints and stumbling blocks. To refuse to cow down and contribute, even in a small, inconsequential manner, within the functional and territorial limits. To contribute to the ecosystem by adopting suitable and corrective measures, by thoroughly understanding the local situation and to deliberately find time to be amidst the people. 'At best, it has to be a question of choice and how to accord priorities before oneself.'

But all good things must come to an end and the calm and quiet of Kheri of 1993 was shattered in June. It came to our notice that Balwinder Singh, alias Kali, originally of the KCF-Panjwar and who had now formed an independent group, was secretly leading a money extortion racket. The Sikh farmers under the Mailani police station and in the border villages were facing the heat of Balwinder's pressure. The Sikhs were relenting out of fear and paying up. Through some sources I came to know about a demand of Rs 1 lakh made by three members of the Kali Gang from a Sikh farmer. The police also found out that two escapees from the Lucknow Jail, Manjit Singh, alias Meeta, and Sukhvinder Singh, had joined the Kali Gang. While the former was from Mohammadi of Lakhimpur Kheri district, the latter was a resident of the village Rampura, Bheera. Both of them knew the area like the back of their hands. During the same period, another name popped up. It was that of the terrorist Deepa, who had ironically been declared killed by the Punjab Police. But some people of the nearby areas were insistent that Deepa was alive and that he had also joined hands with the Kali Gang.

All the pieces of information pointed in one direction—the Kali gang. It had emerged as a major threat to peace in the region. The well-to-do Sikh farmers and their jhalas had become their prime targets. The movement of the gang became a major challenge for the police. The families lived under constant fear and threat. We continued to add to our information and tried to piece everything together. The geographical influence of the Kali Gang kept growing and reports also came in from the village Kishanpur and the adjoining jungles of Bheera straddling the Sharda River. Hazara region in Pilibhit also resounded with the sighting of the Kali Gang. If this was not enough, there was also a rumour about a meeting of the Kali Gang with terrorist Mehtab Singh.

The date of 9 June 1993 will go down in the history of Lakhimpur Kheri as another gory day as eleven innocent people were gunned down by terrorists in three neighbouring villages under the same police station of Maigalganj. The first incident was reported from the village Rahi Paras, where six people died. Three other villagers were injured in the attack. Besides this, three people in Kharhana and two in Chaturipur were mercilessly shot down. A pamphlet purporting the cause of Balwinder Singh, alias Kali, was found by the police. The presence of Sukhvinder Singh as a perpetrator of the crime also came to light. The incident shook the entire region and an atmosphere of terror, which seemed to have waned, started to envelop the psyche of the people again. As the news of the massacre rolled out, the Governor of the State, Motilal Vora, made an impromptu visit as UP was under President's rule at that time, post the Babri Masjid demolition in December 1992.

The police investigation revealed an altogether different angle. The lone Sikh family in the village of Rahi Paras had one Labh Singh as its head. The Sikh family was troubled by other people in the village. To make matters worse, Labh Singh and a few others had a transactional deal that went sour. So far, the matter looked straightforward, but this is where it got complicated. Balwinder Singh, alias Kali, was the grandson of Labh Singh and Hardeep Singh Deepa was the son of Labh Singh. Deepa was also a member of the Kali Gang. The insult to Labh Singh was not taken well by Balwinder and he, along with Deepa, Sukhvinder and an additional mate, wreaked havoc in the village and around.

Regardless, the sound of the bullets and the accompanying terror reverberated in the entire region. As luck would have it, a day before the incident, UP had got a new DGP, Ved Prakash Kapoor. The new DGP expressed the feeling in an interview with a magazine, 'The terrorists through this act have given me a reminder that terrorism is alive in Terai.' Kapoor also sounded miffed with the outgoing DGP, Prakash Singh, who in his farewell speech had also made a remark about terrorism in the region. 'Terrorism in Terai is practically dead. There are just a handful of inconsequential terror groups; they'll meet their end soon.' Kapoor found the above statement responsible for the extreme action of the terrorists.[19]

The Maigalganj shake-up

'I'll be gone for a while,' I said to Neelam as we sat outside under the shaded veranda of the bungalow. It was more of an announcement.

'For how long?' The question had a tinge of resigned acceptance.

'I don't know. I really don't know. But it will surely be a while.'

The mass killings at Maigalganj had egged me to double our efforts. I had decided to camp at Maigalganj police station until the police made a breakthrough.

'I know this is your job and that you're totally committed to it, but you have a family too. Two growing up kids.'

Honestly, I wasn't prepared for this. I wasn't available to the family the way I should have been. It had been almost a year since we shifted to Kheri. And I had . . .

I couldn't even complete the thought. There was a call. We had received another tip-off.

I had ordered the mobilization of forces in the entire district. I was keen on a massive combing operation to flush out all existing terror outfits. I wanted its scale and scope to be humongous. Raid the possible hideouts of the terror groups. That was the plan. People with suspicious antecedents were to be detained and interrogated. A coordination committee under Padman Singh, an IPS officer who was a senior commandant in the nearby PAC battalion at Sitapur, had also been constituted. The SPs of two more border districts, Pilibhit and Shahjahanpur, were asked to be part of the team. That evening's phone call and the information it brought hastened the entire exercise. Time was the key, and I could not offer any explanation to my partner.

Members of a terror group had been sighted near Mailani and Pilibhit and the suspected area was cordoned off. The police too surrounded the area. Though we were cautious, a suspected terrorist on guard duty got a whiff of our presence and opened fire. All hell broke loose. When the exchange of fire, which lasted more than an hour, cleared, we only found smoke and a few AK-47 cartridges. The terrorists had escaped. I refused to bracket the operation as a demoralizing happening. Instead, I invoked the forces to see it as a sign that the terrorists were on the defensive and this provided us the perfect time to hit them hard. Everyone was raring to move ahead.

We pressed for a massive combing operation covering Mailani, Bheera, Gola, Palia, Sampurna Nagar, Phoolbehad, Tikonia and a few more areas. The agenda was clear: to nab the perpetrators of the Maigalganj massacre. Monsoon-crazed nullahs, swamps and sticky, slippery terrain notwithstanding, the CRPF jawans, the battalion of PAC and our district police force undertook 15–20 km of combing operation every day. The operation had all the trappings of thrill, drama and adventure. It matched the size and tenor of an army manoeuvre. A cash award was also announced for any who could provide vital clues. We also maintained constant touch with Punjab Police for any leads on Kali and his gang.

On 9 July, exactly a month after the Maigalganj killings and post the previous encounter, we entered the dense forest of Dudhwa National Park. In this entire operation, the commitment of a young IPS officer, Avinash Chandra who was posted as ASP in the district, was remarkable. Another officer, V.K. Singh, station house officer (SHO), who had become a thorn in the flesh of the terrorists since 1991 and was on the hit list of the Khalistan terrorists, showed his grit and bravery during the entire operation.

Rain and the resultant road blocks only added to the adventure. The police party crossed Ambedkar Nagar and other villages and reached a gurudwara in Gola after a ninety-minute walk. The Granthi, ceremonial reader of the Guru Granth Sahab, of the same gurudwara had been caught a year back, for he was a terrorist masquerading as a religious head. About a hundred metres away was the farmhouse of one Sikh, who had been brutally burnt alive along with his wife by militants, barely a month before my posting in this district. The police personnel covered every village, each farmhouse, and would only leave after a thorough search. A forest guest house deep inside the forest area was also searched. The guest house had no approach road and had to be accessed after the police party constructed a bamboo bridge across the Sutiya Nala. One jawan at a time, every individual's trousers tightly tucked inside their shoes and wrapped with a covering to wade off the poisonous bite of *jaunk*, leech, a blood-sucking menace. The guest house was secured, and the party moved forward, but despite the precaution, many jawans had painful bites and experiences with jaunk. There were no other alternatives and there was no going back. We continued and crossed numerous waist-high nullahs, and after the entire day trek, reached the jhala of one Vooksha Singh. The jungle was fast losing light, and the entire day-long operation had come a cropper.

'Sir, nothing today either,' it was ASP Avinash Chandra. 'I'm not demoralized though. They seem to have vanished. Have they shifted base?'

'I don't think so, Avinash. I don't think so,' I was lost deep in my thoughts. It had been more than a month since the launch of the massive hunt without even a single terrorist being found or eliminated. This was a definite disappointment.

'Sir, they are terrified and on the run. We must continue with the operation.' V.K. Singh stuck out his neck for the situation.

The operation had not yielded the expected results, but it was successful in instilling confidence in the people of the region and pressurizing the terrorists.

Gallantry outing

27 July 1993 saw the gunning down of the dreaded terrorist Sukhvinder Singh, alias Punjabu, in an encounter in the forests of Mailani.[20] He was one of the terrorists who had escaped from his cell in Lucknow Jail. When the credible information came about Sukhvinder, it was clear that instant action was needed. We drew personnel from Palia, Maigalganj and Mailani, besides the force from Kheri. Each SHO led his team. Leadership is always tested in such tight situations. I took the frontal attack team from the northern end of the hideout. We had anticipated the terrorists

to be adequately armed and the surprise element was the key. The chosen hideout was well camouflaged with thick and dense grass. We had three sides covered. My team mounted the assault. We were returned with indiscriminate firing. Calls to surrender were returned with more fire. AK-47 ruled the scene as bullets whistled through the greens. The dangerous drama went on for about forty-five minutes. Finally, when the bullets fell quiet, one dead body was recovered—that of a terrorist. The remaining terrorists had escaped. Sukhvinder Singh, alias Punjabu's, sinful life ended that day. Good triumphed against evil, again. A Gallantry Award and a citation followed for me. Despite the glorification, it was yet another day at the office.

A similar fate awaited Dheera around the same time in 1993. We wanted to nab him alive, but his own desperate self brought death quicker. Although the area was cordoned off, and the police party announced on the Public Addresses system for Dheera to surrender, he had other ideas. Dheera opened fire on the police party like crazy. The crossfire riddled his body. A much-feared terror maker had been felled.

Cynics might ask about the futility of extreme violence, death and gore, but I humbly reiterate, when you have donned the colours, and are in the line of fire, saving lives and protecting the honour of the land supersedes everything. Apart from these encounters, terrorists were nabbed by the Kheri police in dozens in quick succession. A mountain of AK-47, carbines, stick bombs and other illicit weapons were recovered. Suddenly, the entire picture had changed. There was a reversal of the situation. The disappointment of the combing operation was behind us. We had caught terror and its propagators by its neck.

Time to pack up

The terrorism, especially that associated with Lakhimpur Kheri, had one positive outcome.

Kheri is endowed with 2 lakh hectares of thick deciduous forest land. The forest area includes two famous national reserves dedicated to 'Project Tiger': Dudhwa National Park and Kishanpur Wildlife Sanctuary. While nature lovers thronged the forest reserves for their wealth and solitude, the forest also attracts people with dubious intentions. Illicit felling of trees and poaching of wild animals were organized crimes in the area prior to my taking over as police chief. The land and timber mafia, which included local goons and politicians, in connivance with corrupt officials, had depleted the forest wealth. The 1980s saw an alarming rise in the poaching of animal hide. Government records stated the recovery of ten tiger skins, three leopard skins, twelve swamp deer skins, seventy spotted deer skins, fifteen sambar skins, fifteen jog deer skins, eleven jackal skins and two python skins by the law enforcement agencies. Imagine the trade that would have slipped the attention of the enforcement agencies. The actual numbers could possibly have been a 100 per cent more or even an unimaginable number. We will never know. Palia, near the Nepal border, was considered the hub of dealings in illegal skin, which was then transported to Calcutta (now Kolkata) and Delhi markets.

But the onset of Khalistan terrorism instilled fear in the minds of the poachers and soon the jungles were devoid of them. These jungles had once been a safe haven for the terrorists as they became their shelter spots. As a consequence, the same areas became out of bounds for the timber and poaching mafia. The interior parts of the jungle were freely accessed by the terrorists and the police went after them with the intent to hunt them. This got us twin rewards, as our raids in the jungles caught the poachers by surprise. It was in the course of pursuing some terrorists that our police party ran into four poachers who were involved in the illicit business of skin. A panther's skin worth over Rs 10 lakh was seized from their possession. In another instance, the local SHO masqueraded as a customer and struck a deal for the purchase of a panther's skin. The poachers were arrested at the time of exchange and the skin was recovered. If that wasn't enough, during interrogation, the poachers provided another lead that led to the recovery of a tiger's skin. More arrests followed.

With the poachers either arrested or blocked and the tourists shying away from the jungles out of fear, the jungles wore a deserted look. I think the wild animals were the happiest lot. But now the decade-long turbulent period in the beautiful Terai region was finally drawing to a close, bringing down the curtains on an era of unrest. The success of the Kheri police can be directly attributed to a simple factor—we stuck to our task with self-belief.

Moreover, the police of Lakhimpur Kheri achieved success in their mission without in any way harassing the innocent Sikh populace or any other individual. The bonhomie with the locals was no flash in the pan. The sustained efforts of the police to reach out and to win their hearts did not go unrewarded. I will always cherish the day of 30 July 1993 when a delegation of UP Sikh Pratinidhi Board came from Lucknow. The group of representatives had come to felicitate me on behalf of the Sikh community. I was honoured at the gurudwara and was presented a *saropa*, a treasured gift for an officer on duty. The accompanying commendation letter said that my efforts not only provided relief to the community by dismantling the edifice of terrorism in the region but also assisted innocent youth to join mainstream society. Senior IAS officer Vijay Shanker Pandey, a no-nonsense and hard-to-please DM of Lakhimpur Kheri, endowed us with another accolade. The DM's commendation cited our proactive endeavours to crush terrorism.

It wasn't just counterterrorism that kept us engaged. Effective policing along with the standard operating procedures remained concurrent. There was another responsibility we had to undertake—that of capping the smuggling of goods to and from

from Nepal. During the early 1990s, electrical goods, including VCR, VCP and other audio-visual devices such as cameras, torches, calculators and medicines would find their way through the borders, skirting the enforcement machinery. The collusion of the government officials was undeniable. Not just collusion, the smugglers were offered protection by these devious traitors. The illicit traders in return were handed over sugar, vegetables, kerosene, salt, soap, agriculture machinery, cloves, cardamom and almonds. It was also the same period when the menace of drug trafficking raised its ugly head. The transfer of the banned substance began with small quantities, and it was *charas* and hashish that found favour with the dealers. The wild forest path, the railways and the heavy transport vehicles, especially the trucks, were extensively used to provide closure to the deals.

My district posting in Lakhimpur Kheri was thus extremely varied. My memory often travels back to the frightening chill of the terror-filled dusks of the Terai district of Kheri where paramilitary forces could be seen patrolling with their SLRs mounted menacingly on open Gypsies. The Terai's long winter season, with warm sunny days and cold nights, has stayed with me as a rich experience. It was a bliss, away from the noise and pollution that various metropolises represented. Once, the happiness of my children knew no bounds when they saw a black buck grazing inside our official sprawling bunglow. It so happened that during one intensive combing operation in the Terai jungle, I sighted this beautiful deer which had been captured alive by a poacher as he attempted to make good his escape. Deviating from my mission for a while, I chased the vehicle and thus, the black buck found a safe abode on my campus. The black buck remained a cynosure for all eyes. My daughter, Avni, would chortle to herself with delight while my son, Apoorv, with his black shaggy mane covering almost his forehead, would glance at the wild animal with popping eyes. In the Terai terrain, with the Kumaon hills only a few miles away, the wildlife had become thinner and perhaps human's animal instincts predominant.

Factually, my double-pronged endeavour in crackdown and sowing goodwill reaped a rich harvest. My superiors, the general public and the media, all were in unison in their praise and applause. The police efforts to herald a new era of peace and prosperity had yielded the desired results. I can say with a great degree of pride and humility that terrorism in the Terai region is dead and buried.

As I look back to that time, and my tenure pans before my eyes, I cannot help but find a smile on my visage. I was a young officer, married, with my two children barely six and four years old. I was unmindful of my own safety and even my family's. I braved my own countrymen who came with such suffixes as dreaded terrorist, militant, smuggler, poacher, mafia, you name it. I am deeply privileged, as a police officer to have found the opportunity to serve my state, my nation and my people in those challenging times.

6

The Tsunami Years

The date of 31 December 1993 was my last day in Lakhimpur Kheri as the district police chief. I was received as senior superintendent of police (SSP) in Bulandshahr with much fanfare. What awaited in my new district and beyond was the worst nightmare a police officer can expect.

Mira Bigha was my home, but the plains and the hills of UP had become my *karma-bhoomi*, my workplace. The last nine years had been a roller-coaster ride. Allotted the cadre of the Hindi heartland, I had covered quite a bit of ground, literally. Moradabad, Varanasi, Aligarh, Prayagraj, Almora, Special Protection Group (SPG) and, till a day before, Kheri.

'UP cadre is baptism by fire, you'll realize quite soon.' It was a remark that was specifically meant for my ears, and it emanated from a senior police officer. It was an honest sermon for a budding officer with zeal and zest. To me, it had sounded Greek.

Having now completed thirty-seven years of dedicated service, which I am extremely proud of, I would humbly state at the outset that choosing to be a policewallah in India is an unforgettable challenge. One swims with the sharks and hunts with the lions. I know this requires more elaboration, but please exercise some patience and read on. If Bihar, my playfield, sensitized and oriented my early learnings, it was UP that taught me lessons in religious sectarianism, caste calculations and political dogmatism.

The training at the NPA is extremely objective and thorough. It really prepares an officer for police work, both mentally and physically. Crime, criminals and the law are all our nemeses and, at the same time, our saviours. Police officer trainees are attuned to adopt a thorough approach towards absorbing the Indian Constitution, the Indian Penal Code, Indian Evidence Act and every other law incidental to their work profile. We did exactly that—we crammed all the laws and revered them as our Gita and our Bible. But while training prepares you for your work, one aspect that is missed or ignored is the dynamics between the political executive and police officers. The equation becomes all the more important when you diligently stick to the book. The police are subordinate to the political executive, but should they be subservient to them?

UP is a huge state with a complex caste equation. Even within the state, the eastern part has a different caste conundrum than the one that exists in the central or western part. The dynamics are far removed from the idealism of an egalitarian society. Your professional ethics and excellence can go for a six if you're caught up in the *chakravyuh*, or trap, of caste, underworld and politics, sans any protective layer. It is tough for a police officer to be answerable for what they have done on the field, away from the cozy confines of the space called 'office'. The simple, straight-forward advice to all young officers would be to remain on the right side of the law and leave the rest to your god, if not the one sitting above in the hierarchical order.

Political Roulette

I found myself in a tough spot right at the beginning of my new responsibility at Bulandshahr. A dreaded Gujjar warlord,

Mahendra Fauji, was the reason for it. Fauji was a terror in the western part of UP, a region where the gangsters owed allegiance to their respective castes. Fauji's terror was so rampant that the UP and Delhi government announced a cash reward of Rs 2 lakh (a big amount in 1994) on his head. He was wanted for many heinous crimes not only in UP and Delhi but also in Haryana, Rajasthan and Punjab. Other gangsters who belonged to the Yadav and Tyagi castes would be in the crosshairs with him, leading to brazen violence on frequent occasions. He was associated with the Maan Singh gang, whose members included the notorious Satbir Gujjar. The late 1980s saw various permutations and combinations of gang members involved in a spate of heinous crimes. Subsequently, the Maan Singh gang split into two formidable gangs led by Mahindra Fauji and Satbir Gujjar. Due to strong rivalry, the two gangs kept killing their counterparts and created a reign of terror around Delhi. Fauji was wanted for the sensational murder of UP MLA Mahendra Singh Bhati and his former associate and younger brother Rajbir as also for the killing of Jagmal, manager of Inter College, Meerut at the UP–Delhi border in 1989.[21] Fauji was facing trial in several cases in Meerut courts. A resident of Ghaziabad district, Fauji was known to live a fugitive's life and took shelter in remote hamlets and forests of UP. It was precisely because of this that he succeeded in eluding arrest for a long time. He was involved in thirteen murder cases, four cases of dacoity and road hold-ups, five cases of kidnappings and twenty-two cases of other serious crimes. In 1992, Satbir was gunned down by the Delhi Police. Then, on a fateful day in April 1994, Fauji was gunned down by Bulandshahr Police in a chance encounter. I was then SSP of the district. Open and shut case? It should have been, but that was not meant to be.

On the political front, UP was facing a watershed moment. The demolition of Babri Masjid led to the coming together of new forces and a formidable coalition was formed between the Samajwadi Party (SP) and the Bahujan Samaj Party (BSP). The coalition had a doughty and diminutive Mulayam Singh Yadav as its chief minister. The BSP, although a fledgling Dalit party, had the towering presence of Kanshi Ram as its leader and Mayawati as its general secretary. While the district celebrated the end of terror, Fauji's death created a new trouble for me. I had simply performed my duty, of stopping a criminal from committing a crime and providing succour to lakhs living under fear. How was I to know that it would lead to harakiri of sorts? The criminal had locked horns with the law and the police, and he got killed.

Apparently, the Gujjar community had lent their support to the BSP, and the party had a lot of support amongst them.[22] The party claimed that the killing of Mahendra Fauji had upset the equation. The timing of the encounter further upset the apple cart, for the Hastinapur Assembly seat, part of Meerut district, was going for a bypoll. It was piquant situation and a big political question (no matter how ridiculous) emerged.

* * *

The BSP party was so riled up with the encounter that Kanshi Ram, also known as Bahujan Nayak or Saheb, and Mayawati demanded my suspension from their coalition partner, the Samajwadi Party. Not just the timing of the encounter, but the encounter itself began to be described as ingenuine. I was not shattered but I was definitely disappointed.

Despite there being a massive strain on the coalition government, Samajwadi supremo CM Mulayam Singh Yadav refused to concede the demand of my removal from Bulandshahr. It goes to Yadav's credit that he remained firm in his stand and stood by the happenings in Bulandshahr. A grassroots leader, he displayed exemplary courage in this case in taking a bold decision despite the government being a coalition one.

The political theatre of absurdity

The month of May 1994 brought a new development, and rather a bold one. Till date, I don't quite know what prompted Mulayam Singh Yadav to take the decision of posting me as SSP Lucknow. Yes, Lucknow.

One day in May 1994, I got a call from the DGP headquarters to present myself for an audience with the CM the following day. Unknown to me, two more calls were also made. The first was to another IPS officer Jagmohan Yadav, my batchmate who was posted as SSP in another district, and the second to Satish Chandra Yadav, a state police officer promoted to IPS. Both the officers were given identical messages: 'Present yourself for an audience with the CM in Lucknow the following day.' The irony of the situation was that all three of us checked in at the same Police Officer's Mess in Lucknow and had separate meetings with the CM on the same day, oblivious of the fact that the meetings were interviews of sorts to pick an officer for the coveted post of Lucknow SSP. Chandra walked out of the meeting as SSP Prayagraj, Yadav as SSP Kanpur and I was asked to join as SSP Lucknow. Personally, it was an assurance that good work always gets recognition. On the political front, Mulayam Singh's move caused a storm. Considering the political dynamics and expediency, it made no sense. The consequence? This move further incensed the coalition partner, the BSP.

To add to it, four Dalits with criminal antecedents were lynched in a Thakur-dominated village of Bulandshahr. It was an unfortunate incident where mob fury took precedence over sanity. The victims had gone to the village with the intention of committing a crime but had been caught by the villagers. The tragedy had happened in the thrashing that ensued. The police had nothing to do with the incident, but the incident was used to clobber me.

The BSP had already lost the Hastinapur by-poll and the defeat was being attributed to the Gujjars deserting the party, angered by the encounter of Fauji. The BSP was completely rattled. Instead of the CM suspending me under pressure, I was given an important posting.

One thing led to the other, and in a web of developments, a high-octane press conference was held by Kanshi Ram and Mayawati in Lucknow on 10 June 1994. In the press conference, Kanshi Ram and Mayawati demanded not only my transfer but also my suspension by the government.[23] A flawless career of a civil servant was blemished for no fault of his. It was an uncalled-for, below-the-belt attack. I had never even met Kanshi Ram and Mayawati, yet I was dragged into the political tussle between the two parties. I had not built my professional edifice on the basis of caste configurations. A civil servant has his limitations, and I lamented that fact. Like numerous other things, I swallowed my pride, tucked things in the corner of my heart and moved on.

The CM, who had till the moment withstood all the pressure against me, was shaken. Barely two weeks later, and on the thirty-seventh day since my taking over as SSP Lucknow, I was called by the CM at his residence. It was past 11 p.m. and I was at my desk completing my paperwork. By the time I was ushered into the living area at the CM residence, it was almost midnight. Mulayam Singh Yadav often met visitors in the plush drawing room of his Vikramaditya Marg residence. The room had a massive window overlooking lush lawns with seasonal blooms and trees. On the walls were framed portraits of socialist leaders: Ram Manohar Lohia, Madhu Limaye, Jayaprakash Narayan and Chandra Shekhar. Seated near the CM was a journalist of a Hindi daily, whom I did not recognize. Greeting the CM, I too took a seat. Mulayam Singh Yadav asked the journalist to leave the two of us alone. The grim expression of the CM, after the journalist left, did not enthuse me, but what happened next completely bamboozled me.

'*Aapko suspend nahee kar rahe, transfer kar rahe hain* [You're not being suspended but being transferred],' the CM said.

'Sir, I feel things are fairly in check here in Lucknow, but if the government wants me to go somewhere else, I will.' I answered with a straight face.

'SSP saheb, if I don't transfer you, the BSP will withdraw support and my government will fall. We have to undergo this drill,' the CM said with his eyes no longer meeting mine, I continued to sit there, near numb. I had never seen a powerful leader in such a helpless state. In his second term as CM, Mulayam Singh Yadav, the undisputed leader of the SP, was one of the tallest of socialist stalwarts from the heartland. As an officer, I was a witness to the strange dynamics of politics. Dynamics in which I was being tossed around like a hapless chicken. I felt flattered and bemused at the same time to become a reason for the fall of a government. It was complete absurdity the idea that a small spoke had the power to stop the giant wheel of the system.

'Where would you like to go?' The CM's question surprised me. I thought he would be ruthless. Instead, he wanted *me* to make a choice. I liked that in my heart. The man had stood by me till that day and was himself disappointed at his own helplessness. He was seeking to make amends. I treaded carefully.

'Sir, I'll go wherever you direct me to go. I have always wanted to serve the Kumbh Mela. It's my lifetime dream, Sir.'

Mulayam Singh Yadav looked up at me and, without saying anything, reached for the bell. Minutes later, an attendant handed him the receiver of the landline phone. The DGP was on the other side.

'*DGP saab, sarkar ne faisla liya hai SSP O.P. Singh ko Kumbh Mela ka SSP niyukt kiya jaye. Aap uska notification jaari kar deejiye*

[The government has decided to post SSP O.P. Singh to the Kumbh Mela. Kindly issue a notification to that effect].'

Under normal circumstances, the conversation should have ended with an affirmation and greetings, but that did not happen. The DGP was saying something. Obviously I couldn't make out what, but the CM's reply let the cat out of the bag.

'*Nahee! Aap unhe mana kar deejiye. O.P. Singh ko Kumbh Mela bhejne ka notification jaree keejiye* [No! You answer him in the negative and issue a notification for O.P. Singh's posting as SSP Kumbh Mela].'

That was that. I rose from my position, saluted the CM and walked out of the premises, fully aware that I was no longer the SSP of the state capital.

The morning brought with it amusement galore.

The DGP spoke to me, and he waxed eloquent on how he had convinced the CM that I would be an ideal officer for the post of SSP Kumbh Mela at Prayagraj and not any other insignificant posting. For the second time in the last twenty-four hours, I aced the art of keeping a straight face. Obviously, the guy had no idea that the 'officer' himself was with the CM when his 'objection' came and not any 'imagined help'. I kept mum. I was maturing as a civil servant.

A few years ago . . .
(Aligarh, August 1987)

Unnecessary and uncalled-for interference from political masters was a malaise that I became grimly aware of, for the first time in my career, in Aligarh. It was my initiation into the murky world of politics—my first brush, or a run-in with the political establishment, whatever expression one might prefer to use.

I had become one of the few police officers in the state cadre to be promoted to the senior scale directly to the city level, instead of being routed through the rural level. I was elevated to the post of SP (City), Aligarh, on my promotion to the senior scale. The then DGP of UP had informed me personally that my competency and dedication had led to the scenario. It was a prestigious posting, but the city was highly sensitive to religious and communal flare-ups. I realized it was a test of a different kind. I was all geared up to meet the challenge. The situation in the city had deteriorated considerably for a long period between 1978 and 1980. Communal rifts and frequent incidents of violence and riots had ripped apart the social fabric of the area. For me, it was just a different law-and-order situation. My brief as a protector and enforcer of the law was straightforward. I had a job to do. Nothing else mattered.

Aligarh has had a chequered past. The history books record its name as Kol before it was named Sabitgarh in the sixteenth century, then to Ramgarh in the eighteenth and finally to present-day Aligarh. The Aligarh Fort is an important fixture of the city which largely rose to prominence because of the central university status of Aligarh Muslim University. Initially, Aligarh enjoyed a demography that had a mixed presence of Hindus and Muslims, and the population was interspersed. However, communal strife took its toll and communities became concentrated in specific areas. I went to Aligarh with this back story in mind but was confronted with an unimagined situation instead.

It was the menace of land grabbing that came to the fore. The criminals operated with brazen defiance, and they were generally aided by junior government functionaries, and more often than not shielded by unscrupulous elements in the police. To top that, the thriving business of land grabbing was happening under the indulgent shield of a few political leaders. Post-independence, large estates had been abandoned as their owners migrated across the border, to the new state of Pakistan. The huge properties left behind became the focal point of protracted legal battles among their remaining heirs. Touts and land sharks abounded in the city. Land grabbing turned into an organized art, where the tenants would be forcibly evicted, and then slush money would take over to convert and transform the illegal acts into 'legally, fool-proof deals'. I took on the challenge head-on and made it clear that the administration would not hesitate to use even the National Security Act (NSA) against any professional land grabber.[24]

In March 1988, one night when I was patrolling the city, I came across a group of men and women crowded together, and a sense of tension was palpable. I anticipated serious trouble and stopped to inquire. A frail man who looked to be in his late seventies approached me: '*Sahab, pachees-tees gundon ne ghar mein ghuskar mujhko aur meri biwi ko peeta aur hamare ghar se buhar nikal diya. Hum iss ghar mein tees saalon se reh rahe hain* [Sir, some twenty–thirty ruffians forcibly entered our house, battered me and my wife, and then kicked us out. We have been living in this house for the last thirty years].'

Further inquiry confirmed that the man was actually a tenant of that land for the last three decades, and he belonged to a scheduled caste. A case for eviction was filed by the owner in the court. The owner, on realizing the long time required for judicial settlement of the matter, had already sold the land to a doctor, who, in turn, wanted the land for the construction of a nursing home. The doctor had hired musclemen to get the tenants evicted.

My chance presence at the crime scene resulted in the arrest of some of the miscreants. Of the arrested, two names were quite interesting. One was of Raghunandan Singh Chauhan (an alleged relative of the UP Minister of State for Home, Surendra Singh Chauhan) and the other was another local leader of the Congress party.[25] The rowdy elements were led by Chauhan, a resident of Aligarh. Their plan was simple: to forcibly evict the couple and take over possession.

What followed was my first brush with the whims of the political executive. I had done my job. I had done the right thing. I had performed my duty as per law. The reactions were to the contrary. The minister was angry with my action. For me, the case was simple. I would have arrested Chauhan even if I had known he was related to the minister. I always strove to stay on the right side of the law. Nothing else mattered. Although I earned the displeasure of the ruling dispensation, I also earned unprecedented support from the general public.

The arrest was a major embarrassment for the minister personally and also for the ruling party too. Soon, the members of the party began demanding my transfer from the post of SP (City), Aligarh. On my part, I briefed my superiors about the incidents leading to the arrest. I elaborated on the fact that I had done no wrong and had followed every rule by the book. I vowed before my superior officers that I would not budge from my position irrespective of the extraneous considerations. I would not let any external factor or pressure hamper my professional work.

The reaction of the political masters was somewhat expected and understandable, but the behaviour of some of my seniors disappointed me, to be honest. Instead of a pat on the back, one of my seniors sent a vague report to the headquarters. It was a report that had no praise for my work but attempted instead to tarnish my image. My senior gave in to the pressures of a few local leaders of a political party. It was a sad day in my professional career. Instead of a bouquet, I was assured of brickbats. As a consequence, within a few days of the incident, I was given a marching order to relieve myself of my responsibility as SP (City) Aligarh. I got a transfer order as commandant of a PAC battalion at Gonda. What happened next was equally baffling. The public, the opposition parties, NGOs, the media and others rallied behind me and demanded the reversal of the decision.[26] It was an impromptu show of support for an honest officer. Articles in newspapers, demonstrations, slogans, conversations and opinions of the public at large overwhelmed me. Although I was in the dumps professionally, the support that came from unexpected quarters served me as something far bigger than any bravery award. And then, wonder of wonders, the student union of Aligarh Muslim University (AMU) came out in support of my action in protecting the rights of the downtrodden and weak. (I call it the wonder-of-wonders because I had once faced the students' ire inside the AMU campus when I had gone to investigate a hit-and-run case of an AMU hosteller.) The student union even met the DIG Range with the demand to cancel my transfer order. They also demanded a fresh inquiry into the incident and the antecedents of the culprits, especially those affiliated with any political party. The local media opined that the city had become a haven of anti-social elements who masqueraded as netas.

If this was not enough, what transpired next bolstered my faith in my convictions and belief. The state government reviewed the earlier order and cancelled the transfer order. In a miracle of sorts, I was retained as SP (City) at Aligarh. The incident worked as an elixir for me that rightful work wins laurels, and a police officer should adhere to the law, come what may. The underlying principle that I adopted and sustained in my entire career, and I would like to offer to all my fellow officers, young and not so young is: in the conflict between law and justice, you must forget about everything and simply stick to the law of the land. Justice is abstract and not in your hands, but to abide by the law is a fact and will always remain in your control.

One fact that irked me for a long time and remained a sour point in my career was the unsettling aspect of a few of my seniors. I had, with due respect, wished for high standards from my seniors. Unfortunately, that was not to be, and I let the incident remain an education for me for the rest of my career, and always. I say this with all my responsibility and humility. When your juniors look up to you and support you, it speaks volumes about you as a leader. I ensured, right through my career, that officers and ranks under me got their due and their rightful actions always found my support and appreciation. Using the baton of 'transfer' or 'suspension' on untenable grounds demoralizes the force and sends a wrong signal. It should be used sparingly and with extreme caution and due diligence.

I rest my case here and take the reader back to Lucknow 1994, when I was asked to quit as SSP Lucknow even before I had completed forty days in my office.

The ticking bomb: Lucknow State Guest House incident

I had a fulfilling posting as SSP, Kumbh Mela at Prayagraj. It was a dream come true to be responsible for the biggest open-air theatre of religious congregation on earth. A congregation, a belief, a festival, a faith where all classes of society become classless. I was truly blessed to have facilitated the uninterrupted flow of people coming together at an appointed time, again and again.

In another surprise move, I was given the posting of SSP Lucknow again. The political scene in the state capital was rapidly changing. The BSP, a coalition partner in the state government, had withdrawn its support from the SP. At the outset, it must be said, I was not keen to come to Lucknow. The grapevine in the forces was, if one does a successful stint at Kumbh, one can ask for a posting of one's choice. I made no such request yet I landed the job. In fact, as the rumour was, I was going to be posted as SSP Kanpur, and that too after a three-month waiting period. It was only much later that I came to know it was the then principal secretary of CM Mulayam Singh Yadav, who had come in with the suggestion that I should be brought to Lucknow again. Mulayam Singh then gave his final nod.

I was not only not keen to join, but I had a strange premonition of an imminent mishap. My instincts were playing on my nerves,

making me uneasy. I had no option, though. The discipline in the
forces prepares one for all responsibilities at all times. In reality,
what unfolded next was beyond my wildest dreams. I refer here
to the infamous 'Guest House Incident' of 2 June 1995.[27] An
indecorous political drama in the history of modern-day India
which not only changed the politics of UP but impacted the
politics of the country as a whole. The incident that transpired
on the fateful day of June shook me from within. Although as
a bureaucrat and police officer I was not servile to my political
masters, the circumstances entrapped me in a situation that only
I and my God could understand. As I relive those moments blow
by blow, minute by minute, I have just one prayer, one request:
may such pernicious and insidious moments never befall anyone.

2 June 1995
12 p.m.

I proceeded towards the SSP office and took charge from the
officiating SSP Rajiv Ranjan Verma. An outstanding young IPS
officer working as SP (City) Lucknow, Verma had taken over
the charge from the previous incumbent Gur Darshan Singh, an
officer of the 1984 batch. I then reported to the DGP headquarters.
I returned to the SSP Camp Office and had a meeting with the
district police officials to apprise them of the law-and-order
situation in the city. The all-important mourning period of
Muslims, Muharram, figured prominently in the agenda for the
meeting. Muharram has always been a sensitive proposition in
Lucknow, and its error-free arrangement has been the top priority
of each government. Precisely a year ago, my short tenure in the
same post had my department manage Muharram arrangements
to near perfection. In fact, the peaceful and foolproof handling of
the period found resounding appreciation all around. But that was
a year ago, a fresh start had to be made. Next on the agenda was
a meeting with the Deputy Inspector General of Police (DIG),

Lucknow Range. DGP V.S. Mathur had forewarned me to take extra precautions about police arrangements for Muharram, so that became a prelude for the meeting with the DIG Range.

I returned to the SSP camp office, only to find the media waiting for my official byte. As the new SSP, my name was flashed to the various SHOs and SOs—to remain put in their resolve and continue with their respective duties instead of giving me any courtesy calls.

2 p.m.

I got a call from DGP that he has received some complaints regarding disturbance by unlawful elements at the Meera Bai Marg State Guest House. I instantly commanded the Circle Officer, Hazratganj, under whose jurisdiction the guest house was. A team was dispatched to the guest house.

2.30 p.m.

The Circle Officer (VIP), stationed at the State Guest House, informed me that everything was normal and nothing was amiss. What was the basis of the apprehension in the first place then, I wondered.

4.15 p.m.

I reached the residence of DM Rajiv Kher, an IAS officer, for my call-on meeting. Again, the focus of the discussion was the maintenance of law and order and the maintenance of peace on account of Muharram.

Approximately 5 p.m.

The meeting with the DM was interrupted by telephonic messages from the Principal Secretary, Home and simultaneously from the DGP about some unlawful elements present at the State Guest House. We both promptly directed ADM (City) Madhusudan

Raizada and SP (City) Rajiv Ranjan Verma to reach the State Guest House immediately and take necessary action.

5.09 p.m.

A few minutes thereafter, I received a distress message of a disturbance taking place at the State Guest House. Both DM Kher and I rushed to the spot. We rode together in the DM's ebony-black Ambassador and my official car followed.

5.20 p.m.

We reached the spot at Meera Bai Marg of Lucknow city. There was a huge gathering near the reception area and in the lounge of the guest house. We were informed about the presence of a few MLAs too at the gathering by the police officials present at the guest house. The entire gathering seemed divided into groups and they were raising different slogans. Some people complained that the MLAs of the Bahujan Samaj Party (BSP) were being detained forcefully. They demanded free and unhindered movement of the MLAs. Others contradicted them. The UP government was a coalition of the BSP and the Samajwadi Party. The political climate then was thick, with the possibility that the differences between the coalition partners had gone beyond repair and the BSP had already withdrawn support to the Mulayam Singh Yadav-led government.

In the ensuing chaos, some claimed to be the party workers of the BSP, out there to meet their leader, Mayawati, who was staying in suite number one and two. Others posed themselves as the bodyguards of the MLAs. The situation was quite precarious for the power supply was down and the telephone lines were dead. There was complete chaos.

'We need to clear the place of all these people,' DM Kher and I concurred. We both swung into action and appealed to all present there to leave the premises, which we accomplished in doing with some effort.

'Make sure suites one and two are doubly secure,' I directed the officials to beef up the security. A sudden commotion erupted and we noticed one person being whisked away. He was literally being carried away in the grip of arms. He was later identified as BSP MLA, Mewa Lal Bagi. The DM, SP (City), ADM (City) and I tried to free him from the clutches of the motley crowd, but the crowd power prevailed and Lal Bagi was carried away in the melee. I, along with DM, immediately directed the SP (City) to stop them.[28] Visibility was poor as the electricity supply was also down. Snapped deliberately perhaps?

'This is an extreme situation. We have to take more firm steps,' I confided in the DM.

SP (City) resorted to lathi charge. The hard cane had its effect. There was confusion in the ranks of the crowd, and they ran helter-skelter. We focused on the group that was still holding the MLA with them. The SP (City) and a team of policemen charged towards them. In the ensuing melee, we got a body grip of Mewa Lal and retrieved him from the group's clutches and vacated the area. The officers transferred Mewa Lal Bagi to the meeting room of the guest house, where other MLAs were also present.

We also evicted all the outsiders present in the meeting room of the guest house. One police officer was posted at the gate of the meeting room to prevent the entry of any outsider. I remained there till the time normality was regained. Eventually, it became clear that the withdrawal of support by the BSP had caused the piquant situation. While Mayawati was trying to protect her MLAs from crossing over to the other side, the Samajwadi Party was claiming that some BSP members had expressed allegiance to Mulayam Singh Yadav, but they were being detained by their leaders. The BSP supporters were contradicting that.

The situation could have been much worse. Stories and rumours ran wild all around. Sample this—at around 10 p.m., that same day, the divisional commissioner and IG (Lucknow zone) visited the state guest house. The former had a word with Mayawati on the intercom. She expressed her desire to have tea. The estate officer, in charge of the guest house rued there was no cooking gas cylinder in the kitchen. A cylinder was arranged from a nearby residence. The sight of the cylinder as it was being rolled towards the kitchen area, and the grating noise caused by it, sparked a rumour that there was an attempt to set Mayawati on fire. This was but another addition to the shock and misery that awaited me.

3 June 1995

The following day, I received a copy of a letter dated 2 June 1995 addressed to the Governor of Uttar Pradesh by Mayawati. The letter alleged that certain members of the Samajwadi Party unlawfully gathered at the State Guest House and attacked the members of BSP and also took away some MLAs with them.[29] And all of that happened right under the nose of the police and district administration officials present.

I was rather surprised because during the entire guest house episode or after, none of the BSP members or Mayawati had made any such complaint nor had anyone alleged any kind of police inaction. Another falsehood in the form of an FIR. was lodged by one Umakant Yadav, legislator BSP, at the Hazratganj Police Station at 8.35 p.m. on 2 June, alleging that he along with other BSP MLAs had been detained and tortured in the meeting room of the State Guest House, against their will.[30] As a police officer, I was again caught in the crossfire of the insidious kind between two political parties, playing their power games. I instantly directed the SP (City) to review the situation and provide security to Mayawati. I wrote another letter to the DM, with a request for a magisterial probe into the incident since the role of the police was commented upon in the complaint. I did this to keep the slate of my role clean and my actions above doubt. The developing political situation in the state capital took another shift, and on the night of the same day, at around 9 p.m., the Governor dismissed the Mulayam Singh government and Mayawati was sworn in as the chief minister.

4 June 1995

Gur Bachan Lal, SSP Bareilly, met me at the Camp Office and dropped a bomb: 'I was informed the night before that I have been posted as SSP of Lucknow.' My transfer order came a short while later and I had no choice but to hand over the charge, which I did. If one were to think that my ordeal was over, one is wrong. Very wrong. A short while later, I received another order. This time, of my suspension. I was shell-shocked. 'Why me?' was the question that repeatedly returned to me.

Why me?

There were four of us. Three besides me, the DM, the ADM (City) and the SP (City) and only I was suspended. That, too, for simply performing my duty. It was obvious that I had been 'chosen' to be suspended. *What could I have done differently in the given situation?* The ideal action in a similar situation is always to apply the basics: apply crowd access control measures, keep outsiders out, personally request all the members and senior leaders to maintain order and allow safe passage to those legislators desirous to enter or leave. As SSP, I had ensured that dispassionately and with complete impartiality. It was a rare case, probably, of a police officer being gripped with anguish rather than embarrassment. Sympathy calls poured in from all sides. Vendetta-of-Mayawati was the resounding call. But, for me, nothing mattered. Mahendra Fauji's encounter, the demand to suspend me, transfer, reversal of transfer, my posting as SSP Lucknow, face-saver Kumbh posting, and return to Lucknow—all flashed before my eyes. It was a crude culmination to a political drama.

Once again, more than the politicians, it was my seniors and their submissive demeanour that disappointed me. I had been a witness to lily-livered seniors in the past, but this time, it was even worse. It was a detestable example that my seniors had set for juniors like me. I can never forget the body language of a senior IPS officer when I called on him post my suspension. He was very uneasy with my presence in his office, and he ensured I realized that I was the most unwanted person around him. Such was the terror of Mayawati in those days that no officer wanted to be seen with me. Overnight, I had become a pariah. This senior was so rude to me that he literally turned me out of his office. When misery knocks one down, it squeezes you from all sides. Even my close friends from the services began to avoid me despite being aware of the circumstances leading to my suspension. It was a predicament for other officers, who had to decide whether to follow their spineless seniors, who sought to be on the right side of the fence to please their political masters, or to simply disregard them. My resolve was not broken, but I was surely heartbroken. What a shame it was to be treated like an outcast to appease the new ruling dispensation!

I was slapped with two cases,[31] both related to the events of the State Guest House. In each of them, I was named the villain, the villain who was nursing a grudge against Mayawati and was also involved in the kidnapping of legislators. With due regard to the then DM and other officers present at the site, on the eventful date, my moot and open question was: 'Why was no other officer suspended for laxity of command or impartiality in his duty?' As per Para 7A and 7B of the then UP Police Regulation, the DM was the final authority in such a situation, but the only officer facing the flak was the SSP. My argument fetched me no answer. The brute reality was that I was present on the scene along with the DM and other officials and performed what was best suited to the situation. All the decisions were collectively taken by me and DM on the spot.

Commenting on the report of the investigating officer, the district and sessions judge of Lucknow affirmed my viewpoint that: 'If the SSP was responsible, the DM, ADM, City Magistrate, SP (City) and other police officers ought to have been equally responsible. This having not been done, the investigation cannot be said to be fair.' The court went on to add, 'There is no evidence of his connection with the incident which took place on 02.06.1995. There is no evidence, whatsoever, of his complicity in the commission of the offence as alleged. It is not clear as to what has prompted the investigation agency to find him involved.' The District and Sessions Judge of Lucknow passed the final order in one of the cases while observing, 'The report does not contain any specific allegation against Shri OP Singh, the then SSP Lucknow, even though it has been lodged two days after the alleged incident and [the] removal of Mulayam Singh Government.'[32]

As was expected, the situation prompted me to seek relief from the Central Administrative Tribunal (CAT). To cut a long story short, the government reinstated me on 30 October 1995, about 150 days after I was suspended. I was given a posting as Assistant Inspector General of Police (AIG) of Provincial Armed Constabulary (PAC) Headquarters. All the cases and the attached inquiries against me were subsequently withdrawn.

Those five months gave me enough time to ruminate. I read and wrote copiously. Philosophy and theology assisted me in finding answers to many profound questions that came to my mind. Why are we punished for crimes we don't commit? Are we mere puppets in the hands of destiny? Are we manipulated by the strings of our karma? If everything is predestined, what control do we have over our actions? I can distinctly recall reading the *Matsya Purana*, which narrates an interesting conversation between Satyavrata Muni, a great king and sage in ancient times and Lord Matsya, an incarnation of Lord Krishna. Satyavrata Muni asked, 'O Lord, which is superior, fate or one's own exertion and effort?' Lord Matsya explained that three elements—fate, effort and time—conjointly affect the course of one's life. I was no Satyavrata Muni, and languished in the dark, eager to elicit answers to the questions arising in my mind. Where did I lack? Regardless, with or without any answer, I emerged from my own ashes, a far more formidable self with a steely resolve to never compromise in a situation, come what may.

I may not be so spiritually or intellectually evolved as to find answers from the Supreme Power, but I nursed a deep desire to meet one mortal on planet earth—Mayawati. I wanted to ask her: What led you to form such a negative narration about me?

It was in 1998 that I got an opportunity to meet Mayawati. She was out of power and had come to Azamgarh, UP, where I was posted as DIG Range. She was in town for a party meeting and was housed at the state PWD guest house. I directed my DSP to fix a meeting with her. It was gracious on her part to accept my request.

It was a sunny day, I can distinctly recall, as I drove to the PWD guest house situated in the heart of the city. The driveway and the front compound were crowded with people, mostly *karyakartas* (party workers). I was ushered inside the waiting area, which again had more people awaiting an audience with her. In no time, I was led to a private suite. Mayawati was there, but she also had company. I recognized the face, it was the local MP, Akbar Ahmad Dumpy. We exchanged greetings.

'Dumpy-ji, please leave us alone.' Mayawati directed. '*Bataiye*, DIG saab,' Mayawati threw the ball at me once Akbar Dumpy had quit the scene.

'I have nursed this feeling for a long time, Madam. To meet you and clear some concerns. With all due respect, I have some direct questions for you,' I was upfront and direct.

'*Aap poochiye* [You ask].' Her wide eyes and direct eye contact were a clear indication that she was all ears.

'These thoughts have disturbed me for a long time, and I seek answers for them,' my voice was quivering, but I pulled myself together.

'Madam,' I continued, 'what do you say to an officer who is punished for doing his job? I took extreme steps on the fateful day of 2 June to prevent the situation from getting worse. Protected life and property. Even saved your MLA from being kidnapped from the scene. I took the extreme action of resorting to lathi charge to keep the rowdy elements away . . .' I paused. There was no change in Mayawati's expression. I was in no mood to let go of the opportunity.

I continued, 'I conducted myself as per the code. You know there was no dereliction of duty, yet adverse cases were filed against me. Only me when there were other responsible officers at the scene. In fact, all the decisions were made collectively with the DM, who even stated that in his written report. There's not even one mention of my name to the contrary. Madam, why? Why was I singled out? I'm an apolitical officer. My entire service record will tell you that. Was that the reason? Was the punishment a reward for doing the right job . . .' I stopped again. I was shivering. I lowered my eyes to collect myself. Mayawati didn't say a word all this while. By now I had a feeling that I wouldn't be getting a clear answer.

'An upright officer lives by his promise. The promise of integrity, the promise of fairness. I have always operated above political affiliation or caste considerations. That is me, nothing else.' I looked up again. I had nothing more to add. The words were enough to keep faith in one's actions and beliefs.

It was time to move on.

7

My Lesson

I especially write this chapter to share with you my biggest learning as a police officer. We are a civil police force and we function and operate to serve the people. We dedicate our lives to the safety and security of our nation. As I completed my training and stepped into the real world, I realized that maintaining close coordination and transparency with the general public can greatly facilitate the smooth running of the police machinery.

My successful stint at Lakhimpur Kheri, despite the challenges, substantiated the need for effective communication. My outreach to the community, especially the Sikh community, served as a balm and eased their concerns. The daunting task of controlling the situation of terror was made easy by the support of the populace. Small steps, such as keeping the victims of any crime informed about the development of the investigations, gave them a sense of confidence in the khaki and the belief that the police mean well. The community became my eyes and ears. Half of my intelligence came from not just alert and conscientious people but individuals who were committed to the cause of peace and stability.

Later, I experienced how the general public can become your strength during disaster management operations. Information forms one of the key saviours during difficult situations. Time is sparse and the flow of information makes the difference between life and death. Setting up quick deployable mobile antennas, establishing dedicated lines for communication and spreading them nationally as well as utilizing different social media platforms has become the SOP today.

During my career, I ensured outreach at all ends, from the lower ranks to seniors and bosses, was fair and transparent. I stuck to the basics and discovered the wonderful world of ingenuous communication. I encouraged team meetings, reporting, regular feedback and face-to-face exchange of ideas and information, brainstorming and ideation. One incident in my early days at Aligarh particularly drove home the importance of outreach and communication.

The university town has had the tradition of police never entering the university campus. I found the proposition strange and did try to find a reason for such an extreme stance but found no concrete or satisfying answer. I was told that AMU was a mini town and they didn't like any interference in their workings or operations. I found this answer even more strange and baffling. However, fate took an interesting turn and the unwritten protocol had to be breached on 14 March 1988.

I received information over the wireless about a young student having been hit by a speeding truck on Anupshahr Road in front of Sulaiman Hall in the university campus. I rushed to the spot. The injured student turned out to be a resident of the Sulaiman hostel of AMU. The accident had resulted in the victim, Qamruddin's thigh bone breaking. He was immediately rushed to the hospital. The truck involved in the incident was seized by the police and the driver was apprehended and taken to the Civil Lines Police Station. While an FIR was being registered by Qamruddin's brother at the police station, we received further information that following the news of the accident, a mob of unruly students had reached the Vice Chancellor (VC), Syed Hashim Ali's, lodge and were indulging in violence. For the second time in the night, I was headed in the same direction. The DSP in charge of the area and a few other police personnel accompanied me.

As we entered the VC's lodge, scenes of destruction greeted us. Broken windowpanes and flower pots lay scattered. An emergency siren was hooting in full blare. We had barely entered the lodge when a huge crowd of students converged on the scene. They were aggressively shouting slogans. They wanted to know why the VC had summoned the police. The situation was quite grim and in the growing din, no one was willing to heed counsel. I had already directed the DSP to keep back-up teams ready. Meanwhile, the agitated students demanded to meet the VC and forced themselves into the premises by breaching the gates. In the mayhem that ensued, the students indulged in brick-batting. That was followed by the complete destruction of windowpanes, flower pots, bulbs, generator sets, air conditioners, tube lights and notice boards. The students continued to demand the audience of the VC.

I impressed upon the VC the need to comply with the students' request and he conceded. The anger of the students was fuelled by the rumour that the injured student had died while on the way to the hospital. The reality was otherwise; Qamruddin had his leg in the cast and was safe in the hospital. The rumour-mongers did not stop at that, it was further alleged that the university authorities showed apathy and slackness in the situation. The angry students continued to demand answers from the VC. With his official residence gheraoed by the unruly mob, the VC had no option but to dial the police. The situation continued to worsen: the gate, the gate lamps, mercury lights, nothing was spared. If that was not enough, the students-turned-rioters set ablaze my official vehicle. I would have easily called for additional forces to enter the campus, but I chose restraint at that moment.

The following day, the VC sent a detailed account of the events as they unfolded in the evening and the night. Another official letter from the university was received by the SSP Aligarh, expressing regret over the students' behaviour and the loss of the police vehicle to vandalism. I immediately seized the moment and assured the VC of my continued support and cooperation in the matter and beyond. I told him specifically to keep the communication channel going. Reciprocating the move, the university invited me as their chief guest for their sports event a few days later.

As I've mentioned in the previous chapter, things moved to the contrary when my dedicated action of ridding the city of Aligarh from the malaise of land-grabbing found me in a tight spot. My actions rubbed the powers-that-be the wrong side and my tenure as SP (City) was threatened. On that occasion, the student union of AMU rose to the occasion and to my support. Positive public support backing my actions led the government to reverse the order and my transfer was cancelled.

More than three decades later, the wheel of time renewed my association with the institution. I was again on the guest list of Prof. Tariq Mansoor, VC AMU, for an engagement with the students and this time around he wanted my name inscribed on a plaque for times to come. A new block of a girl's hostel had come up and the students, faculty and administration wanted me to inaugurate the new facility. They also wanted me to address the students on 'Youth and Nation-Building'. As far as I can remember, no police officer's name has been inscribed on the portals of AMU. I was initially skeptical, for there is a dialectical equation between the protest politics of the university and the imperatives of law and order. My team was also wary of the possibility of a black-flag demonstration by some sections of the students during my address on 'Youth and Nation-Building'.

Whenever faced with a dilemma, the senses of a policeman are auto activated, and conviction and courage come to the fore. I kept my word and the exalted honour of the UP Police, as usual, snubbed the skepticism and indecisiveness.

The warm welcome given by the VC, academia and students was unprecedented. I exhorted the students to become agents of change, to inculcate a scientific temper and to be curious. My words were well received. There was not even a whimper of protest on the campus, even though AMU and the local police have a history of having locked horns on numerous occasions.

The image of the police needs a makeover. We need more heroes, ideals, inspirers and idols in the force. I hope and expect the young architects of UP Police to rise above the ordinary and take bold initiatives in the interest and sake of the UP Police and for the people we have vowed to serve.

8

Tackling Disasters:
Leading from the Front

I list below some of the major disasters that occurred during my command of the NDRF as its DG. I have deliberately laid out these troubling scenes of distress and pain to highlight the fact that our security and armed forces are also engaged in duties and tasks that contribute immensely and tirelessly at the humanitarian level. The forces have to literally fight battles at various fronts to serve the nation and society. At a personal level, my association with special forces such as the NDRF opened diverse vistas of crisis and disaster management. This exposure yielded dividends not just in my skillset but served to greatly temper my mindset.

September 2014. Kashmir Valley witnessed heavy torrential rains that caused widespread destruction and severe distress to the state of Jammu and Kashmir. The floods, which crippled Srinagar and the adjoining areas, resulted in several fatalities and a large section of the population was displaced. The NDRF, making its presence felt in Kashmir, had the first-ever experience of handling urban flooding on such a massive scale. Personally leading this rescue operation in Srinagar, I witnessed thousands of people stranded on rooftops, upper stories, mounds and knolls—all dependent on defence personnel and the NDRF to bring them food and other supplies or to move them to safer locations. Heavy rain had inundated the flat vastness along the Jhelum and the Tawi in the region where the two rivers drained into the Dal and Wular lakes. I had gone to Srinagar and Jammu on 6 September 2014 along with Union home minister. The PM visited the state on 7 September. It was a major national disaster, bridges were swept away, roads subsided or disintegrated under water, and landslides and mudflows caused dangerous and messy blockages. The scale of disaster was unprecedented and gargantuan, the worst in almost eighty years. It was against this backdrop that the NDRF worked tirelessly in localities of the Valley.

With twenty-two NDRF teams and nearly 150 inflatable boats, we penetrated areas where the water level was initially almost 14–15 feet.[33] In some areas, the locals created hurdles in the rescue and relief operations damaging some of our boats demanding to be aided first. They even tried to assault our jawans by pelting stones, as a consequence of which one of our jawans was severely injured and had to be airlifted to Chandigarh for treatment. We rescued CRPF personnel from one of the camps in a night-rescue operation lasting till the wee hours. The Valley seemed choked with the stink of garbage over a week as water began to stream into the houses. The NDRF set up medical camps and treated patients deep inside various mohallas in what we called boat hospitals. There were some of the areas where carcasses of cows and dogs could be seen floating. I felt proud of my teams for braving waterlogged lanes, submerged houses and marooned people to provide humanitarian services. During the operation, NDRF teams evacuated 50,815 persons, retrieved fifteen dead bodies, distributed 88.22-ton relief materials, established medical camp and attended 10,145 flood-affected persons.[34]

October 2014. Cyclone Hudhud hit the eastern coast of the country. More than a lakh people were directly affected. Forty-two teams of the NDRF were pre-positioned in Odisha and Andhra Pradesh. The teams evacuated 15,596 people from vulnerable areas.[35] The proactive deployment of the NDRF along with excellent coordination with the affected states was the hallmark of this operation.

April 2015. An earthquake devastated Nepal and stunned the entire world. It was a Saturday. That day, the plates of a geological fault slipped somewhere deep in the earth and caused the ground to convulse and contort. These movements brought about widespread, but highly irregular, patterns of damage to property and life across the country. Hundreds of villages were reduced to rubble and poorly built houses collapsed in the faraway city of Kathmandu. The worst-affected areas included parts of Kathmandu Valley, Bhaktapur, Lalitpur, Sindhupalchok and Gorkha. The scenes were remarkably haunting. In the affected places, a mix of grief, alienation and anger ruled.

The first international response and assurance to the Nepalese people came from the Indian Prime Minister Narendra Modi, who discussed the situation with the political leaders of the ravaged country and promptly dispatched a strong contingent of the NDRF as an Indian Search and Rescue Force. Swift and coordinated rescue efforts made a difference in coping with the aftermath of any disaster, natural or otherwise, in terms of saving lives and minimizing property loss. Constrained by limited resources, Nepal simply could not cope alone and, therefore, the assurance given by PM Modi provided succour to the grief-stricken people of that country. India's first seven rescue teams, comprising 305 multi-skilled and internationally trained NDRF personnel, reached Kathmandu within six hours of the tragedy and started round-the-clock rescue operations in the affected areas.

December 2015. Chennai was hit by one of the worst floods. Heavy rains pounded several parts of Tamil Nadu and inundated several parts of Chennai and its suburbs covering more than a

4-km radius around the Adyar river, which flows through the heart of the city. Normal life was severely disrupted. Electricity supply was cut off to avoid accidents. The people were in the grip of great anxiety and fear as the communication system was affected. Their homes submerged, vehicles swept away, and no drinking water and food further added to the misery. As the city faced more torrential rains, the NDRF was pressed into service. The use of technology by the NDRF during this urban flood was one of the highlights of sticking to basics by managing a disaster under severe conditions. The NDRF established On-Site Operations Coordination Centre (OSOCC) commanded by DIG NDRF. The Centre was provided V-SAT connectivity through Quick Deployable Antenna (QDA), which was in turn connected to the NDRF headquarters at New Delhi. My team at the headquarters was managing the Twitter and Facebook accounts and a #NDRF was created for 'Chennai Flood Operations'. The extensive use of social media as a major communication channel helped people immensely. During the operations, several precious lives were saved and 22,450 people were evacuated from flooded areas.[36] A large number of medical and relief camps were set up and managed by NDRF personnel during this rescue operation.

May 2016. Forest fires engulf Uttarakhand. The fire spread roughly over an 1800-hectare area including Chamoli, Almora and Pauri districts.[37] Though the NDRF was not trained in firefighting operations, we were instructed to deploy our teams in this severe forest fire disaster. Acutely aware of the NDRF's inadequacy in the situation, I decided to put in all our efforts to manage this crisis. Fire tenders and such other heavy machinery are handicapped in operation due to restricted terrain within the forested confines. In the case of the Uttarakhand fires, the difficult situation was further compounded by limited road connectivity. Consequently, any rescue and response in the situation entailed an extensive planning and drawing in huge manpower. The teams in Pauri district covered more than 60 km of the mountainous terrain to subdue the raging fires in the district. In Almora, the teams worked for almost six days continuously covering about 148 km to accomplish their tasks. Similarly, the teams at Chamoli remained occupied for five days at a stretch and covered a distance of about 45 km to completely douse the fire in the district. Although it was the NDRF's first response operation involving forest fires, the teams with their extensive and varied experience in the field of disaster response could achieve the best in spite of their lack of experience in firefighting in such difficult circumstances. The NDRF had once again exhibited its dedication in service to humanity in distress.

June 2016. In one of the biggest rescue operations of its time, an under-construction tunnel collapsed in Bilaspur district of Himachal Pradesh. One tunnel worker died while a few others were trapped inside. It was an incredible mission. The tunnel had caved in and detecting the ones buried underneath without wasting any time was key. A team of engineers, drilling experts and geologists worked round the clock to dig a 1.3-metre-wide hole to enable the NDRF to do the rescue operation. The trapped men survived for nine days on biscuits, dry fruit, glucose and water supplied to them by the rescue team through a narrow duct after a contact was established with the help of a microphone-linked webcam dropped into the cavity. They were finally evacuated through a 1.3-m-wide and 40-m-deep vertical tunnel that was drilled in a span of four days using a super-speed machine. It was a unique and successful operation in a confined space in the midst of loose rocks and water seepage.[38]

The Himalayan disaster

India, true to its principles of Vasudhaiva Kutumbakam, rose to the challenge of the Nepal disaster and delivered a stellar, empathetic relief operation to its neighbour and friend. This is no self-praise, but the relief operation, code-named Operation Maitri (Operation Amity), won hearts and appreciation the world over.

The United Nations Office for the Coordination of Humanitarian Affairs (UNOCHA) led the international laudatory note for NDRF and its endeavours.[39] The NDRF, established in 2006 in the wake of the 2004 tsunami, has grown into the world's single-largest dedicated disaster response force with the best technology and highly trained personnel. Its capabilities matched the most stringent international standards, and the force was in line to get certification from the International Search and Rescue Advisory Group (INSARAG), a global network of rescue forces under the United Nations.

It was a matter of great pride to lead and supervise the entire NDRF operation. It was also a unique opportunity for me, as the head, to make an on-the-spot assessment of my own team. Believe me, the team made the nation proud. During our operations, we received much encouragement from India's national security adviser, Ajit Doval, who came to Kathmandu along with the then foreign secretary, S. Jaishankar (current External Affairs Minister) and P.K. Mishra, the then additional private secretary to the prime minister of India. I was in regular touch with the Union home secretary and members of the National Disaster Management Authority (NDMA) particularly two of the members, R.K. Jain and Kamal Kishore who were approachable and guided me. I received tremendous help from Kamal Kishore, who personally came to Kathmandu on behalf of the NDMA. Prof. Santosh Kumar, the then executive director, National Institute of Disaster Management, prepared a report in which he lauded the efforts of NDRF in tackling this humanitarian crisis. My batchmate and in-charge of the disaster management domain of the MHA, B.K. Prasad, an IAS officer, was a strength for me and my teams throughout rescue operations in Nepal. As a seasoned officer, he would take every problem as an opportunity. We would often discuss how NDRF capacities could be gainfully utilized over the coming days to meet some of the urgent and immediate needs of the affected people. While interacting informally with Nepal officials, we would indicate some of the critical areas where NDRF capacities could potentially be used.

As Nepal lay buried under the rubble of devastation, NDRF rescue personnel started working round the clock to reach out to the victims affected by the earthquake. The NDRF, over the years, had been trained in Collapsed Structure Search and Rescue (CSSR) capabilities, which gave its personnel a lot of knowledge on the mechanical behaviour of concrete buildings that might have suffered a total collapse. Being a specialized response force, the NDRF always factored in the presence of empty spaces beneath the ruins that could support survivors, as well as the ability to create access tunnels in reaching trapped victims during rescue operations. NDRF teams carried equipment which were needed in such a scenario: lightweight and not vulnerable to dust and water. The NDRF already had the experience of working in Sikkim in 2011 when an earthquake of 6.7 magnitude struck.

During the search and rescue (SAR) operations in earthquakes, the position of the trapped victims in the ruin, the way the building has collapsed, and the building materials used, all create a great variety of situations and therefore the rescue operations may require a few minutes to several days. The way a building has collapsed dramatically differentiates the demands in personnel, supplies and effort. When a building collapses completely, rescue operations are often time-consuming and involve the need for a larger labour force. On the other hand, when a building collapses partially, the victims have, in most of the cases, no injuries and are in fact able to contribute to the rescue operations.

The rescue workers from the NDRF were deployed at different locations in the Kathmandu Valley. They were working closely in coordination with Nepalese authority, especially with army officials. Within the first twelve hours of their arrival from India, night operations were conducted by them in Lalitpur, Sitapaila and Gongabhu areas besides Bhaktapur. These locations had suffered greatly and the Nepal Army had requested the NDRF teams to help locate and rescue victims trapped under the debris. Nearly thirty-five rescue personnel led by its team leader Inspector Raj Kumar reached Lalitpur at about 11 p.m. guided by a liaison officer of the local army. The team was successful in recovering the body of a male victim from underneath the collapsed building of the income tax office. 'The casualty was trapped beneath a collapsed frame, pinned down by a lot of rubble,' recalled Raj Kumar later. 'The rescuers had to use hand tools and light machinery to extricate the dead body very slowly. It was a complex process, but the team pressed on and managed to get the body out in less than four hours.'

I wish to cover in detail the post-disaster happenings, for they reflect the true picture of such a relief operation. Moreover, such overwhelming situations also offer us heartwarming stories of human grit and hope.

The first news

'Sir, the ground shook quite violently some time back. There seems to be an earthquake of a severe magnitude. We have reports coming in from Bihar. I will give you details once I collect more information,' my NDRF control room called me to say this as I was returning from Dwarka, Delhi, after attending an official function on 25 April 2015. 'Please contact the India Meteorological Department [IMD] immediately and get in touch with emergency operation centre (EOC) at Patna to collect more information,' I told the officer on the phone.

Very soon, I was informed about the magnitude of this tremor by the IMD which was initially pegged at 7.3. The news of some casualties in Bihar also started pouring in and, subsequently, Nepal was mentioned to be the worst sufferer of this earthquake. The NDRF control room informed me that the epicentre was at Lampung in Nepal, about 80 km north-east of Kathmandu.

While in the car, I talked to the Union home secretary and briefed him about the situation. I also told him that we might have to send a few CSSR teams to Bihar once the details were known. 'Sir, I have instructed all my NDRF battalions to be on alert for any eventuality,' I said to the Union home secretary. DIG (Operations) S.S. Guleria, a competent officer who had already done his homework, called me and gave slightly more detailed information about this earthquake. He suspected hundreds to have died in Nepal, where a quake of 7.8 magnitude had struck the country at 11.56 a.m. on 25 April 2015. This earthquake was followed by three major aftershocks measuring 6.1, 5.3 and 5.5, on the Richter scale, respectively. In India, the earthquake affected parts of eastern UP, Bihar, Gangetic West Bengal, Darjeeling, Sikkim and the Delhi-NCR region.

I rang up the cabinet secretary and narrated the entire information available to me and briefed him about my preparedness in sending the Search and Rescue teams to Bihar. He told me that he would immediately convene a National Crisis Management Committee (NCMC) meeting and have talks with all concerned members to discuss the rescue and relief measures in the wake of the earthquake. After this meeting, there was another meeting called by the prime minister in which the then finance minister, the late Arun Jaitley, also participated, along with all concerned top officials of the Government of India. I represented the NDRF and was given the instruction to lead my team for a Search and Rescue operation in Nepal. That is how my team reached Kathmandu within six hours of the tragedy striking Nepal.

On the morning of 26 April, I was scheduled to catch an Indian Air Force Ilyushin Il-76 from Palam to Kathmandu. In the meantime, our teams were successful in saving a few lives in the Kathmandu valley. I wanted to be there well before 10 a.m. as there was an urgent need to coordinate our efforts, not only with the Nepal Army but also with other agencies coming from different countries. As I started to prepare for the journey, I received information regarding the delay of the flight to Nepal. Sensing further delay, I boarded an 11 a.m. Indigo flight to Kathmandu. As I reached Delhi International Airport, the atmosphere was buzzing with the news of the earthquake. The TV screens there were displaying pictures of the Nepal tragedy. As images of a devastating earthquake kept trickling in across television screens, the death toll quietly climbed close to 2000 by the wee hours of the morning. With Nepal's government overwhelmed by the scale of the disaster, India flew in medical supplies and relief crews. The news channels reported that hospitals in the Kathmandu Valley were overflowing and soon running out of medical supplies. The visuals on the television showed bodies being brought to a hospital in Kathmandu, where a police officer was telling the media person that his team had brought in more than a hundred corpses in one night. Both private and government hospitals had run out of space and the patients were shown being treated outside, in the open. Debates were going on across many channels and experts were of the opinion that unplanned growth, despite the region being quake-prone, had led to massive destruction. Kathmandu had grown and expanded into a congested and dense concrete jungle. Though there were official building codes to make them quake-resistant, there was hardly any adherence to them. According to some experts, a series of scientific studies of this fault line had adequately warned of an impending earthquake. 'Going by past history, Nepal is expected to have 1934 range earthquake every 80 years,' one of the experts said.[40]

All TV channels, however, were praising PM Modi for his swift decision. India was doing a credible job of providing Nepal with the much-needed relief and in evacuating tourists stranded there. But much more needed to be done.

After boarding my flight, I quickly checked my phone once before turning it off. It was inundated with video clips forwarded from Nepal. The first one was a 55-second film shot by an Israeli tourist while he was in the compound of the Pashupatinath Temple complex. The phone camera panned the space and captured the terrified tourists who numbered about sixty. The shaky images gave a clear indication of the intensity of the earthquake. The terrified souls were holding on to each other, even extending their arms sideways to keep their balance over the toppling impact. Moments later, the northern wing of the temple could be seen crumbling, raising a mini storm of dust. Within seconds, the temple structure directly opposite the first met the same fate. The tourists continued to cower. The next video was that of an undisclosed intersection somewhere in Kathmandu. It was shot from the first floor of a roadside building. The huge roundabout had cars of all sizes stranded. The statue and its cenotaph at the centre of the roundabout suddenly collapsed like a pack of cards. The streets were filling with people rushing out of the nearby buildings. The person foolishly continued to film. Another structure, which seemed like a police post turned into rubble. The debris fell horrifyingly on two people who were slow to react, or in hindsight, got no chance to evade near death. The third clip was from a CCTV camera mounted on to a building overlooking a two-way street. The visibility was five hundred metres. At precisely 11.57 a.m. local time, on 25 April, the tectonic shift of earth plates was clearly captured by the camera as the wavy street brought a halt to the traffic.

Due to extremely bad weather conditions, we were informed by the pilot that it would not be advisable to take off as it was rather impossible to land in Kathmandu. We were also informed that three IAF aircrafts, tasked to supply stretchers and other medical aid for earthquake victims, returned after encountering bad weather, or in technical terms a squall line. A squall line, we learnt later, is a line of thunderstorms that forms along or ahead of a cold front. Apart from the bad weather, the lack of parking space at the Kathmandu airport also compounded these aircraft's return. Another aircraft, which had two teams of NDRF and its dog squad, however, was the only aircraft that could land in Kathmandu that afternoon. Our pilot kept hovering over the airport and finally the plane landed at around 8 p.m. When we finally landed, it was raining and completely dark. The weather forecast predicted widespread rain and thundershowers over Nepal for the next twenty-four hours.

When I entered the airport, the first thing I saw was a long, narrow waiting room packed with hundreds of passengers peering out at the incessant rain and the flights taking off. The crowd gathered inside this waiting lounge comprised mostly Indians and Chinese, with some Europeans and Americans as well. Flights getting into Nepal was having a hard time landing, though as I got out of the plane, I did see two flights taking off in different directions. Inside, past the deserted arrival lounge, nearly 300 people were waiting in the baggage claim area, listless eyes fixed to the conveyor belts.

DIG R.K. Rana, Commandant P.K. Srivastav and a few other officers were present at Tribhuvan International Airport to receive me. Rana, who had come to Nepal a day earlier with the NDRF teams, briefed me about the situation in the valley. According to him, more than 2500 people had lost their lives within a few hours of the earthquake. The aftershocks of varying intensity had kept the Himalayan nation of 26 million on the edge. Rain was the last thing Nepal needed, as hundreds were feared trapped or missing in parts of the country and around Everest, where a fresh avalanche struck a portion of the base camp that served as a staging point for those looking to scale the world's highest peak.

Incessant aftershocks continued throughout the day on 26 April and the major one—a 6.8 magnitude jolter—recorded in the afternoon as I was still airborne, was felt across northern and eastern India and Bangladesh. 'These have slowed down the rescue efforts and temporarily closed the airport where thousands, mainly tourists, have gathered to catch a flight out of the ravaged nation,' said Commandant Srivastava, whose NDRF teams were still sifting through rubble amid fresh tremors. I decided to go to the Nepal Army headquarters first to obtain direct feedback about rescue works undertaken by NDRF personnel since their arrival a day earlier. It was a scary drive from the airport. Panic-stricken Nepalese people were running helter-skelter on the streets of Kathmandu dreading another catastrophe. Massive crowds could be seen lying on the grounds outside buildings of the shattered capital, several people with intravenous drips, trauma writ large on their faces. With all sorts of rumours flying around in the near-absence of a phone network, wary people prepared themselves to spend their second consecutive night under the open sky. Heavy rains added to their misery, disrupting relief operations. All day long, smoke billowed out of the ghat of the Bagmati River, forming a dense cloud as hundreds of bodies were consigned to flames. Most areas were without water and power. The first seventy-two hours would be critical for Nepal, I told my officers.

On my arrival at the army camp, a short briefing was arranged by the Nepal Army. I was told that the army had mobilized its personnel soon after the earthquake struck despite limited resources and equipment. The Government of Nepal was leading the response through the National Emergency Operation Centre (NEOC), with additional coordination and liaison set up at the airport with the Reception/Departure Centre (RDC) and with the Multi-National Military Coordination Centre (MNMCC) in Kathmandu. The MNMCC, established on 25 April, became the hub of coordination activities for all local and international search-and-rescue teams. Our team leader was already establishing appropriate liaison with Nepal functionaries through the NEOC and the Nepalese Armed Forces via the MNMCC. Emergencies of a certain magnitude involve a great number of humanitarian actors—actors already present in the country or those coming from abroad to provide assistance. In this earthquake of 7.8 magnitude, the Office for the Coordination of Humanitarian Affairs (OCHA), under the United Nations Secretariat, was responsible for bringing together humanitarian actors to ensure a coherent response to the emergency. Soon after the disaster struck, the Government of Nepal formally requested international assistance. Several international urban search-and-rescue (USAR) teams had indicated that they were going to deploy.

There was, however, a lot of uncertainty as to when those USAR teams would be able to depart for Kathmandu from their home bases given the rapidly expanding backlog of flights attempting to land. As such, during the first days of the emergency, numerous USAR teams and relief flights were delayed or diverted in the air to other airports. Indian USAR teams were the first to reach and started their operations immediately upon their arrival. On 27 April the decision was made by the Government of Nepal that no more USAR teams were needed. Despite this, the influx of USAR teams remained high. Tasking of the teams was conducted in a meeting taking place every morning at the MNMCC where national authorities went through geographical sectors. Following each day's operations, the results were shared, summarized and prepared.

One week into the earthquake, an On-Site Operations Coordination Centre (OSOCC) became fully functional, staffed by OCHA and the United Nations Disaster Assessment and Coordination's first responders, together with staff from the EU Civil Protection Team, MapAction, International Humanitarian Partnership, Assessment Capacities Project, UN Volunteers, the UN Resident Coordinator's Office, Danish Emergency Management Agency, Swedish Civil Contingencies Agency and the World Health Organization (WHO). OSOCC staff meetings were held daily at the OSOCC, wherein I participated regularly.

National and international media was also rushing in to reach the disaster-struck Nepal. Big names from the world of media, medicine, hospitality and other fields joined me on the same flight: Rahul Kanwal (India Today), Rama Lakshmi (*Washington Post*), Tripti Nath (Asahi Shimbun, Japan), Dibang (ABP News), Michael Ernst (team deputy, DART), Umesh Saraf (MD, Hyatt Regency Kathmandu), Padma Shree-awardee Dr Ashok Gupta (Mumbai-based plastic surgeon), Kartikay Mehrotra (Bloomberg News), Ziv Bilaus (Minister Counsellor), Manogya Loiwal (TV Today), Lalit Agrawal (chairman, Himalaya TV Nepal) and Sébastien Farcis (Radio France).

Alisha is reborn

A sixteen-year-old girl, identified as Alisha, was one of the first few survivors of the Nepal earthquake. Alisha became the hope of the Indian NDRF rescue team on its arrival at Kathmandu, barely twelve hours after the first shocks hit the region. Alisha was buried for over twelve hours under a four-storey building that had collapsed. The building was located in a narrow passage that was blocked by the rubble of collapsed houses on both sides. A few walls still stood but those were severely hit, and the entire structure looked like a hanging building. After assessing the situation, the team, led by Kuleesh Anand, assistant commandant, NDRF, came up with the plan of drilling a hole so that the location of the trapped victim could be ascertained. It had to be done in such a way that the structure was not affected on account of vibration. After illuminating the work site and ensuring the safety of the personnel, the team shredded some load from the site without disturbing the heavy rubble to prevent any vibration. They then stabilized the debris and made a 3–4-ft foxhole to confirm the victim was alive and conscious. Unfortunately, both her legs were trapped in two different directions, and she was hanging upside down. Two wooden logs were jutting in front of her: one near her face and the other close to her chest. Digging them out or cutting them was not possible as these logs provided shoring to the debris. The opening, on the other hand, proved to be narrow. Taking her out without releasing her legs looked difficult, rather impossible. Hence it was decided to prepare another entry towards the direction of her trapped legs. Since the available digging tools proved to be of no use, improvised tools of iron bars had to be made on-site. Sensing that the removal of big rubbles was not possible, the rescuers tried to dig them out in small pieces with those tools. After trying for nearly three hours, the team finally succeeded in making another foxhole of around 4 feet towards her trapped legs and released them without hurting her. This was audacious work that was impeccably executed. Another challenge lay in making a proper opening from the front and it became essential to cut the two wooden logs. It was done with the shoring of wood and bricks to stabilize the front foxhole. Covering the face of the victim with a pillow, the rescuers managed to cut both the wooden logs and made the victim totally free to be dragged out. Taking all safety measures, the NDRF team managed to place a flat board under the trapped victim and safety dragged her out of the debris. After giving her first aid, Alisha was handed over to her parents, who then shifted her for advanced medical assistance. One of the eyewitnesses present on the scene appreciated the efforts by saying that the NDRF team from India was the first foreign rescue team he had met and expressed his gratitude in one of the personal conversations with a team member.

Midnight joy

Throughout the night of 26 April, my teams were assessing buildings that had totally collapsed, looking for signs of survivors. Finding the exact position of trapped people was of primary importance and for that the NDRF teams relied on sound-detecting devices, trained dogs, information and on-the-spot examination.

Working with small, medium and heavy sophisticated technical equipment, one of the teams zeroed in on a building that was reduced to rubble and located a live victim. This was close to thirty-six hours since the disaster. Chances of people surviving were diminishing. The personnel broke layers of concrete, iron and rocks to reach the victim: a woman trapped underneath the ruins of her meat shop. Forty-three-year-old Tanka Sitaula had given up hope when she suddenly heard the noise of rescuers sifting through the rubble. Of the fourteen people trapped under the debris, Sitaula was the only survivor. 'Before I was discovered by a joint rescue team led by Indian rescuers, I had lost all hope of seeing this world again,' she recalled. She was doing the dishes—her husband and sons had left home after lunch—when the building collapsed. 'Before removing the debris we had to confirm her location. We told her to knock something close to her so that we could trace her,' Inspector Karan, team leader of the NDRF, later told me.[41]

On the second day of the operations, five people were pulled out from under what was once a shopping mall. Observation holes were made and cameras with a 360-degree view and night vision inserted through them. Aftershocks and tremors continued to make our job difficult and risky, but hoping for more miracles, my teams nevertheless continued with their efforts.

As I boarded the Air India flight back to India, with my rescue teams preparing to withdraw from disaster-stricken Nepal, the memories of people experiencing the survival of a natural disaster filled my mind again. I had seen a society in mourning, further alienated by conditions of uncertainty and despair. I had witnessed arguments about the preparedness of such disasters. As people were putting things back together, they also knew that future earthquakes were inevitable. As Edward Simpson writes, 'An earthquake does not conclude. It lives in metaphor, and history, passing in and out of popular consciousness . . . Earthquakes are remembered, but in other ways, they are forgotten; occasionally forgetting and remembering touch one another.'[42]

Gongabhu

Close to Ganesh temple, the wife of an army personnel was trapped under a collapsed structure. One of the NDRF teams was deployed there. The woman was in trauma. She was in no position to free herself. Her left leg was stuck between two heavy pillars, and on top of that, an iron rod had penetrated her other leg. She was sprawled between the roof and the floor. The team tried to pull her out with the help of a rope, but in vain. Airlifting bags too failed to lift the slabs. Continuous tremors further made their task challenging.

Post a collective survey, there was quick change of plan. The team decided to make an approach from the rear side of the building. Two bodies were extracted from under the rubble. Two precariously hanging floors also collapsed. Rain continued to pound the scene and the agitated crowd added to the tension. The brave men of the NDRF continued undaunted. They had the dual task of securing the place and continuing with the tricky operation. They inched forward, using chipping hammers and other equipment. It was 5 a.m. when the lady was visible again. By then exhaustion gripped our men.

At around 7 a.m., a fresh round of tremors hit the valley. A chunk of rubble came crashing down, injuring one of our team members. The rescue operation had to be halted for a while till the tremors subsided. The operation commenced at 12 p.m. Meanwhile, the husband of the trapped woman was convinced that amputation of her leg was the only way to free her. A team of army doctors was also called in. They ruled out the amputation.

It took another three hours for the NDRF bravehearts to cut the pierced iron rod and the pillar crushing her legs. Thanks to the tireless efforts of the team, she was finally released by 4 p.m. and rushed to the hospital. It was a miracle of sorts. The team had put in nearly seventeen to eighteen hours of work, sans proper rest and food.

Tanhu Hotel

It was another dreary sight. Several people were trapped under the New Bus Park, Tanhu Hotel. The Israel and Chinese rescue teams were the first to arrive at the site. They found the site too precarious to handle. The risk involved was too high. I reached the site along with my men to make a quick survey. Only the sixth floor of the hotel was accessible, the rest was crushed and completely buried below. The hotel was further compressed by adjoining buildings. An NDRF team was deployed there too, under the command of Inspector Hira Lal. We decided to drill from the wall of an adjacent hotel. The operation began at 7 a.m. on 27 April. An L-shaped 30-feet-long corridor was created after working for hours at length. Fresh tremors added to our woes. The team then made an attempt to enter from behind the hotel. Incessant rain hampered our strategy and even that attempt had to be abandoned midway. The front entry was the only option available. Work began afresh, and after rounds of drilling, soaring and chipping, two bodies were finally discovered. It is nearly 7.30 p.m. when the work stopped because of exhaustion. The entire day had yielded six dead bodies. There were many bodies still buried under the debris. The team returned the following day to retrieve the dead. They worked tirelessly, under much stress and were successful in getting out all the dead bodies by 6.50 p.m. The team then moved on to the next site.

The list of sites kept mounting: Namuna Toll, Suryamadhi, Bhaktapur, Machhapokhari, Sobha Bhagwati, Brijeshwari, Sitapaila and Balaju Bypass.

The NDRF was the first international rescue agency to respond to the calamity. As many as sixteen teams of forty-five members each were airlifted to the affected areas of Nepal. Our swift action saved lives and retrieved 133 bodies. It was all rack and ruin when I reached Kathmandu. It was hard to imagine all those who had a cover over their heads the night before had been rendered homeless. The ashen faces stand out in my memory. One does become philosophical in the face of such calamities, but it was a race against time for us.

Our relief and rescue operation turned out to be one of the landmark relief operations launched on any foreign soil in recent times. As the largest-ever Humanitarian Assistance and Disaster Relief (HADR) intervention abroad by India, the NDRF had the clear, compelling and challenging task of saving lives. The initial seven to eight days saw regular meetings coordinated by the Indian embassy from the beautiful garden in front of the Chancery. The embassy officials, under the leadership of Ranjit Rae, Indian ambassador to Nepal, worked day in, day out and played a critical role in coordinating Indian agencies with local authorities. While I attended the meetings on behalf of the NDRF, Major General J.S. Sandhu, a very competent army officer, was from the Indian army. Three military commanders, led by Major General Sandhu, were in Nepal to coordinate its stepped-up relief operations as well as evacuation of Indians stranded in the quake-devastated nation. My friend Prabhat Singh, who was posted at the Indian embassy in Kathmandu, provided excellent cooperation to me. I recall vividly how important these meetings turned out to be in rolling out our activities of humanitarian assistance on a day-to-day basis and also to avoid duplication and confusion. While coordinating with the Nepal Army, I interacted with Nepal Army Chief General, Gaurav S.J.B. Rana, who was appreciative of the role played by the NDRF. In fact, he visited NDRF locations to witness the indefatigable efforts made by our jawans to extract bodies from under the rubble. It was a simple case of nature's fury versus the tenacity of the NDRF jawans. The prime minister of Nepal too applauded the stellar work of the armed forces.

Despite the commendable speed and scale of India's response to the Nepal earthquake, the efforts were marred by the excessive and sensationalist coverage by the Indian media. Journalists, initially instrumental in revealing the tragedy's magnitude, found themselves criticised for pursuing sensational news, displaying insensitivity, and projecting arrogance. The disaffection caused by the Indian media was evident through the trending #GoHomeIndianMedia hashtag on Twitter. As one national daily aptly noted, 'While rescue effort has been praised, media's wall-to-wall coverage of the calamity and that of the relief operation seems to have left a bitter aftertaste among Nepalis.'[43]

Each disaster presents its own unique challenges and the response of the humanitarian agencies and systems are usually tailored to the context. In the case of any disaster, an understanding of the topography, institutional policy, and the legal, sociocultural and political context is key to ensuring efforts are effective. The same is also important to building resilience and sustainability of agency/capacity of institutions and communities to respond to future disasters. The Nepal earthquake of 2015 was a salient reminder of this fact.

A reluctant start

I had been a reluctant starter for my NDRF posting. In the first week of January 2014, the MHA, Government of India issued an order for my deputation to the Central Industrial Security Force (CISF). I was ADG (Security), UP, at that time and had worked as ADG (Intelligence) and ADG (Meerut Zone) in the last two years. The then DG CISF, Rajiv, an IPS officer from the UP cadre, had recommended my name for the post of ADG in CISF but by the time the order came, he had already retired and DG NSG

Arvind Ranjan, a Kerala cadre officer, was holding the additional charge of CISF. After a few days of my joining the CISF, I was given the charge of the Airport Sector, which had the mandate to look after the aviation security of airports in the country.

During the same time, on the recommendation of the NDMA, the MHA downgraded the post of DG NDRF to the ADG rank and bifurcated the NDRF from Civil Defence and Home Guards. Mahboob Allam, an IPS officer from the Tamil Nadu cadre, was appointed DG NDRF in the rank of ADG. The Civil Defence and Home Guards organizations were looked after as an additional charge by a DG-rank officer of a Central Police Organization. Allam had only a few months left for retirement, therefore it was expected that some officer of the ADG rank would be appointed as DG NDRF once the current incumbent retired.

I happened to meet a member of the NDMA, K.M. Singh, also a former DG of CISF, at an official gathering. An IPS officer from the Maharashtra cadre, Singh was known to me, and we had kept in touch even when I was in UP after my repatriation from the CRPF in 2008. An accomplished intelligence officer, he is renowned for his profound understanding and expertise in matters pertaining to national security and the intricate realm of intelligence operations. During the conversation, he suggested I join the NDRF as it would unfold another domain of my professional career. He narrated to me the historical background of how he had played an important role in setting up the NDRF from scratch. Frankly speaking, I was in no mood to leave the CISF and showed no inclination to join a small organization such as the NDRF. I was gradually settling down in my new responsibility of aviation security management and was enjoying my role in the CISF. The work demanded a lot of critical thinking, planning and resourcefulness and I was truly measuring up to the task. As a senior police officer, I was bringing my unique micro-detailing perspective and strong understanding of aviation security operations and management to key decisions. Being new to this area of policing, I was constantly looking for ways to improve the activities and process of aviation security. But Singh was of the opinion that the NDRF would be professionally more rewarding for an officer such as me (he had heard about me being the first IPS officer in the country to have successfully completed an MBA in Disaster Management in an executive programme). Besides, I had been organizing and conducting various programmes connected with disaster management in UP as well as in other parts of the country. On a few occasions, we both shared the platform as panelists or guest speakers in discussions on issues related to disaster risk reduction.

Not long thereafter, the MHA gave me the additional charge of the NDRF along with the CISF assignment. Thus, my innings with the NDRF began on 1 September 2014 after Allam's retirement from IPS. Looking back, I am grateful to Singh for pushing me into the disaster management domain and guiding me, on and off.

A fledgling body

The apex body for disaster management in the country is the NDMA, with the prime minister of India as its chairman and the MHA the nodal ministry. In the federal structure of our nation, the primary responsibility of disaster control and management rests with the state governments. The central government lays down the policies and guidelines and provides technical, financial and logistical support, while it is the district administration that carries out most of the operations in collaboration with the central and state agencies.

When I joined the NDRF, it was eight years old. As a wise guardian, I was fully aware of the ingrained qualities of the elite force as well as its shortcomings, and that both had to be taken care of in equal measure. The NDRF was conceptualized as a specialized response force to a threatening disaster situation or an actual disaster under the Disaster Management Act, 2005. It is a mandated response force positioned in an operational mode to be a proactive educator, as well as a responder to any natural or man-made disaster.

I have been a witness of human suffering on many occasions that I have lost count. One might consider me as most unfortunate to be in the midst of so much pain and suffering, and even death, but I look at it not from the prism of negativity and despondency but from the rainbow of hope and service. We brought hope, life and smiles to countless individuals caught in the powerful jaws of fate and nature. I am extremely proud of being there at the forefront of calamities such as the Jammu and Kashmir floods, Chennai urban floods, coastal cyclones and the Himalayan earthquake. Although I would leave it to others to assess my team's and my effectiveness, I can say with all humility that there was a gumption to lead and meticulously galvanize the response team and carry out daring rescue operations to save the lives of thousands of distressed and marooned victims.

In India, the number of people directly affected by disasters would surprise anyone—nearly 1 billion people have been affected by different disasters in the last two decades ending 2010 and this number is expected to grow up to 1.9 billion by 2030. Because of its unique geography and climatic condition, our country is among the most disaster-prone regions of the world. As much as two-thirds of the population here is vulnerable to hazards of different kinds. We are exposed to windstorms from the Arabian Sea and the Bay of Bengal. Over 50 per cent of our total landmass falls in the tectonic zones of earthquakes owing to the Himalayan plates. Twelve per cent of our total area lies in the zones where floods happen and 68 per cent of arable land is exposed to droughts. India also has a coastline of 7600 km and Tsunamis are a major threat.

Disasters come in many forms and have multitude causations. However, all disasters need mobilization of resources, right assessment of the situation, a defined policy and strategies for their control and mitigation. Often this task is undertaken by the Armed Forces, paramilitary forces or the local police along with the assistance of NGOs and the local population. But all of this often results in a delayed response, confusion and inefficient utilization of resources. A substantive policy of disaster management with a pragmatic approach is the answer to control and reduce the losses occurring at regular intervals, both to lives and property.

The NDRF turnaround

It would definitely not be out of place to mention the systemic changes I brought about in the intrinsic management of the Force. In 2013, during the Kedarnath disaster, the common perception was that the NDMA's and NDRF's presence was mere tokenism, as written by Hridayesh Joshi, a prominent journalist, in his book *Rage of the River: The Untold Story of the Kedarnath Disaster*.[44] However, following various disasters I dealt with, I tried to instil the kind of innovative practices and dynamism required by a prime organization such as the NDRF. Joshi goes on to say: 'When I covered Cyclone Hudhud, which struck the east coast of India in 2014, and the earthquake that devastated Nepal in 2015, there was a perceptible change in the way [the] NDRF functioned.

They were better equipped, better trained and better prepared. I see this as a positive outcome of the Kedarnath tragedy.[45]

It is said, 'If you go solo, you go faster, but if you take your team together, you go far.' As the leader of the NDRF, I was determined to know the way, go the way and show the way. The Force had begun to conduct breakthrough operations to save both lives and property. The sanction of two new battalions from Sashastra Seema Bal (SSB), NDRF Academy at Nagpur, the institutionalization of the NDRF Response Medal, expeditious procurement of response equipment, raising the built-up accommodation for personnel and their families and quick mobilization of the NDRF teams during disasters were some of the milestones achieved under my tenure.

With my experience of field postings and having worked with the ranks and file of the police department, I had a fair idea about the need to have training for the Force in uniform. Moreover, training plays a crucial role in effective disaster management. The only way for the Force to be abreast with the latest methods of disaster response is by way of developing core competency through training. The training at the NDRF was still being conducted based on the training regime prepared by the NDMA in 2009. I pushed for a revision of the training model keeping in mind the dynamic disaster landscape and of course the changing training needs of the NDRF as well. Apart from the personnel training at our designated centres, we also roped in disaster response trainers from the Swiss Development Corporation (SDC) to update the skills of the uniformed men. For once, we were going beyond the rule book.

One of the critical factors for the Force to be wary of was the need to respond swiftly to an emergency. For a Force to be International Search and Rescue Advisory Group (INSARAG) External Classification (IEC) certified, it is required that it be deployed within twelve hours of help sought by a disaster-affected country. A key factor causing delay in our deployment was the waiting time for the air force aircrew. There was a system in place of keeping two teams in a battalion as disaster-response-ready round the clock, meaning, the teams and their equipment were loaded on to vehicles (called team-on-wheels). The response time for the two teams was twenty minutes. This was regularly practised and stressed upon. Through effective coordination with the Indian Air Force, for the first time ever, NDRF teams began to be deployed with zero delay. This was no mean achievement.

To meet the challenges and make the NDRF a multidimensional disaster response force, the exploration of new possibilities and ideas became imperative. Thus, we started some new initiatives in the organization whereby it could hone professional competence to achieve excellence in disaster response to make India disaster resilient. Expanding its role in regional cooperation, on the initiative of the Government of India, the first-ever South Asia Disaster Management Exercise (SAADMEx) 2015 was organized in New Delhi where delegates of seven SAARC member nations actively took part in a three-day mega exercise. This exercise proved a step ahead in regional alliance to meet the challenges of disasters among the SAARC member nations. A programme of capacity building, already in vogue with the SDC, was enlarged to include veterinary doctors and a canine squad to meet international standards. In order to recognize the contribution of a responder to the cause of the Force, a Disaster Response Medal was instituted for the first time in 2015. We also took an initiative to start the NDRF Wives' Welfare Association to support and enhance the official welfare efforts within the NDRF, focusing especially on the welfare of families and children of NDRF personnel.

In view of the ever-increasing role of social media, I always felt the Force needed to foster an organic relationship with the citizens using a media interface. Therefore, at the NDRF, we started an initiative to connect extensively using the social networking sites. We opened NDRF's Twitter page (NDRFHQ@Twitter.com) and a Facebook page to receive regular feedback on its operations and important activities. In fact, an area that needed a strong focus was the NDRF's visibility for humanitarian assistance. In the Jammu and Kashmir flood of 2014, the public of Kashmir, for the first time, saw for themselves the extent of support provided by the NDRF. In the Nepal earthquake, we did outstanding SAR work but because our personnel wore uniforms with a logo that did not mention India, the visibility was impacted. We needed to think of rebranding the NDRF. We amended the logo as NDRF-INDIA.

A dedicated team at the centre used social media channels effectively by creating a hashtag #ChennaiFloodOperation. The team worked 24/7 to ensure help reached on time. The use of social media and information technology (IT) helped us overcome the language barrier, and unlike regular phone lines, there was no issue of busy or clogged lines. This was the first such operation for the NDRF where crowdsourcing was used to receive and disseminate information.

The NDRF began collaborating with pioneering, specialized agencies in the country to upgrade information and data, its skills, training and preparedness for potential disasters. We signed an MoU with the Jai Prakash Narayan Apex Trauma Centre (JPNATC) AIIMS, New Delhi, in January 2015 to develop and implement mutually beneficial training programmes in capacity building for emergency medical support. An MoU was also signed with the National Remote Sensing Centre (NRSC), ISRO, Hyderabad. Through this understanding, the NRSC was mandated to provide earth observation data from space and aerial platforms, develop technologies for the management of natural resources, support disaster monitoring and management as well as capacity building for the utilization of earth observation data. It was also mandated to facilitate the NDRF in Disaster Management Support Services. Another MoU was signed with Navodaya Vidyalaya Samiti to carry out Training of Trainers (ToT) programmes to sensitize children of such schools located in the highly seismic zones.

Documentation was another field I found to be in need of immediate attention. To bring uniformity as well as standardization into the process, there is always a need to develop SoPs on response methodologies and techniques for different types of disasters. These SoPs also present the framework of NDRF's response in providing support to local authorities when struck by a major disaster. The police have the Blue Book to follow for any operational occasion, deliberating, analysing and documenting every operation so that lessons can be learned from any such disaster for a proper future strategy. SoPs were prepared for earthquake disaster response, to conduct mock exercise and for capacity building of the State Disaster Response Force. Besides SoPs, the Medical Manual was also prepared as an NDRF medical component that is an integral part of each USAR team. The manual provides procedures for immediate medical attention to the victims during disasters.

* * *

My hunger for learning was not reduced to hands-on work. I also wished to utilize my expertise to open new vistas that would not only widen my horizon but also contribute towards my output. My participation in international seminars, conferences and trainings saw a spurt in the intervening period of 2014–17. INSARAG Reclassification of the Swiss Rescue and INSARAG External Classification of the Moroccan USA Team, Geneva, Switzerland (2014) became my first learning in that direction.[46] Soon thereafter, I participated in a seminar on the Chemical Weapons Convention of Chemical Safety and Security Management at Colombo, Sri Lanka (2014), in which I gave a presentation on NDRF's Chemical, Biological, Radiological and Nuclear (CBRN) capabilities. The 2015 World Humanitarian Summit in Dushanbe, Tajikistan, and my participation in it reinforced the all-important need to cater to the weak and the vulnerable. Many more followed, such as the 50th Session of the Programming Committee of SAARC in Pakistan (2015), INSARAAG Global Meeting, Abu Dhabi (2015), the Senior Crisis Management in Washington, DC (2016), Urban Emergency Rescue in Shanghai (2016) and the UN-led Civil-Military Coordination Conference at Dhaka.

A holistic and comprehensive view was taken by us regarding critical deficiencies of the organization which was mainly involved in quick response activities. 'Ease the process of procurement' was the new mantra. The process was relatively simplified with decentralization at field commanders' level for low-value items. Meetings with the Directorate General of Supplies and Disposals (DGS&D) for the purpose of rate contracts of disaster management equipment and their enlistment were carried out. Wide publicity was given to terms and conditions as well as Qualitative Requirements (QRs). Specifications being of international standard, Original Equipment Manufacturers (OEMs) were communicated to enlist their firms with DGS&D. Our team also held meetings with firms to know their difficulties in quoting NDRF tenders. We reviewed specifications after getting feedback from the firms. The most urgent requirement of equipment for the NDRF such as chipping hammer, multipara meter-monitor, secondary battery SMF for communication and rescue boat were finalized by our team. A project for revision and updation of disaster management equipment was undertaken due to which the specification of 112 disaster equipment was reviewed by our team. This resulted in the processing and procuring of equipment such as multi gas detector, rubberized sandal for water rescue, handheld gas detector and generator set. The procurement of operational uniform dungarees was quickened by reviewing the technical specifications with the help of the Northern India Textile Research Association.

* * *

Motivation plays an important role in effective disaster management. I visualized and worked towards institutionalizing a medal in the form of recognition for NDRF personnel so that they were motivated to the cause. Sustained efforts finally resulted in the creation of a Disaster Response Medal by the MHA in 2015, which is now awarded to every personnel who serves the NDRF for more than three years in continuation. In 2013, during the Kedarnath tragedy, when an Indian Air Force chopper crashed in Uttarakhand, a few NDRF personnel, along with a few air force personnel, were killed. While the air force personnel were swiftly acknowledged through posthumous gallantry medals, the sacrifices of NDRF personnel remained unacknowledged for an extended period. However, our tireless campaign for the rightful recognition of these brave personnel yielded results and, in January 2015, their valour and selflessness were finally honoured with posthumous gallantry medals.

I must say, in a short period, the NDRF has proved to be a dedicated force for disaster management in the country. I have consistently believed that a fundamental element contributing to the success of this organization is its members' deep comprehension of the substantial cultural distinctions among people both within the nation as well as outside. Respecting ensuring that the key messages on a difficult and vital domain of disaster response is delivered with sensitivity and empathy. Based on the success of this model, many countries have shown their willingness to set up a similar kind of specialized force for disaster response.

Looking up

My tenure with the NDRF was an exciting challenge, but it was coming to an end. *Leading from the Front: Awarenes, Engagement & Intervention for Community Empowerment*, a case study of NDRF by the Indian Institute of Technology (IIT) Delhi had the following to record:[47]

> Jammu and Kashmir floods, Cyclone Hudhud and Nepal Earthquake got NDRF its visibility not only in the country but also to the international community . . . It has also acquired the image of a truly specialist response force to deal with any natural disaster including CBRN (Chemical, Biological, Radiological & Nuclear emergencies). With the institutional mechanism in place and the continual improvement of technology, India is much better equipped to handle disasters more effectively than in the past.

Hardly the one to rest on my laurels, I further got down to the task of fine-tuning the entire gamut of disaster management mechanisms.

Today, there is only a handful of subject specialists who have an understanding and/or are trained in the subject of earthquake disaster management from the standpoint of earthquake disaster response. The NDRF should consider creating a federal pool of these limited resource persons and from subject-specific resource teams. These teams can be charged to provide necessary peacetime technical support during operations and in the aftermath of earthquake disasters. Hence the timely role of the NDRF is critical to meet the expectations of an effective response.

Today, there's a mechanism in place, with highly competent, conditioned and trained minds and hands devoted to the cause of safety, protection and humanity. The specialized force of the NDRF has a very different role to play, far removed from the traditional law-and-order-related exercises. Even as I pen this, seismic tremors have been recorded in another part of the globe— Turkey. Lives and properties are endangered. True to its words, an NDRF team has landed at Ankara, the capital city, informs the current DG Atul Karwal. The men and their grit had been put to test again. I'm proud and confident. Closer to home, as I write, the Silkyara-Barkot tunnel collapse in Uttarakhand has demonstrated the courage and tenacity of multiple agencies, from rat-hole miners and the NDRF to the Indian Army. The seventeen-day rescue operation mounted in the aftermath of the collapse was not just inspirational but was also an intensive and painstaking exercise to successfully extract the forty-one trapped workers after working through 57 m of rock and debris. Drills broke, rocks cracked and attempts failed several times. The experience of operating in the smallest of crevasses and challenging terrain tells the story of our journey that has a never-say-die attitude written all over it.

Disaster risk reduction measures, as P.K. Mishra, principal secretary to the prime minister of India, an authority on disaster management, recalls in the context of G20 deliberations, can play an important role in preventing such losses.[48] With a population of 4.7 billion, the G20 nations have been greatly exposed—ranging from risks resulting from asset concentration and vulnerability to natural disasters.

The memory of a woman and her words flash before my living conscience. Her child had been pulled out from the entangled mess in the Bihar floods after hours of concerted efforts. The distraught mother's joy knew no bounds at the sight of her rescued child. She hugged me in a tight embrace, then gently placed both her hands on my head and said something that still rings in my mind: 'I will name my child NDRF Singh.' I know the words were said in an emotionally surcharged moment. Possibly she never named her child NDRF Singh, but the joyous relief I saw in those eyes and felt in those words was priceless.

9

CISF: The Nation's Pride, My Tiara

To command a Central Armed Police Force (CAPF) is a dream come true for any police officer worth his salt. The NDRF and my association with it became a precursor for more action when I was offered the charge to steer Central Industrial Security Force (CISF, another CAPF). Memories of my stint as the DG CISF stand apart. If the NDRF got me national and international recognition, the CISF got me opportunities and challenges afresh. A premier, multi-skilled security agency of the country, the CISF was mandated under an act of the Indian parliament on 10 March 1969. Although started with a modest strength and defined objective, the CISF today is not just a public sector undertaking (PSU)-centric force but caters to and secures major critical infrastructure of the country. Under its ambit come nuclear installations, space establishments, airports, seaports, power plants and sensitive government buildings as well as heritage monuments. The force also provides VIP security through its elite and specialized Special Security Group (SSG) commandos. The broadening of the charter of duties and responsibilities in the year 2009 has brought private sector establishments under the security cover of CISF too. The geographical spread of the force includes sensitive areas affected by terrorism and left-wing extremism in the states of Jammu and Kashmir, Chhattisgarh and the

North-eastern states. It was a proud moment to walk into the decorated office space of the DG CISF on 26 September 2016. I was convinced about the distinct mark of the CISF as a professional and tech-savvy central police force of the country.

Peculiar features of the CISF

What makes the CISF very different from the rest of the CAPFs is that it is need-based and functions on the model of cost reimbursement by the organizations availing its security services. Thus, for its day-to-day operational and administrative requirements, the CISF depends on the management of the units which it secures. It is thus dependent on the satisfaction of the concerned ministries of the Government of India for its sustenance and functioning and not just the MHA. Certain establishments are directly owned by the CISF, such as the Reserve Battalion, training institutions, Force headquarters and subordinate field formations. In addition, the CISF secures certain establishments directly under the MHA, such as Special Security Group, Delhi Metro Rail Corporation and Government Building Security. For these units, the CISF must procure and provide kit items, vehicles and accommodation by receiving funds for the purpose from the MHA. The need-based model also means that the force must market itself adequately to not only retain its present deployment but to add new units to its cover. Therefore, it is very important that it be perceived by its customers as a highly skilled and capable force vis-à-vis less costly options such as private security agencies. The CISF is also unique in the sense that it is the only CAPF which has its own fire wing deployed in addition to its security wing in some of its units. This highly specialized fire wing has a separate organizational set-up within the CISF.

A clear vision

While addressing a group of senior officers at the National Industrial Security Academy (NISA), Hyderabad, during a training programme in the latter half of 2016, I articulated my perception of the CISF:

> I never compare [the] CISF to other paramilitary forces. We have a different mandate altogether. We are contributing to the macroeconomic development of our country and as the nation's economy grows, we grow with it. We add value to the functioning of the ministries whose units we secure. Because of the changes taking place the world over and because of our nation's progress, the nature of risks to the country's assets is fast changing. Therefore, we as the chief protector of the country's economic assets should be able to recognize, analyse and develop strategies to mitigate these risks. Only then would we be adding value to our client ministries and can expect recognition from them. And it is only by serving our client organizations effectively that we will contribute to the nation's security.

With this exposition of the CISF's role, I not only reminded the officers of the larger role they were playing in the nation's security and economic progress but also cautioned them that if they did not rise to the expectations of the client organizations in the rapidly changing security scenario, they would perish. The CISF officers were aware of the reality of this threat as prior to the induction of the CISF in the airports in 2000, there had been some rethinking in the corridors of power about winding up the CISF as a separate CAPF.

Based on my previous experience of working in a CAPF and my tenure in other organizations, I had formed clear ideas on how to go about leading the force. It was made clear to everyone that we needed to work as a team; to start with, our focus should be operational preparedness and upgradation.

Steps to galvanize the Force

I devoted my first week with the CISF to understanding it deeply. My energy was soon channelized into digging, questioning, probing and conducting collective as well as one-to-one meetings. The idea was to ensure that the state of preparedness of the force remains adaptive to dynamic growth organically. Within months, the communication channels were made seamless and sensitivity and motivation became the hallmark. Excellence was the goal; the difficult, even the impossible, was achieved in the form of expansion of the Force in 2017.

Even before I took charge as the DG CISF, I knew that the CISF had the best of the lot when it came to the constabulary, sub-officers and gazette officers as compared to other CAPFs. I firmly believe that the nature of work undergoes constant evolution as professional and personal lives intertwine due to evolving technology, shifting work expectations and changing environments. Furthermore, the intricacies and challenges of the modern world could no longer be effectively addressed solely through 'command-and-control' leadership; instead, they call for more collaborative, constructive and shared leadership models. I started touring the CISF units across the length and breadth of the country, undertaking as many as thirty-two tours in a year. On each of the tours, my biggest agenda was to interact with the constabulary, share meals with the sub-officers, cut the extraneous grandiloquence and fill their hearts with pride. It was a simple strategy and its impact was felt instantly—the tours opened communication channels that had been hitherto slow or non-existent.

My first visit was to Chhattisgarh, in LWE pockets, where our Force was. I spent time with my jawans over meals. In one informal chat, I was told about the pendency of general provident fund (GPF) transfer cases. This happened because the GPF accounting was not being sent to the respective offices of the personnel. This gave me an opportunity to start a special drive to reduce the pendency and keep reviewing it on a fortnightly basis at the Force headquarters. To our relief, the number of cases pending dropped sharply. Other interactions provided me inputs on the inadequate utilization of vacancies for various Bureau of Police Research and Development (BPRD)-sponsored management development programmes organized at Indian Institutes of Management, NPA and other reputed organizations. These programmes were essential to enhance the professional capacities of police personnel.

Moreover, I ensured my tours were over the weekends. My physical presence in Delhi on weekdays was devoted to ideating, planning, strategizing and completing a lot of paperwork. It was a subtle message; I was willing to go the extra mile to ensure the welfare of the force, at the cost of my personal time and interests. Naturally, the same diligence and commitment was expected in return.

Having worked with several armed forces, I knew the importance of regular training in maintaining operational effectiveness. Traditional wisdom also says that if personnel are left idle, they indulge in all sorts of non-productive activities. Therefore, we decided to observe 2017 as the 'Year of Training' in all CISF formations and units to make the personnel physically fit and mentally alert so that they could effectively respond to any operational contingency. During the year, we advised the supervisory officers to visit the units under them. This was done to monitor and ensure regular training was taking place at the unit levels to achieve physical fitness of the CISF personnel. Tactical preparedness of the units was equally important. Zero tolerance for accidental firing, review and Implementation of SOPs in CISF units, effective connection of the Unit Commander with the Unit personnel, and effective leadership of the Unit by the Unit Commander was also emphasized.

Effective use of social media and technology

We also harnessed social media and technology to infuse a sense of camaraderie and competition among the senior officers. We strongly believed that a free-flowing channel of communication at all levels facilitated better decision-making and faster adaptation to change. Therefore a WhatsApp group was started, comprising all officers of the rank of DIGs and above in the CISF. This worked wonders to activate the thinking and working of these senior officers. It built a community wherein the good work done by one officer was immediately made known to the rest and got appreciated by the superior officers. This led to a chain effect where every officer started doing some good work and projecting it on to the group. The group also became a platform for sharing opinions and discussions about various professional matters. I further encouraged the senior officers to form WhatsApp groups of their own, including their subordinates', so that important decisions taken at higher levels and other information could be disseminated downwards without wasting time. We also insisted that senior officers should always be connected to their personnel and be abreast of the ground realities. We wanted them to use this platform to inform their subordinates about the positive developments in the Force and motivate them to greater action. As chief of the Force, I always saw a value addition in the adoption of appropriate technology and, ensured new technological initiatives in CISF. Additionally, I held the opinion that it was more important to make the Force personnel passionate about their jobs, which would in turn lead to creativity and innovation.

Men first: Tackling personnel issues on priority

Soon after taking charge, I took up the issues plaguing the personnel branch as a priority. First, we got the departmental promotion committee (DPC) for senior officers accelerated resulting in 369 officers getting promoted during 2016–17 compared to only 133 during 2015–16. This sent a message that we were concerned about the promotions of our officers. In addition, during 2016–17, a total of 2627 NGOs were promoted as compared to 1048 during 2015–16.

We also took up the issue of cadre review for Group A officers on mission mode. This had been hanging for over a year and half. The position was reviewed in October 2016 and thereafter we started closely monitoring the progress almost on a day-to-day basis. Such close monitoring paid off and by the end of October 2017, a sanction of twenty-five additional posts including two ADGs, seven IGs, eight DIGs and eight commandants was given. With this, the long overdue promotions of the senior cadre officers could be implemented.

We drafted a new transfer policy after due deliberations with all Sector IGs, field officers and other ranks and files, and decided to implement it. We knew there was no harm in trying it and if the new policy were to fail, we could always revert to the existing policy.

I firmly believed that the organization should be responsive to the grievances of its personnel. Hence, we introduced the system of giving SMS feedback on the action taken on the grievance represented by a person during the request room of the DG on Mondays and Fridays. This was done for the first time in the CISF. Any person who came to meet the DG would immediately come to know about the decision taken on his representation or the reasons for the delay in taking the decision, if any. This greatly increased transparency and hence the satisfaction levels of the personnel. I was ably assisted by IG Anant Kumar, an IPS officer from the MP cadre, and IG Anurag, another IPS officer from the Tripura cadre who formed a robust backbone of the force, displaying impeccable qualities and integrity as consecutive team members, which were unquestioned and commendable. Both the officers made my job way easier, refined and precise.

Justice, even if delayed

I noticed that the number of legal cases that the CISF was grappling needed our attention. Behind every case was a human face who felt that some injustice had been done to them by the Force. It was our responsibility to verify the facts and settle things based on the merits of the case without any consideration of who the person was.

I took this matter up on priority with the legal branch in the Force headquarters in 2017. For the first time, video conferencing was introduced to monitor and expedite the finalization of departmental enquiries and court cases. Some long-pending cases could be disposed of through video conferencing. We wanted infructuous cases to be identified and action thereupon initiated to close them. We were also willing to review old cases and explore if they could be settled at the departmental level itself. I felt that even personnel against whom the CISF had acted in the past were entitled to a consideration of their grievances in an appropriate manner. To educate the staff at the field formations about legal matters so that errors could be avoided, sixteen legal workshops were conducted in 2017. DIG Shyamala, our legal eagle, the brain behind the possibilities and arguments, led from the front. A great mind, Shyamala set high standards of engagement and delivered promptly. I knew that in a disciplined organization like the CISF, change had to begin at the top. Only a vibrant Force headquarters could drive the subordinate formations to perform better.

Provisioning: The essential support

One of the branches that produced dramatic results due to robust monitoring was the provisioning branch of the Force headquarters. In my very first meeting after taking charge as DG, I proclaimed that provisioning would be top priority. To avoid delays in the process of procurement, we introduced the Performance Evaluation and Review Timeline Chart (PERT). This encouraged officers involved to commit themselves to deadlines and subject themselves to review against their own committed dates and outputs.

Regular meetings were held with connected external agencies such as the DG of Supplies and Disposals and the MHA to resolve issues. Prompt response and resolution of bidder's queries ensured wider participation. Sticky issues that had been pending for years were finally resolved.

Advance planning for the entire process of procurement was introduced and the sector headquarters which had to actually do the procurement were also involved in the planning and preparations. The annual procurement plan for 2017–18 was prepared in November 2016 itself and circulated to all sectors. Advance tendering was initiated to reach the stage of placement of supply orders, which were then placed as per priority and fund availability. Workshops were organized at the Force headquarters in January 2017 for all sectors' headquarters to disseminate understanding on provisioning and procurement issues. This was followed up with close monitoring of the work entrusted to the sector headquarters and providing immediate guidance on matters to avoid unnecessary delays. Due to these planned and persistent efforts, the budget was utilized properly.

Focus on airports

From my earlier experience as the ADG of the Airport Sector in the CISF, I knew that the airports were the face of the CISF.

Therefore, we gave a good part of our attention to improving the functioning of CISF at the airports to give a better experience for the air passengers. Due to an earlier stint in the airport sector, I had a good understanding of the operational and administrative constraints in enforcing security protocols.

Based on this experience and my interactions with the officers on the ground in the airports, we introduced several proactive measures based on the adoption of new technologies in aviation security leading to seamless experiences for passengers at the major airports of the country.

One bold initiative was to do away with stamping of tags on hand baggage. Similarly, to ease out congestion in the Hyderabad airport, the CISF in collaboration with airport management, started an initiative of providing a dedicated security check facility for passengers having hand baggage only.

It was during an event organized by the Air Passenger Association of India at Chennai that I was approached by especially abled passengers with their concerns, and I consequently decided to take necessary steps to address their grievances. The resulting measures were put into effect almost immediately and led to training sessions for CISF personnel aimed at increasing sensitization in the Force towards the needs of specially abled and neurodivergent flyers training sessions were initiated at the Delhi Airport, following which a session was held at the Kolkata Airport. The training event saw active participation from CISF personnel from eighteen other airports including Patna, Raipur, Port Blair, and the North-eastern states. Another session was conducted at the Mumbai Airport and was followed by more such sessions in a total of fifty-nine airports under CISF cover. It was an initiative that enhanced the capacity and image of the Force manifold.

Our efforts to improve the functioning of the CISF at the airports started getting accolades from several corners. In 2017, it became the first CAPF to get Quality Excellence Award for Best Airport Security at the World Quality Congress. The same year, the CISF unit at the Mumbai Airport was given the most coveted 'Golden Peacock Award for Risk Management' for organizational leadership and institutional excellence. The award jury was headed by Justice Arijit Pasayat, a former Supreme Court judge, and the CISF was the only government organization to get this prestigious award under the risk management category. K.N. Tripathy, DIG and Chief of Mumbai Airport Security, was the main force behind it and acted as an effective leader to motivate his team with the organizational belief and core values. We started and operationalized a Special Tactics and Training Wing (STTW) at the CISF's National Industrial Security Academy (NISA) in Hyderabad. The STTW became a game changer for Tactics Training in CISF and positioned the Force as one that had capabilities in operating in urban and built-up areas. It also boosted the morale of the Quick Response Team (QRT) members of the CISF tremendously as they saw the immediate relevance of these special tactics to their job context. The idea was to make special teams more capable of responding to any threat that emerged at airports or other critical infrastructure. Adhering to high standards, Rajeev Panwar, in charge of the Wing, displayed exceptional professionalism and supported the operational domains through training as and when required.

Fresh as I was from my experience of heading the NDRF, I started taking measures to improve the operational preparedness of the Force regarding fires and disasters. First, we combined the Fire and Disaster Management branches in the CISF, which was the need of the hour, as earlier disaster management was being handled by the Welfare branch. Then, we got the branch to work on a handbook on operational preparedness during fire and disasters, which was circulated to all field formations. A compendium on major fire and disaster incidents and guidelines for the safe handling of fire equipment was also prepared and circulated. Disaster management plans for 206 of the 336 CISF units were prepared and approved by the local civil authorities.

The frequency of mock drills involving all the stakeholders that is, state, SDRF, NDRF, police, local agencies, etc. on-site and off-site emergencies in the field units was increased dramatically.

I was aware of the superior disaster management and fire-training capabilities available at the FSTI and NISA. In fact, NISA had been one of the earliest training institutes in disaster management since 2002 and had been equipped with costly equipment funded by USAID. So, we wanted to offer these facilities to other agencies to boost the image of CISF as a key player in this area. Accordingly, a fire and disaster management training brochure was prepared and circulated to all heads of CAPFS, NDMA, heads of police organizations, PSUs and state fire services, and I inaugurated the first such course on disaster management for external police organizations in September 2017 at the Fire Service Training institute (FSTI), Hyderabad. As a recognition of the efforts to improve and project these training capabilities in CISF, NISA and FSTI were awarded the FIST (Finest India Skills and Talent) award by Fire and Security Association of India (FSAI) in 2017.

Of all the CAPFs, CISF had the largest number of canines, at around 700. During my visit to the CISF complex in Ranchi in January 2017, I found that though a Canine Training School of the CISF had been inaugurated there around three years ago, it was practically lying dormant as the entire staff was located at the 5 Reserve Battalion in Ghaziabad. Upset at the sheer wastage of such an important facility, I ordered the immediate operationalization of the Canine Training School. Accordingly, within twenty days, the entire staff was shifted from Ghaziabad to Ranchi and the CTS was operationalized.

The challenge of training

The huge intake of personnel threw up yet another major challenge—that of training them. While starting the training programme for the new recruits, the Reserve Battalions, which were co-located with the RTCs, were brought under the administrative control of the respective RTCs and the Reserve Battalions were converted into ad hoc training centres. With this move, within the short span of three months, the unthinkable was achieved in the CISF; the RTCs had prepared themselves for training the expected 20,000-odd constables and the training commenced in the RTCs in April 2017. This was possible only because of the excellent officers we had in the CISF. I counted on R.K. Mishra, ADG Headquarters, an outstanding officer and Yamini Priya, DIG Training at the headquarters, who was meticulous and committed to her work. Fellow officers DIG S.K. Malik, D.P. Parihar, V. Khamo and Inspector General IG Jagbir Singh (who headed NISA) contributed significantly to the whole mission and accomplished the job in an impeccable manner.

Taking up such a huge training load of constables was fraught with the danger of compromising the training quality and the welfare of the trainees. To meet both these challenges, for the first time in the CISF, the system of mentoring, buddy pairing and group monitoring were introduced in the training institutes. For each platoon of thirty trainees, a carefully selected senior was appointed who was responsible for closely monitoring the progress in the training of the platoon. This system, because of the temporary enhancement of several personnel in the training institutes to act as mentors, took a great toll on the existing resources of the units. Initially, no senior officer was in favour of handling such a huge training load. ADG Mishra and I, despite our personal apprehensions, declared 2017 as the 'Year of Training' and exhorted all to cooperate with the mammoth effort never ever attempted before in the CISF. Online evaluation of trainees as well as online examinations were also conducted. The quality of training turned out to be far superior as reported by the Sector IGs who were sent to conduct a third-party evaluation of the training at various RTCs. The training endeavour was ably energized by IPS officers Dharmendra Kumar and M.A. Ganapati. Their zest and commitment to deliver inspired everyone. Both officers brought with them their inimitable capacity and their deep knowledge of police work.

Sharing space and vision with me were dedicated individuals who formed my strength and gave so much meaning to the word 'team'. This chapter would be meaningless sans the mention of DIG Administration, Sudhir Kumar. Courteous to the core and possessing lightning-sharp grasping ability to analyse and deliver on organisational matters, Kumar was simply amazing. His cheerful personality only added to the zest of the system. Another officer, K.P. Singh, AIG Administration, was a warm and delightful personality who was reputed to be extremely resourceful, dynamic, and amiable. Ajay Kumar, a young commandant, was another CISF officer who was very meticulous. His analysis on matters connected to aviation security was very helpful to me during my tenure. My private secretary, Naresh Yadav, a very capable and reliable assistant, handled various tasks with confidentiality and discretion. He managed schedules, handled correspondence and assisted in daily administrative tasks in a professional manner.

* * *

I also knew the importance of making the CISF's presence felt in social media. So, we started the CISF Twitter handle @CISFHQrs in October 2016 and kept a dedicated team to promptly tweet on this handle and respond to tweets related to the CISF. Similarly, the official and verified CISF Facebook page @official.CISFHQrs was launched on 29 August 2017. The awards won by the CISF in the last year of my tenure such as Best Marching Contingent on Republic Day 2017 and 'M-Power App' being adjudged as the best IT project amongst CAPFs by NCRB in the category of empowering police with information technology were a feather in the hat for our team of officers who were already pushing themselves for the force. In 2017, we signed an MoU with National Skill development Corporation (NSDC) for imparting skill training to wards of personnel and families and low medical category personnel for financial independence, resettlement after retirement and empowerment. An MoU was also signed with National Academy of Legal Studies and Research (NALSAR) University, Hyderabad, for awarding a PG diploma to the serving officers and sub-officers who completed their basic training at NISA. This was aimed to equip CISF officers with additional qualifications. In collaboration with the Ashok Institute of Hospitality and Tourism Management under the Ministry of Tourism, we launched a four-month long Hunar Se Rozgar Scheme in September 2017 in New Delhi for the children of CISF personnel. In a similar endeavour, the first Skill Development Centre was established at reserve battalion Ghaziabad.

* * *

This part of my journey might sound cut and dry to you and may lack the adrenalin-pumping action of other tenures, but the period affirmed in me the need to make policing systems fundamentally strong and dynamically futuristic. The agenda for my team and I was cut out for the coming year. It was indeed an honour to be the head of a force which had earned a name for itself on account of its dedicated commitment to high levels of professionalism and remarkable public dealing. The professional acumen of CISF personnel in protecting national assets has been appreciated by every section of society. This has only been possible on account of the consistent efforts and hard work put in by all the officers and Force members.

10

UP Calling

I have taken great pride in each of my postings and responsibilities. Each of them brought distinct challenges and possibilities and I tried my best to do justice to them and come out unblemished and proud. I was wedded to the khaki, and its honour and grace were my utmost intent. I never imagined that my last posting would turn out to be the highlight of my career.

It was December of 2017 and the colourful celebrations of Passing Out Parades (POPs) were taking place at various training institutions of the CISF. It had indeed been a year of splendid achievements, so far as capacity building of the Force was concerned. The training of more than 20,000 recruits in CISF training centres, post augmenting resources of different kinds, was no mean achievement. In each POP, the grounds echoed with the sounds of the coordinated movements of trainees and the inspiring notes of the CISF Band. The demonstrations of the rope *malkhamb*, bicycle show and silent drill by the lady recruits, and a karate demo by our instructors at the Arakkonam RTC left the spectators awestruck. Such a series of POPs, ably organized on such a grand scale, had never been witnessed before. These RTCs had not only accomplished the seemingly impossible task of training more than double their capacity but also raised the bar so high that it would be difficult to beat for years to come.

My deputation with the central government had seen fructuous times as DG CISF. I was aware of the retirement date of the serving DGP of UP but had no clue that a committee headed by the chief secretary, UP government had been initiated to appoint the next head of the UP Police Force. It was a prestigious position in one of the most professional and robust police forces in the country. On 30 December 2017, I got a call from Sulkhan Singh, DGP UP. The conversation was simple and straightforward and honestly, one hell of a surprise—the state government wanted me as DGP after his retirement the next day.

Barely eight to nine months into office, Yogi Adityanath, who was helming the UP government, held a fervent determination to rectify the prevailing law-and-order situation in the state. With an unwavering focus on transforming the state's crime landscape, the new chief minister personally selected me for a prominent role. It was as if he believed my appointment would be the catalyst to bring forth the transformative change he sought.

While the offer came as a surprise, the waiting period was exasperating. It was well into January of 2018, but there was no word from the MHA that my repatriation had been okayed. Then, in the third week of January, I was informed that the order had come through and that I was to join UP 'as quickly as possible'. The three-time SSP (Lucknow) was back as the chief of UP Police. It was an exciting moment, one that filled me with pride and anticipation. ADG (Law and Order) Anand Kumar handed over the ceremonial baton and the office within a few hours after my plane touched down in Lucknow.

It was a momentous occasion. I was left with more than two years of service, and there I was, feted with the most challenging assignment of my career. It was truly an honour, an hour of true calling, a dream come true. Heading the biggest police force of one of the most populous states of India brought me immeasurable pride, but I was also grimly aware that it doesn't take much for heroes to bite the dust and kings to fall from grace. I knew that as UP Police Chief, I would be under constant scrutiny. I would be required to use my skills of gentle persuasion to make the top political bosses see reason. I would have occasions to disagree with the ruling purveyors of power. How would I do it without ruffling too many feathers? It was soon to become the measure of my leadership, expertise and experience. In simple terms, I had got what I had aspired for, and now it was upon me to make it or ordain it otherwise. I was determined to make it.

It is also imperative at this juncture to make you aware that there were certain postings and assignments of my career in the past, which have deliberately not found a mention here. My roles as ADG (Intelligence), ADG (Security), ADG (Special Enquiries) and ADG (Telecommunication) have not found any mention in my memoir because of obvious reasons. The sensitivity and national importance of the work and operations take precedence over anything and everything.

Besides the regular policing task and management exposure in diverse sociopolitical scenarios, I also brought to the table my vast expertise from the areas of intelligence, communication systems, security, disaster management and assets safety systems. In the last leg of my career's journey, I clearly intended to put this to effective use. I was ready with my plan, but before we get into that, it is important to talk about the law and order and the crime scenario in UP prior to Yogi Adityanath becoming the chief minister.

Before Yogi Adityanath became the CM of UP, the state was notorious for its poor law-and-order situation and high crime rates. The state was infamous for incidents of communal violence, caste-based violence and gang wars. According to the National Crime Records Bureau (NCRB) data for 2016, UP had the highest number of crimes reported among all Indian states, with a total of 3.2 lakh cases. The state also had the highest number of crimes against women, with 49,262 cases reported in 2016.[49]

Apart from this, UP witnessed several high-profile cases of crime, including the 2013 Muzzafarnagar riots, one of the deadliest instances of communal violence in the past eight decades of India's independent history. Marked by incidents of brutal violence, including cases of arson, looting and sexual assault, it led to the death of over sixty people and the displacement of thousands.[50]

Similarly, the 2016 Bulandshahr gang rape, a heinous incident of sexual assault, caused widespread outrage and protests due to the state government's inadequate handling of the case. The case brought to light the issue of women's safety in the state and the need for greater awareness and measures to prevent gender-based violence in the state.

Amidst such a volatile social environment, the police force in the state also faced a severe shortage of manpower and resources. Plagued by a high crime rate, with incidents of murder, rape and communal violence being reported regularly, the law-and-order situation was a dire challenge to overcome.

In addition to the issues of communal violence and crimes against women, rampant corruption, as well as organized crime and general political violence, made UP a breeding ground for dangerous criminality. The situation was so grim that 'even the cops have been found to be blatantly violating the law despite a series of suspensions and even dismissals. In some cases, the police were found to be running extortion rackets and looting traders'.[51] Overall, the law enforcement situation in the state before Yogi Adityanath was a cause for concern.

The plan

The Indian Police Force is governed by the Indian Penal Code, 1860. Though the Model Police Act, 2006 brought a fresh burst of oxygen, necessary changes have only trickled in. The political class continues to cling on to archaic policing mechanisms, dealing a heavy blow to the police's effectiveness, and indirectly deflating the morale and the spirit of the personnel.

A constable of the force can aspire for just one promotion in his entire career. At the most, he can reach the rank of head constable. Are we fanning his motivation or smothering it? Police infrastructure, weaponry, vehicles and so on continue to remain abysmally below standards. Recruitment, training, posting and promotions are mired in an unjust quagmire of manipulation. The conviction rate of criminals says it all. And, finally, the public image of the police hangs on the precipice of painted initiatives, exceptional human interface and, of course, fate.

I know I stand the risk of sounding disparaging and negative here. But a spade must be called a spade, and as a committed soldier, sold to the ideals and principles of the police force, I was determined to take on the daunting challenge. Neither did I intend to run away from it, nor did I feel the need to apply a cosmetic filter and pass on the baton to the next incumbent after my term ended. Carrying the baton, I entered the arena with a sense of pride. Now, I was the chief of the Force and not only knew the drill but was equally aware of the pulse of policing.

My plan included six pointed strategies. Number one, overhaul the perception regarding the men and women in khaki and meet the expectations of the common man. This was a big challenge. Perceptions and expectations had to be purposely and sensitively handled. The image of the police in the eyes and the minds of the people needed a refined makeover. Every action that followed must send a clear message to the common man that we meant business. We meant to stop crime and criminals. We meant to reduce road accidents and streamline traffic on the streets. We meant to make the women, the elderly and the weak feel secure.

Number two, while the general public should feel assured about the police, criminals should fear the khaki force.

Number three on my priority list were the police personnel themselves; the foot soldier, the *sipahee*, the constable, the head constable, *thanedar*, the inspectors, all of them needed to be touched, re-trained, cajoled, motivated, provoked, threatened, warned and cared for, to not only bring the best out of them but to give them the self-belief of a cohesive team working for a common objective.

The fourth intent involved using technology to our advantage. The rationale against incorporating the latest technology could only be attributed to the lack of funds and the will to take it forward. I intended to change all of that. A smart age requires smart policing. The old must be gracefully gloved into what is new and more relevant. I was willing to ride any wave of criticism or any roadblock to do and achieve what was right.

The fifth aspect was (and is) very close to me—the style of functioning, the leadership personality that I imbibed from the ecosystem. Any job is run under the influence of and eventually known for the kind of personality the head brings to the table. I believed in my style of functioning, which was/is transparent, persuasive and action oriented. I had a clear idea to use my style of governance and send a clear, effective message down the hierarchy, with all elements of shock and utility alive and kicking.

Finally, the sixth and the last intent, but by no means the least, was that of innovation, of introducing game changers and setting the standards high and making a habit of achieving them.

The big nod

I was confident that the above-mentioned points could be achieved through sustained and concerted efforts. But to achieve that, it was imperative that an ideal state of polity existed in the state, one that did not interfere at any level of management and one that gave a free hand to bring about change. The number-one suggestion of the police reforms proposal mooted in 2006 talks about freeing the police from its political masters. It was a tall order, but I had heard positive things about the new political dispensation. Yogi Adityanath, the UP chief minister, was a no-nonsense politician and was going about governance with a concretized and focused approach.

Somewhere, I was confident that the new chief minister had the necessary mettle to run the state in an exceptional manner.

My taking the helm of the State Police in the beginning of 2018 also coincided with the first major initiative of the new Yogi government, the Global Investors Summit. It was to be a congregation of national and international heads from the corporate world. Investments in certain sectors, specially defence, electronics, agro and technology were targeted. The President of India, Ram Nath Kovind, the prime minister, Narendra Modi and many key ministers' proposed presence added to the prestige of the event. UP had to be showcased in the best possible manner. In the past, major investors had stayed away from the state fearing poor law and order. The chief minister had scheduled a meeting of the core committee at his residence and the entire executive brass had been directed to be present. It would be my first official meeting with the chief minister. The buzz about the head of the executive repeated two words as acknowledgement—straightforward and no-nonsense. At the Secretariat, I was directed towards the ante room: 'The CM wants to meet you before the meeting.' I was both excited and curious; this was unwarranted and definitely not on the agenda. I had barely seated myself when the door across the room opened and the familiar figure, in his distinct attire, emerged. He had his hands folded and a vibrant greeting of 'DGP Saab' on his lips. I was instantly on my feet trying to match the exuberance. He made no attempt to sit down.

His deep-throated voice rose, '*Aapka abhinandan* [You are welcome]. I couldn't meet you earlier. The people of your state welcome you. You have to take care of them, whatever the cost. My government follows a straightforward approach to governance and zero tolerance towards crime and corruption. You have a free hand to do what it takes to keep the state safe and happy. Interact with me directly.'

It was no doubt a straight, no-nonsense meet. His words were full of humility, optimism and vitality. It suited my upbeat spirit from the moment we met. 'Let's go and start the meeting,' the man responded to my overtures.

My first meeting with CM Yogi Adityanath had ended, but it was the beginning of a long and meaningful association with the man and his ways. I had touched the nerve of the leadership and felt just the right intent. I went about my job, as they say, guns blazing.

Although I'll go about describing my strategies and their implementation one by one, in real time they happened concurrently. Which ones overlapped the others, which assumed prominence over the other, is but a matter of conjecture. For the sake of convenience and in-depth review, I have broken down the happenings of my two-year tenure into well-defined headings.

First things first

The case with law and order in UP is challenged by the density of population and the size. At a population of twenty-three crore, the machinery of policing is understaffed and over stretched. I knew structural changes and reforms in the archaic laws would happen at their own pace, we had to operate with the current strength and means at our hand.

On the first night after taking charge, I dispatched two young IPS officers, Himanshu Kumar and Mohit Gupta, in plain clothes and unmarked vehicles, to make unannounced secret checks of all the police stations, checkpoints, field posts, deployments, level of alertness, responsiveness and empathy. 'Mark your areas and give me the report in twenty-four hours,' was the cryptic brief.

Sleep on the first night at the official residence of the DGP came with a strange satisfaction. Each post in the past had been accepted with the spirit of a challenge, and it was no different with my new, albeit last responsibility.

The next day in office saw a barrage of meetings, press briefs and circulars being drafted. I began my review of the law-and-order situation, region-wise and district-wise. By the late afternoon, it was amply clear that the UP Police Force needed a push of a different kind. Although efficient, the Force seemed to have slipped into a 'self-congratulatory' mode. While its perception about itself was satisfactory, even good, the same could not be said about the general belief.

For getting big results, small, even minuscule, formulas work. Starting from mile-zero is always a good idea. I remember an interesting story my father had shared with my brother and me. We were at the dining table when he said, 'Do you both know where the phrase "back to square one" originated?' I looked at him with curiosity, even as my brother continued eating. 'Football commentators in America divide the field into imaginary squares for the sake of convenience for its listeners on the radio. This helps the commentators to easily let the listener know where exactly the ball is on the field. The square from where the game begins is square number one. So, whenever the ball returns towards the centre of the field they say, the ball is back to square one,' my father concluded.

Post lunch, I was alone in my office, a much-needed respite from the flurry of happenings and information. I stared at the open page of my diary. The date on the page seemed immaterial. The page was blank, the steel-body pen lay helpless yet poised. About ten minutes later, my General Staff Officer, Sanjay Singhal (a senior police officer of the rank of ADG) informed me about the return of young officers from their fact-finding tour. They were quickly ushered in. Their fatigued and not-so-happy faces were already a commentary about the report they carried.

Their debrief was on expected lines. Laxity and lethargy had no place in the system, yet it was all over the place. Officers Gupta and Kumar had found gaping holes. They had found absent patrol beats and gaps in highway policing. The system needed a shake-up. I immediately assembled my entire secretarial staff and officers for a meeting.

My assistant's writing hand flew at a furious speed, as he jotted, 'I want the SoPs shaken-up. Inform every thana, control room, that the official phone numbers of the SHOs, inspectors, out post incharge, have to be boldly displayed along with their names at prominent places. I want photographs taken and uploaded on the headquarters command link. Furthermore, a complaint, even if received by an SMS will be looked into and taken up as if it is a regular complaint. All calls to the official numbers will be received. In the event of a call being missed, it will be returned at the earliest. Every complainant must be informed through SMS of the progress made in his/her complaint. Any laxity in any of the aforementioned areas will carry serious repercussions.'

'What's the standard response time to crime in our state, Sanjay?' I asked my assistant, who was of the rank of ADG and was my general staff officer.

'Twenty-three minutes, Sir.'

'We have to bring it down to fifteen minutes, and later to ten minutes. Get me the breakdown of response protocol, post a distress call or emergency.'

I was determined to not let mediocrity come in the way of professionalism, and I had made the first strike. I was also determined to not let this be seen as a starter's-intent before things converge into complacency and incompetence. I was up and away.

Lightning decisiveness

A thana is no ordinary place. It is the fulcrum around which the entire law and order of a specified area circulates. Under the existing system of policing, a thana is commanded by a singular SHO. For a long time, I had strong reasons to believe that a lone inspector was not enough to handle the demanding new-age policing. Besides maintaining law and order, the police must deal with crime and also partake in investigation.

Proposal ready, appointment fixed, I shuffled into the CM's office. I was greeted with the same high octave tone.

'*DGP saab, bataiye* [Please take a seat]. How can I help you?' The CM was right on the money. I matched his zest.

'Sir, I have a proposal to staff three inspectors in each thana across the state. One SHO would be responsible for law and order, the second would focus on crime and the third would be totally dedicated to investigation.' The CM nodded to my proposal.

Thus, in one stroke I was able to make a major decision, on an experimental basis, of separating the tasks of crime control and investigation. This was the clear differentiation the Model Police Act, 2006 talked about.

My bid to strengthen the beat patrol mechanism resulted in the purchase of 4221 vehicles for the UP Police. Of that, 3318 were motorbikes and the rest were four-wheelers. The vehicles were equipped with GPS-enabled mobile data terminal linked with the Dial 100 (now 112) Control Centre. In the occurrence of an unfortunate incident, the victim and the related people need help to arrive in good time. The challenge with the Police Force has always been to reduce the time taken to respond to the cry for help. The UP Police took approximately twenty-three minutes between cry and response. The same was challenged and brought down to the approximate period of fifteen minutes. Bringing down the response time by eight minutes was no mean feat. In situations where every second counts, this was a boon. The law protection and enforcement Force was operating in a concerted manner with a well-defined vision and goal.

But even this was not enough. I wanted to push the envelope by reducing the response time further to ten minutes. The department and its personnel believed it was possible. All it required was the will to achieve it. We had the infrastructure and technology. There was a different mood in the Force. UP Police was a giant on the rise, and ready to sprint. A year into my tenure, I had no qualms about reiterating that UP Police responds faster than a pizza delivery.

The khaki makeover

In the same space where the entire state machinery, including the police, was working assiduously towards a better tomorrow, a petty incident deeply disturbed the conscience of the populace.

In the bazaar of Shahjahanpur, a betel-leaf vendor was thrashed by five constables of UP Police. The vendor, Sushil Kumar Gupta, was beaten black and blue.[52] His crime? Sushil Kumar had asked to be paid for the cigarettes the constables had taken from his shop. The merciless beating of Sushil was recorded on phone by a bystander and soon the video started trending. I immediately ordered a departmental inquiry. The report, without an iota of doubt, found the accused five constables not just guilty of the crime but their act shrieked of a disturbing mind frame. All of them were sacked.

The incident was in sharp contrast to what had happened on 23 February 2018, in Saharanpur. Constable Bhupendra Tomar (57) was on duty when he received information about a man lying on the road, with multiple stab wounds. Tomar rushed to the spot. However, in a strange coincidence, he received another call regarding the sudden death of his twenty-seven-year-old daughter. You can imagine the dilemma Constable Tomar must have been in, but he made the most difficult decision of this life—choosing life over death. He, along with his team, rushed and rescued the man from the threshold of imminent death.[53]

Contrasting incidents indeed. Both happened within the first fifty days of me being the Chief of Police. While one made our chests swell with pride, the other put us in the dumps.

The khaki had acquired unwanted stains. It needed a thorough wash. Thus began a mammoth exercise of training the police personnel's behaviour. How could the khaki serve the people without discipline, concern and empathy for the victim? The police definitely required a makeover.

The police wasn't just a force; it had to embrace the all-pervading cloak of 'service' and 'smart'. (SMART Police. S stood for strict and sensitive, M for modern and mobile, A for alert and accountable, R for reliable and responsive, and T for tech-savvy and trained.)

On my way to the police headquarters one morning, I sighted an accident victim lying by the roadside, unattended. Two- and four-wheelers whizzed past him. No one stopped to help him. There were no beat police either. I arranged for emergency help and got the victim hospitalized. The newspapers went crazy about it.[54] The act wasn't meant for publicity, but a positive message did go out. A couple of days later, I made a surprise inspection at a prominent traffic crossing in Lucknow. The police personnel were missing at the police-booth. I donned the role of a ticket checker and issued challans of erring drivers.

The 'smart cop' challenge

'How's your day going, Papa?'

It was my son Apoorv on a long-distance call. A son calling in between work or study without a specified purpose is rare. Perhaps I'm being cynical, but I would assign that attribute to the treasure of a daughter's heart. Regardless, there I was indulging in a rare moment of camaraderie with my son while I was at work.

'I'm sure you're enjoying work.'

'I am. I am.' I wanted to say more but an upcoming meeting loomed in my head. It was an inaugural event. Keeping in mind the challenges of the new millennium, especially in the context to the growing threat of terrorism, a specialized wing named SPOT (Special Police Operation Team) had been formulated. The SPOT headquarters was established in the vicinity of the Lucknow International Airport and was being inaugurated that day.

'Papa, make your cops smart.' Although I muttered something incoherent in response, my mind was racing away. 'Like, every time you see an army guy, it gives a different feel. You don't feel the same . . .' his voice trailed away. Possibly he avoided stating the obvious. My mind was racing away, and I found myself replying, 'I will, I will.' I sat there for a few seconds rushing for the inaugural meet and speech.

On the way, I asked my general staff officer to call a meeting of my staff and the district police officials. 'Circulate the agenda of three Es: Energetic, Enthusiasm and Empathy. Circulate to them that they need to come out with their ideas of making the three Es the guiding factor for the personnel of the police force; ways in which we can push a more humane policing idea which can be adopted as a way of life.'

The three Es would also become the starting point of a massive orientation and training exercise for thousands of police personnel in the days and weeks to follow. Additionally, we also tied up with the Indian Institute of Management (IIM) Lucknow, for training the police officers under a customized management programme.

My system of operation was fixated on information, planning and time. I had given clear instructions to my subordinates at police headquarters that my official worktime would begin thirty-five minutes prior to the designated office hour. They were further informed that I needed a heads-up on all police activities planned for the day, reportage and review of the ongoing operations and any other matter that might come up. I would be at my desk at 9.25 a.m. and my office would be populated with the heads of all the branches, including the media cell officer and officers looking after crime, and law and order. My system was conditioned to not only move with time but also to respect it. Rain or shine, the DGP headquarters would begin its day at 9.25 a.m. sharp. Of course, policing is a 24/7 exercise and in moments of need the clock becomes irrelevant. I did face opposition and dissent, especially related to my adherence to time, but it did not affect my resolve. I would be there, on time, staff or no staff. It would have an impact, a deep impact.

My day would begin with briefings about the crime reporting of serious nature of the last twenty-four hours, the progress about the ongoing investigations of important crimes and the resultant feedback about the progress achieved. The pros and cons would follow later. The first thirty minutes of the morning was reserved for everything connected with crime management, law-and-order scenarios, operations, trial management in Protection of Children Against Sexual Offences Act (POCSO) cases, briefings on intelligence and social media analysis. The phones would buzz, or we would connect with the district officials. This small measure ensured the entire police machinery being under close watch and minimizing slip-ups. For me, it was a major strategy. I was majorly aware of the happenings across the state.

I firmly believe that a police officer has '*ashtang bhuja*', eight arms and hands, and each hand holds a tool or responsibility. With a police officer it's not a single hand or a pair of hands in operation at one point of time but invariably all the four pairs simultaneously.

On my part, I completely changed the rules of the game. I was a 'walking-office', an office on the move. I required information in real time. Instructions, commands and decisions had to be made whatever be the time and engagement of the day. Phones had to be answered. The outcome was a lesson in seamless communication. My office was alien to bureaucratic hiccups; they were simply non-existent, and the status was religiously pursued. It was a small, possibly an inconsequential idea, but this innovation became an impactful decision which went a long way in transforming the dynamics of quick communication in the State Police.

The weekend grill

My love for travel was well known, but travel for work found a new meaning, especially when I ensured I travelled on weekends. I called it the Weekend Grill, for it set in motion preparedness and alertness across the state. It was crucial to give a clear message that the headquarters meant business, and mediocrity and callousness would have to be relegated to the darkest of the prison.

Every weekend, an impromptu itinerary was prepared and concealed. Meaning, it was kept a secret to ensure the element of surprise and uncertainty kept everyone in the zones, range and districts on their toes. When the tour and review of a zone concluded, all the other zones were alerted, without disclosing what was next in my itinerary.

Within five months of my arrival to the state, I embarked on extensive journeys across various police zones and ranges. I traversed the landscapes of UP, seizing every opportunity to halt at police stations along the highways and adjacent areas, engaging with our personnel at all levels. On one occasion, I undertook a visit to the Agra zone, conducting meetings, inspecting police units, only to return to Lucknow. The next day I repeated the arduous routine, unfazed by the consuming length of the journey. Upon my arrival at the camp office, I received an unexpected message summoning me to the CM's residence. As I stood before him, he fixed his gaze upon me and inquired about my tireless ventures. His astonishment was palpable when he discovered the consistent nature of my weekend expeditions in the line of duty.

In all sincerity, he advised me to avail myself of the government's aircraft for district visits, emphasizing his concern and extending his benevolence, leaving an indelible mark on me.

The impromptu visits and surprise inspections had the desired impact. It kept the Force alert and vigilant. The spontaneous gatherings with the officers and all rank and sundry enhanced our outreach in relaxed and informal settings. The idea was to send an assuring message that the last in the rank and file is as important as anybody else. The sweat and blood of doers and performers would find validation and support. Loyalty and deliverance were expected in return.

Crime and punishment

Criminals are an integral part of a policeman's life. Criminals, I know, are meant to be put away in prison, but trying to understand how their mind works can be very useful. In-custody criminals are an extremely viable source to understand criminals' mindset, the modus operandi and how they are indoctrinated into the fold. My strategy of being on top of things also manifested in the need to interrogate the criminals caught during operations or otherwise.

Once, the ATS caught a young man who had been recently indoctrinated by Islamist radicals. He was apprehended while he was on the verge of joining the ISIS. The ATS chief called me to let me know about the catch. I expressed my desire to interrogate the man.

'There's no point, Sir, I have already interrogated him and he has revealed whatever information he had, including his handlers and their influence on him. We'll put him through the process of de-radicalization,' the chief said.

'No, I would still like to interrogate him,' I insisted, and my superiority of rank got the better of the situation. I got to question that man for two hours. It might have seemed like a futile, repetitive exercise, but it offered me a first-hand understanding of the ways and means adopted by radicals to influence a young mind. My direct involvement in the happenings kept me completely updated and well informed.

* * *

I found in CM Yogi Adityanath a man with excellent levels of devotion towards duty and idealism. During the period of slightly more than two years, I developed a chemistry that was not just organic but also a rarity.

As the head of the state, it was a stunning display of upright leadership, when CM Yogi Adityanath in a series of meetings and conversations set a clear road map for the executive, 'I want a corrupt-free, crime-free, mafia-free State where every individual feels and lives fearlessly. The government wants you to do whatever it takes, to bring down the edifice of fear, destruction and negativity. You all have my full support.'[55]

It was a huge break in the system, a tectonic shift, to give the police the space to operate freely, without fear or prejudice. Soon a task force was constituted under the stewardship of the principal secretary to quickly monitor and decide the outcomes of corruption cases held up since the last twenty years. Especially on the scanner were the cases filed by the vigilance department and the economic offence wing of the UP Police. Many cases had simply not received the departmental nod and had not even progressed to the investigation stage. Meanwhile, many officers and personnel had retired. Nobody was to be spared. 'Even if it's a politician or their kin, don't spare anyone,' was the clear diktat.

In case of the UP Police, challenges have acted as catalysts for creating new capabilities. Perhaps the unabated crime scenario before 2017 set the stage for changing the mindset to constantly stretch the boundaries of the possible. We were using technology, innovative strategies and human interventions in police activities to tackle crime challenges and working towards building a safer UP.

We went after organized crime in a big way. Land mafia, mining mafia, dons, hardened criminals and their ill-gotten wealth. Illegally acquired land and unauthorized buildings were identified. Then unauthorized structures were demolished or sealed, and the land was reclaimed. The intent and strong follow-up on the ground got us dramatic results. Quite a big number of hardened criminals applied for cancellation of their bail amount and came forward to surrender.[56] A year after my appointment to the rank of DGP, the following facts stood out. The 'zero-tolerance' policy adopted against crime and corruption got us many neutralized criminals (when fired in retaliation), along with many surrendered on their own accord.[57]

In 2018, our objective was to go for proactive policing towards crime prevention, crime detection, women's safety, tackling of cybercrime and traffic managements. In my discussions with field officers, I always stressed upon reducing response time, improving service delivery, enhancing the police–industry interface and making additional SPs nodal officers in order to attend problems connected with traders and small businessmen. There was a concerted effort to prepare a police force that would cater to the needs of modern society with efficiency and also empathy.

By September 2019, the UP Police's massive anti-crime operations put more than 20,000 criminals and dons in jail to cool their heels.[58] The backbone of crime and criminals was severely broken. Likewise, heinous crimes began to get a seal-proof investigation, summary trial and prosecution. A case in point is of a rapist in Auraiya, his arrest, investigation, followed by a trial in the special court of POCSO (Protection of Children from Sexual Offences Act), which lead to him being convicted took precisely nine days.[59] It was one of the quickest prosecutions in the history of UP. In another case in Hamirpur, conviction in a POCSO case was achieved in twenty-nine days (eighteen working days) in the Chikasi Police Station. It was a case wherein two three-year-old girls were molested by their neighbour.[60] This was achieved despite there being a lawyers' strike and the pressure on law enforcement agency owing to the Ayodhya judgment. These cases stand out as most memorable achievements of my career since I maintained speedy prosecution in cases of crime against women as my utmost priority.

As a rule, I have disliked the term 'police encounter' and the connotations a procedural police action receives in certain sensational reporting. But semantics apart, controlling crime and maintaining law and order require the Force to strategically go after perpetrators of heinous crimes, whether gangsters, murderers or the mafia who run a nexus of terror, killings, coercion and fraud.

As a state policy, we were clear in our approach and strategy that we will go after organized crime sans any bias or prejudice. The police, as per legal mandate, is bound to arrest such elements and take action. Encounters between the police and criminals are inevitable only if the former take on the might of such audacious criminals who have nothing but contempt for law and then bring them to book. We ruthlessly went after organized crime. It was a golden period in the history of the state and with more than Rs 200 crore worth property seized,[61] our zero tolerance towards crime was showing effective results. All police encounters wherein death occurred had to undergo the test of legal scrutiny as envisaged in the Supreme Court judgment and National Human Rights Commission guidelines. The guidelines laid down in the *PUCL [People's Union for Civil Liberties] vs State of Maharashtra*[62] are exhaustive and well-enunciated, comprehensively outlining the mechanism and mandatory steps to be taken by the state government in the event of deaths in police encounters.

The peaceful celebration of major festivals like Holi, Eid, Muharram, Diwali, etc., which was always considered a daunting task, received an overwhelming positive response by the public. The flawless policing management and the preceding planning and strategizing had begun to show dramatic results. Zero riots since 2017, for the state of UP, was no mean achievement. Robust law and order facilitated the state's performance in ease of doing business rank from twelve to two towards the end of 2019[63] and there was increasing visibility of police and handholding with industries in places such as Noida and Ghaziabad. Regular interaction with industries provided confidence to the industrialists.

In another first of its kind, the CM directed the Police to conduct the UPMSP High School and Intermediate Examination under a foolproof security net.[64] A comprehensive plan for the safety of question-and-answer copies was prepared, which included their printing, logistics and storage. ADGs, IGs, DIGs, SSP and SP rank officials were directed to ensure regular inspection of the examination centres and their surroundings to ensure a just and fair examination was conducted.

* * *

A simple task effected by me right at the commencement of my tenure was to create a WhatsApp group of all DGs and ADGs of UP Police. The idea was an extension of a practice I initiated in the initial weeks following my induction—inviting the senior officers based in Lucknow for a meet-up over tea. Thus began an organic way of cross-fertilization of ideas. My idea was to treat the entire UP Police as one family and share with each other our joys and concerns, highs and lows, achievements and failures.

A forum for constant exchange of thoughts and dialogues was essential. This was the opening message that I posted in that WhatsApp group of senior officers:

> I have decided to formally launch an official group of all DGs and ADGs of UP Police, so that I can share important information, policy decisions of the Government/DGP Headquarters, information about important meetings,

proposals, and so on. All of you can also share the best practices pertaining to their work spheres. My only request to all of you would be not to reduce this group to a platform for exchange of trivial information, verbatim reproduction of PRO's forwarded messages, etc. If taken seriously, this group can also act as a springboard of fresh and innovative ideas which can act as critical inputs for growth of UP Police. After all, we must ask ourselves what it will take to bring our organization successfully into the twenty-first century.

The core group of senior officers was formed informally and named Police Planning and Advisory Group. The group was formed primarily to deliberate on matters related to administration, investigation, sports, healthcare, compensation benefits and training issues. Proposals such as weekly reserve day for district police staff, uniform of traffic police officers, compendium of instructions, treatment at CGHS rates in private hospitals and diagnostic centres, new sports policy and payment of pensionary benefits, among others, were deliberated and acted upon. An initiative that was taken up by the UP Police related to the new practice of starting reunion of IPS officers promoted from the PPS. This is a practice in vogue in directly recruited IPS officers' batches which is organized by NPA at Hyderabad almost every year. I was glad to see an overwhelming response from the officers who had gathered along with their spouses at UP Police Academy in Moradabad. The officers, who had been trained together in one batch, brainstormed over critical issues and gave their input which were valuable in the light of wealth of experiences they had.

Vaama Saarthi was an initiative launched by the UP Police for the well-being and welfare of police families. Set up and spearheaded by my wife, Mrs Neelam Singh, in her capacity as President of UP Police Family Welfare Association, this endeavour aimed to provide support, assistance and resources to the families of police personnel. It strove to address the unique challenges faced by police families and ran several drives for the welfare and upliftment of women and children. Some of these included the popular Summer Camp for Police Children, Mahila Suraksha Jaagrukta Vyakhyan, Career Counselling and Health Carnival events.

The splendid launch event of the Vaama Saarthi song and Navras Dance Drama unfolded in Lucknow in 2019, captivating the attention of distinguished citizens, past and present police officers, their families and the media. Led by the President of Vaama Saarthi, the affair embodied a remarkable display of collective effort, harmonious synergy and unwavering dedication. The performances, flawlessly edited, evoked a range of emotions, leaving the audience entranced. Notably, the portrayal of an acid attack victim stood out, making a profound impact on the audience. The event was graced by the esteemed presence of the Hon'ble Governor Smt. Anandiben Patel, who lauded every performance and bestowed blessings upon the esteemed police fraternity. The opulent auditorium of Dial 112 brimmed with prominent personalities, lending an exquisite touch of glamour to these memorable police gathering. It was also graced with the presence of prominent classical singer and recipient of the Padma Vibhushan Award, Pandit Chhanulal Mishra. The entire Vaama Saarthi team, under the proficient leadership of its president, deserved heartfelt recognition for their invaluable contribution to the public domain. Through various programmes, initiatives, and outreach efforts, Vaama Saarthi enhanced the quality of life for police families and strengthened the bond within the police community. It exemplified the commitment of the UP Police to not only protect and serve the public but also to support and uplift their own police personnel and their families.

We established a subsidiary canteen for the staff. Such canteens in twenty districts and eight master canteens boosted the morale of the Force. It was a small gesture that should have found a place a long time back. The subsidiary canteen in the basement of the police headquarters catered to more than 2500 personnel from the new police headquarters building, the UP 112 building and those coming to the headquarters.

In September 2019, I inaugurated the Central Government Health Scheme (CGHS) for the welfare of all serving and retired police personnel and their dependents at prescribed rates. Within two months, 948 police personnel in 142 hospitals of fifteen districts of UP benefited from this scheme. Through our painstaking efforts, we convinced all these hospitals to sign an MoU with the UP Police to provide health care services for the police personnel, their dependents and pensioners at CGHS rates and norms. This arrangement covered out-patient and in-patient health services. The initiative, taken after collectively brainstorming, was officer-driven and could see the light of day in a short span of time because I did not route it through the babudom of either UP Police or the government. It underscored the importance of 'bold decision-making' in the interest of organization.

Another very significant policy decision was to give pensionary benefits to any police personnel who has receded into coma due to any eventuality. The genesis of it lay in a case in Agra district that came to my notice in the initial few months of my assuming charge as DGP. After an accident, a constable succumbed to injuries and the other went into a coma. The deceased constable's family availed of the pensionary benefits, whereas these were denied to the family members of the other constable who was in a coma for several years. The harassed family members ran from pillar to post for years in the hope of some relief but in vain. Unfortunately, there was no express provision for the same and the senior officers did not realize the need to make appropriate amends to the ossified rules. When the constable's wife approached me, I was immensely pained to see their plight and I moved a letter to the government to accord the same benefit to a comatose constable as the deceased one. I personally took the matter up with the CM and he was kind enough to give his consent for the proposal. The extension of the CGHS medical cover to state police personnel on the lines of CPOs and CAPFs, as well as extraordinary pension to the family of a police personnel languishing in a state of coma, resultant of any action during discharge of his official duty, spoke volumes of the compassionate approach to recognize the problems faced by our personnel. It was indeed a milestone in the history of UP Police and was only possible because of the extreme humane and benevolent personality of CM Yogi Adityanath.

* * *

The modernization of UP Police got a fillip during 2017–19. The setting up of the SDRF was finally activated, in record time, during 2018–19.

A state-of-the-art police headquarters was inaugurated in Lucknow in the first week of September 2019, with the CM asserting how the law-and-order situation and machinery had contributed towards investors, both national and international, thronging to invest in UP. The CM, on the recommendation of the core policy group, also agreed in principle that the state needed a forensic university and another police academy to train and orient recruits and officers. A command centre to overlook the monitoring of fifty high security prisons of the state was also established in December 2019.

* * *

In all of the controlled and uncontrolled hoopla happening around me, it was equally important to indulge in unknown or untried experiments which had the potential of turning out big. Regret is banished for life if you begin to trust your instincts and give a chance to chance! Policing, for me, was a mix of traditional elements and cutting-edge technology to keep one ahead of the game. Police forces across the country are today increasingly adopting technology to help them offer their multidimensional and often-complex services. In the first phase, the focus was on digitization and making services IT-enabled. In addition, the unique nature of policing demanded that any service we launched had to be made universal and equitable from day one. Our user base is also as diverse, as one might imagine. The constable who was technology-shy and the farmer who was technology-excluded are all equal stakeholders and we must somehow find a way to ensure that simple delivery and consumption coexist with complicated add-ons. Thankfully, we saw some great results in the first phase that gave us the confidence to venture into the next phase of applied Big Data Analytics. I shall take the liberty of briefly mentioning some of these successful projects:

1. 112, our flagship technology project, has now become a benchmark of integrated emergency response. Towards the end of 2019, it was adjudged the third-best call centre in the 'Police' category, after Singapore and Sharjah.[65] In terms of the number of people the project served, it was one of the biggest emergency services in the world. Its core was built on getting accurate caller location using a wide array of technologies. It had an average response time of ten minutes and forty seconds and a caller satisfaction percentage of 81 per cent, two indicators which sufficiently captured its effectiveness. All critical services such as fire, medical, Government Railway Police (GRP) and disaster response were integrated with it. By attending to issues when they were still in progress, we were redefining police intervention.

2. While 112 took care of emergencies, for twenty-eight other police services, we had an app built on the backbone of CCTNS, called UPCOP. Its USP was the facility of registering e-FIRs in a wide category of cases, without the need for any intervention with the police station.

3. We also run the country's premier woman helpline called 1090—a model emulated by most other states. In addition to resolving cases of telephonic, cyber and physical harassment, as swell as stalking, with a robust success rate, it was also implemented as a part of the Safe City Project in Lucknow and other cities.

There were several other projects such as a community policing app that had over 13 lakh members, Twitter Sewa with over 35 lakh followers sharing their problems and suggestions via social media and one of the largest setups of virtual classrooms that connected over thirty police training centres across the country. These examples showed our openness to adopt and push new technologies without compromising on the constitutional burden to deliver democratic and world-class services. Following this, we were upon the second phase of technology adoption. Although this phase continued to have elements of the first phase, the acquisition, processing and visualization of big data distinguished it from the first phase. The learning for this came from the 112 Project. We realized that we handled more than 60,000 calls daily and sent our emergency vehicles to over 15,000 events every day. On each of these events we were capturing a wide range of data, which included personal data, location data, crime-type data, GPS data, resolution status and so on. It only made sense that we used these to reduce response time, help other departments such as revenue and social welfare, and even proactively prevent crimes if we could. This latter idea is often termed 'predictive policing' in the West. To explore the possibilities, we entered into an MoU with IIT Kanpur whereby it would help us optimize the route charts of our vehicles—it was indeed a promising idea.

Collaboration with IIT Kanpur was an important development as it marked the strides that the UP Police and its leadership had made in ushering in greater professionalism and technology applications for policing of the state. We had been talking about making research integral to police functions and now the UP Police had made a formal commitment to it. While the benefits the project would accrue to IIT Kanpur were clear— research and publications on a new frontier that would win laurels for the faculty and students, the gains to the police were equally significant. Associating with researchers would change the working culture and organizational ethos of the department as well as improve the knowledge and skills of its police officers. Working together, the researchers began to understand the hardships and difficulties faced by the police force. They helped improve policing by asking new questions, challenging assumptions and ushering scientific methodology in police functions. Prof. Arvind Verma, a former IPS officer and an outstanding academician currently on the faculty of the Department of Criminal Justice at Indiana University Bloomington, said in a private conversation that when a police department is willing to open itself to external scrutiny, it symbolizes a high level of professionalism and self-assurance in its administration. Cross-sectoral partnership is essential in order to achieve transformation as each stakeholder brings to the fore their complementing competencies towards achieving a bigger goal. The MoU sought to pledge cooperation for joint research in order to develop tools and processes for better law enforcement, management of public order and traffic, as well as joint use of research equipment and facilities for research in new technology frontiers such as big data analytics, artificial intelligence, geographic information system and video analytics.

An MoU was also signed with IIM Indore for leadership programmes. The objective of the MoU was to strengthen the beat policing, develop tools for better law enforcement, traffic and strategic patrolling as well as exploring ways to improve the efficiency and morale of the police personnel while reducing their stress. Long awaited, and probably a first by any state police department, the UP Police launched the web-based Budget Monitoring System designed in-house and a software developed by Omni-Net. The mPassport Police App was aimed at smothering the corruption reigning in the name of 'police verification' for individuals seeking a passport.

I never hesitated to adopt a good practice or system if it ran a decent test. Our efforts brought about the setting up of an Advanced Computer Forensic Laboratory in the state capital in March 2019. It gave a major fillip to solving crimes such as digital fraud, cyber stalking and child pornography. The period of collecting evidence fell sharply from more than a month to a matter of days! Data lost from social media platforms such as WhatsApp and Twitter can now be recovered with ease using this new technology. Proving a crime in a court of law thus took a giant leap forward. Similarly, in mid-2019, an e-Prosecution web portal was launched in Lucknow and Moradabad as a pilot project. Now the investigation officers can seek legal advice from the state prosecution officers by uploading their investigation papers on this portal. The police authorities related to technical services were tasked with starting Inter-operable Criminal Justice System (ICJS) which would act as a search engine for police. The integration of all portals like e-FSL, e-prosecution, crime and criminal tracking networking system (CCTNS), prisons and courts would help police to get status and details of crime and criminal on a click, was emphasized. By the end of 2019, UP created a new identity by securing top position in the e-Prosecution portal's number of data feeds—the number of entries being more than 13 lakh. Gujarat was a close second, followed by Rajasthan. All this was achieved due to the professional contribution made by Ashutosh Pandey, a very competent and forward-looking IPS officer of the UP Police. He was always inspired and rejuvenated while doing his job and, as a professional, transformed the entire set-up through his visionary leadership, technical know-how, and skills. In December 2018, UP Police launched a mobile application called 'Trinetra', meaning the third eye, which was equipped with artificial intelligence and face recognition technology over and above other advanced features to identify and track criminals within the state. The mobile-based application held the database of an estimated five lakh criminals which was collected through inputs from district police, prison department and the Government Railway Police (GRP). It contained photos, addresses, criminal history and other features and served as a complete dossier on criminals. This information, which could be accessed on a real-time basis by any police officer using the mobile application, was updated on a daily basis.

The role of communication can never be discounted. I never shied away from first-hand verbal outreach with my audience on several occasions. It was the mandatory circulars and information that required the written format. My exchanges with the staff and the media always had a personal touch and focus.

Lastly, every organization requires new systems and strategies. The redundant has to give way to the new as the ecosystem requires innovative and technologically savvy interventions. I wanted my Force to be the best in the world. That should be the top priority for any police chief and I was no exception. Systemic solutions to the problems were always the answer. Quick-fix solutions were never part of my functioning style. Judicious usage of social media to one's advantage was the obvious answer to many situations. Cybercrime is real and we can no longer afford to ignore it. The state's first Cyber Forensic Laboratory and Training at UP

112 Headquarter was set up in order to train police personnel about speedy and effective investigations of incidence related to cyber stalking, cyber harassment and other crimes carried out through internet and mobile phone communications. Looking at the challenges of cyber crime in the state, the UP government announced the setting up of eighteen new Cyber Police Stations at all police ranges. I fully implemented the learnings of my experience with the NDRF, and a state-level Disaster Response Force was activated and operationalized in no time. Fast and sturdy police response vehicles (PRVs) were duly positioned all across the state. And to back it up, a centralized Control Room, with a single three-digit emergency number for the entire state (112) was provided in its swanky yet organic avatar. Today, 112 has become the symbol of trust, hope and excellence. We also took steps to take our 112 emergency service to the next level by introducing citizen registration, quality controls and software-driven patrol charts. An initiative was introduced to escort unaccompanied women, on their request, to their destination by Police Response Vehicles (PRVs) between 10 p.m. and 6 a.m. According to directives that I issued, the PRVs sent to assist unattended women would compulsorily have two women constables, besides a driver and a male constable. As many as six women travelling alone in different districts such as Ambedkar Nagar, Lucknow, Lakhimpur Kheri, Mathura, Mahoba and Unnao, were safely dropped off at their destination on day one of the launch of this initiative. We decided to train 1800 women constables over a period of eighteen days for deputation to PRVs at night. These constables were taught tactics, self-defence, arrest procedures and human rights in their training modules.

Every policing activity now generates a large amount of data. Points of data capture would only increase in the days to come. Data quality will gradually improve—much of it with learnings from industry partnership. Managerial decision-making will need data on portable devices in formats that consume less bandwidth and those that can work in low-network remote areas, too. Great emphasis must be placed on accuracy so that false positives are not generated. Else these will cause inconvenience to the public and engage scarce police resources.

I would like to share a success story of our AI-based facial recognition software where we worked closely in the design phase and populated it with data in mission mode. In 2019, we had over 6 lakh criminals' photos, history, details and connections. As CCTV cameras became ubiquitous, the 'hit rate' only improved. That is the beauty of thoughtful development. Technologies positively reinforce each other through seamless integrations. A case of motorcycle loot was worked out in Ghazipur when the number plate was captured during routine vehicle checking. This chance discovery led to looking at the rider's photo captured during enforcement. When it was matched with our facial recognition software, a match of a criminal from another district was thrown up. Physical inquiry finally led to his arrest as well as that of his associates.

The ability to capture, process and visualize data—both from the surface web and the dark web—is becoming a need now. Quick and exhaustive results are preferred, especially in profile searches. Another desirable need is strong CCTV camera analytics. Integrated Traffic Management System (ITMS) and Safe City components are expected to see many cameras deployed and these will be invariably connected to police control rooms and emergency centers. Faces, vehicles and crowd build-up are expected to send alerts to the prescribed agents. Kumbh Mela 2019 was an early test case and we saw very encouraging results with crowd management.

Towards the end of 2019, we were seriously thinking of establishing a Cybersecurity Research and Training Centre for the UP Police in Noida as the police was facing difficulties in handling the growing spate of cybercrimes. The UP Police needed to focus on a range of activities such as cybercrime information collection, awareness creation, training, research and dissemination. As these activities were not well coordinated, desired results could not be achieved. It was felt that several initiatives suffered both from a lack of adequate facilities as well as properly trained manpower. With the help of police officers such as Sujit Pandey ADG, Shahab Rasheed Khan and Triveni Singh, both SPs, and many others, we came forward to conceptualize an idea of establishing a dedicated centre which would provide continuous advance training in a modular format, developed in cooperation with law enforcement and industry targeted at the cybercrime forensic investigators. After a couple of meetings with industry partners at the level of ADG Pandey, a template for establishing such a centre outlining the infrastructure requirements, staffing arrangements (technical/support manpower), equipment and tools was arrived at to ensure that the law enforcement was empowered to undertake technology-crime investigations and at the same time create awareness among the masses on criticality of cyber and mobile security. The proposed centre was to be located at Command Control Centre, Noida and would act as a technical support and training centre for the police forces. The Data Security Council of India's initiatives of Centre for Cyber Crime Investigation Training & Research (CCITR), Bengaluru, had been taken as the reference model to prepare the Public Private Partnership. The existing cybercrime cells of UP Police would function in coordination with this centre and would have been provided the required support. I wish this initiative could have seen the light of day during my tenure.

Transfers and postings

Ah! The famous sport that bureaucrats love to indulge in. The sport popularized both as a punishment and reward. Perfected in the corridors of power and nurtured and developed in government files. The sport is played over phone calls, assurances and orders. A signature seals your fate—for the next three years or three days.

Well, the sport had a new captain, and I wanted none of the nonsense. In a quick and a decisive move, I put a stop to the lobbying that went around for postings and transfers. I completely turned off the tap of such indulgent happenings. Competence became the new criteria for postings and transfers. Additionally, the roles and the performance of the officers had to be regularly assessed and reported, by self and by the seniors, as well.

Being upright and apolitical is not a challenge, provided you make it a way of life. I was lucky, for I was exposed to the worst kind of political high-handedness early on in my career. It was difficult, and far from being a cakewalk, but the importance of it has to be indulged. Chief Minister Yogi Adityanath's style of working impressed me. He reposed complete trust in me. It was a scenario that the DGP Office had not seen in a long time. The CM stuck to the diktat that he laid on his own—all postings and transfers to be made on the DGP's advice and on operational issues, the CM would talk only to the DGP.

The previous administration dealt a heavy blow to the authority, command and control of the state's police chief, rendering it a mere shadow of its former self. During Akhilesh Yadav's tenure, the position of DGPs was in a state of constant flux, with approximately eight or nine changes.[66] The home department of the state was heavily involved in the affairs of the police force, leading to an unwelcome and pervasive influence. Unfortunately, most police chiefs enjoyed brief and fleeting tenures. The crux of any state police set-up rests in the strength, acumen and personal relations of the police chief with the head of the state government. I had the good fortune of establishing an unmediated rapport with the esteemed CM and winning his unequivocal trust. We had candid and productive discussions about police organization, and he allowed me the freedom to run the administration as I saw fit. This is a testament to his leadership and commitment to effective governance.

As the CM of the most populous state of the country, Yogi Adityanath demonstrated remarkable administrative skills that enabled us to develop a diligent work ethic and pay attention to crucial details. It was one of the 'coolest' tenures of my career. I had the toughest of jobs, but it was also a breeze. I could go on to elaborate more in detail about what transpired in the short yet long years of my tenure as chief. Instead, I have picked a few defining moments in the last two years of my career, which will always dwell, like many others, in the lap of my memory.

11

My Gems, My Impeccable Pride

Kumbh 2019

The magnificent energy of the *akharas*, the millions of pilgrims reflecting the colourful patterns of Indian life and culture and a sprawling township of makeshift tents blossoming upon the beds of the Ganga and the Yamuna—this is the site that greets one at the Kumbh in Prayagraj. For centuries, this Mela has been one of the biggest congregations in the world. However, what set Kumbh 2019 apart from all the previously organized ones was its sheer scale, methodical organization, the cleanliness embodied in the idea of Swachh Kumbh and, above all, a 'Surakshit Kumbh', with incident-free management from the police point of view.

My biggest joy came from the responsibility of hosting and securing the Kumbh Mela of 2019. With millions participating from around the globe, the humongous open-air theatre would see unimaginable crowds and, of course, dignitaries and VIPs. It was quite a challenge and one that had to be met with impeccable planning and deft execution.

The history of Kumbh has had its fair share of tragedies and also restrictive practices by the government in pre-independent India. Stampedes occurred in Kumbh in 1840 (Prayagraj), 1906 (Prayagraj), 1954 (Prayagraj), 1986 (Haridwar), 2003 (Nashik), 2010 (Haridwar) and 2013 (Prayagraj). The worst Kumbh Mela stampede recorded till date took place on 3 February 1954, in Prayagraj, which led to a colossal loss of human lives.[67] 'Despite elaborate government arrangements, stampedes occur at the Kumbh regularly. About 600 pilgrims died in three stampedes in Hardwar during the 1980s. The worst stampede was in Allahabad in 1954, killing 800.'[68] The risk of a stampede during such a massive gathering was immense. After all, we are talking about one of the biggest gatherings in the world. As chief of UP Police, I needed to make organizational management and structures simpler and more impactful, helping the police respond faster.

'Safety and service . . .' CM Yogi Adityanath reiterated as I sat facing him in his office. We had roughly eight months to prepare for the spiritual extravaganza. The CM's hands rested on the edge of his desk. There was never a flourish of his hands, a common trait I found amongst many leaders with power. The purpose and intent always came to the fore. The upcoming Kumbh was close to his heart, and it was evident in his involvement and concern. 'We are not only there to protect and keep the citizenry safe, but we are also going to serve them, help provide them the most memorable spiritual experience of their lifetime,' the CM concluded.

Inspired by Prime Minister Modi's vision of organizing a Kumbh that remains unsurpassable in terms of its magnitude and grandeur, Yogi Adityanath resolved to make Kumbh 2019 glorious and mishap-free. The prime minister himself reached Prayagraj well in advance, on 16 December 2018. Besides reviewing the preparations, he gave valuable direction and encouraged the Kumbh team to work harder. He also inaugurated the state-of-the-art Integrated Command and Control Centre. The world-class sanitation arrangements witnessed at the Kumbh (Swachh Kumbh) had their genesis in the Swachh Bharat Abhiyan of Prime Minister Modi, who donated Rs 21 lakh from his personal savings to the corpus fund for the welfare of the sanitation workers of the Kumbh Mela.[69]

The UP Police took upon itself the seemingly insuperable task of making the sea of humanity safe and secure though a multi-pronged strategy. Conventional policing with a judicious mix of state-of-the-art technology, including geotagging, aerial surveillance, deep data mining and analysis helped the UP Police successfully complete the challenging assignment.

An MoU was also signed between Motilal Nehru National Institute of Technology, Prayagraj and the Kumbh Mela Police to generate crowd-density alerts periodically at strategic locations and bathing ghats to flag an emergency. This was the first-ever use of a video analytics-based crowd management system to preclude and prevent stampede at the Kumbh. For the first time, this Kumbh saw a fully digitized lost-and-found centre supplemented by a traditional public address system. Till 2019, the task of finding missing people was done by two centres, namely the Bhule Bhatke Shivir of Bharat Sewa Dal, founded by Raja Ram Tiwari and Bhule Bhatke Shivir for women and children, run by H.N. Bhaguna Smriti Samiti. The two rendered great service in uniting lost families and friends at the Kumbh and earning people's trust, but they relied on manual data. While this method helped reunite people, data of lost persons could not be classified nor was it amenable to any meaningful analysis. The Digital Khoya-Paya-Kendras introduced in 2019 were manned by trained professionals who provided round-the-clock assistance. All the fifteen centres, interconnected by a sophisticated server, had waiting areas, hand over sections, refreshments, medical rooms, lodging facility for lost pilgrims. Information of lost-and-found pilgrims were broadcasted with photos on LED screens at each centre. Social media platforms were used to re-unite the pilgrims.

Apart from the core police duties of ensuring security, crowd control and traffic regulation, the Kumbh required the police officers to act as guides and facilitators for pilgrims. A comprehensive training module was devised, and a full-fledged training wing was set up under an additional SP. The policemen deployed were not only familiarized with the geography, history and culture of Prayagraj but also given behavioural and soft skills training by professional psychologists so that they behaved politely with the pilgrims. The logistical arrangements of the police and other security forces were supervised by senior officers to make their stay comfortable.

Considering the expected global participation in the Kumbh, it was decided well in advance that the Kumbh Mela Police should have a sound communication plan in place, which encompassed print, electronic and social media. The UP Police has had a robust presence on social media for the last few years, which proved to be an added advantage for the Kumbh Mela Police. The social media cell of the Kumbh Police started functioning as early as June 2018. It was perhaps the first temporary police district to have a verified Twitter handle and a Facebook page. An additional SP-level officer with sound experience of media and social media handling was posted from October 2018 to supervise it. The social media cell also produced its own in-house regular news bulletins, which were uploaded on social media. The Twitter handle of the Kumbh Mela Police earned millions of impressions between August 2018 and April 2019. Regular advisory and awareness posts from the social media handles of the Kumbh Mela Police started as early as mid-2018. As a curtain-raiser to the main event, a short film titled *The Making of Kumbh* was produced, which highlighted the sound preparatory arrangements made by the police to instil confidence among the pilgrims. The film was shown to the heads of mission during their visit to the Kumbh Mela. The police launched a dedicated website for the ease of pilgrims, with sections on route navigation, event calendar and regular updates. A truly digital mela with global reach. Animation videos, using the voice of popular Bollywood stars, were produced by the Kumbh Mela Police to sensitize pilgrims about security, traffic diversions and fire safety.

In a first for any police organization, the Kumbh Mela Police launched its own bilingual video-news bulletin named Suraksha Bulletin.[70] With celebrities and volunteers turning newsreaders, the bulletin became an interesting medium of information for people interested in the Kumbh.

Despite threats from terrorists and anti-national forces, exponential increase in population and vehicular density, the successful organization of Kumbh 2019 in a safe and secure manner is a global case study and has no parallel worldwide. It will remain a marvel for governments, civic bodies and police administration, and a veritable laboratory for researchers on urban planning, hygiene and entrepreneurship worldwide. Kumbh 2019 serves as a shining template for all such future Kumbh Melas and large-scale public gatherings across the world.

It indeed was a humongous event and perfect coordination among different departments of the state government was essential. Divya Kumbh, Bhavya Kumbha (Divine Kumbha, Magnificent Kumbha) was in the making. Chief Secretary Anup Chandra Pandey constituted an apex committee, in 2018, which reviewed every department's progress on a fortnightly and monthly basis. Pandey was always prepared to accept challenges and had, in the past, as industrial development commissioner, successfully conducted the UP Investors Summit 2018 in Lucknow. My association with him dates way back when he was information director of UP and I was SSP of the state capital. As a passionate, strategic and evolved officer, Pandey always contributed positively towards the development of the state. We often travelled together to different parts of the state and interacting with him was a great experience. We had a team of vibrant and dedicated police officers including ADG S.N. Sabat, IG Mohit Agrawal, SSP K.P. Singh, ADG Law and Order Anand Kumar, IG Praveen Kumar, ADG B.P. Jogdand, ADG Ramasashtry, ADG Asim Arun, IG Navneet Sikera, SP Devranjan Verma, SP Mohd Imran, ASP Neeraj

Pandey and ASP Rahul Srivastava, who were determined to make Kumbh Mela the most *surakshit* (secure) Kumbh. Divisional Commissioner Prayagraj Ashish Goel, SSP Prayagraj Nitin Tiwari, DM Kumbh Mela Vijay Kiran Anand, DM Prayagraj Suhas L.Y. were exceptional officers who contributed to a Divya and Bhavya Kumbh.

The planning for the 2019 Kumbh had nuances and details that were firsts in many sense—vegetarian and non-alcoholic police personnel were to be given preference for Kumbh duty, and hi-tech and smart policing would be used extensively. About 30,000 police personnel underwent orientation and training in soft skills, during the major part of 2018, with emphasis on empathy. Post a prompt exchange and some deliberations later, we attempted to tie up with an Israeli security company for safety and crowd management. NSG and CISF commandos were effectively deployed. More than 10,000 police personnel, backed with their digitized avatar, were trained and ready to deliver. ATS and the intelligence personnel became the eyes and ears on the ground. The entire mechanism was put on high alert to stop any misadventure on the part of any devious elements thwarting the smooth conduct of Kumbh. The security plan and execution were painstakingly deliberated and decided in tandem with the Traffic, ATS, STF, GRP, Telecommunication, Home Guards, UP112, Provincial Armed Constabulary (PAC) and Prayagraj Zone and Range officials. Our task was simple: the holy dip for each had to be facilitated most effectively and with utmost safety.

It is also pertinent at this juncture to mention the strengthening of the SDRF for UP. Its constitution was mandated by the National Disaster Management Act 2005, but little effort had been made in this regard. December 2018 was the deadline set for the construction of the administrative and residential blocks for its headquarters to be readied, the Force personnel housed and to be ready for any eventuality. Three companies and 369 trained police personnel were housed in the campus.

Meanwhile, UP112 services were integrated with the emergency services of GRP for a unified management. The Indian Railways was expected to logistically manage almost 15 lakh pilgrims on a daily basis. November 2018 also saw the recognition of the endeavours of the UP Police in utilizing the telecommunication services with bold and innovative initiatives. In a grand event organized at Vigyan Bhawan, New Delhi, the Wireless Planning & Coordination (WPC) Wing of the Ministry of Communications, the Government of India duly recognized and appreciated our efforts. It was a proud moment to receive the award. It was an affirmation of the fact that we were on the right track in taking the UP Police to its pinnacle.

By 15 January 2019, the first day of the Kumbh Mela, more than 20,000 police personnel, 6000 home guards, forty police stations, fifty-eight police pickets, fifty-eight fire stations, eighty companies of para military and twenty companies of PAC were spread across nine zones and twenty sectors into which the entire Kumbh area was divided. Mankind's biggest extravaganza was on, and nothing could be left to chance. The world was watching us, and 6 crore individuals had to be given not just safe passage but an experience to remember.

Hosting the heads of missions from as many as seventy-two countries, NRIs from fifty nations and foreign delegates from 182 countries—Kumbh 2019 truly turned out to be a global event. Appreciating the mela arrangements, the high commissioner for Canada to India wrote: 'The challenges were enormous, but the planning, details, specifics were all in place, be it safety, security or health. I loved the two-wheeler fire bikes as well, which could be used to navigate through some of the terrain. The safety arrangements on the river, security cameras, counter-terror units, as well as the commandos, all instil a very strong sense of security.'[71]

Kumbh 2019 will also be remembered for the efforts made by the UP Police for proactive academic engagement. In a first-of-its-kind initiative, the Kumbh Mela Police signed an MoU with Govind Ballabh Pant Social Science Institute, Prayagraj, to conduct exhaustive research on the pilgrims' experiences. Another study was conducted by the Kumbh Mela Police in collaboration with the Bureau of Police Research and Development, IIM Lucknow, IIT Kanpur and Lucknow University. This research focused on critical areas such as leadership, behavioural issues, motivation, team building and reasons for the success of the Kumbh Mela Police. A study was also done by UP 100 (now UP 112), the states police emergency management system, on the pilgrims who availed the emergency services. The findings of their rigorous empirical research provided valuable inputs for improvements in any future policing arrangements in handling crowds of this nature and magnitude.

The astounding success of the UP Police in managing such a huge gathering was no quirk of coincidence. It involved strategic planning, painstaking efforts, contingency measures, adequate deployment of manpower, use of state-of-the-art technology and resources and constant supervision. I can say with immense pride and satisfaction that Kumbh Mela 2019 will go down in history as one of the finest examples of police management.

Lok Sabha elections, 2019

If the management of law and order during Kumbh 2019 was not enough of a responsibility, the Lok Sabha General Election in the months of April and May further stretched the capacity of UP Police. The Election Commission of India directed us to wind up preparations for election duty by the end of February. This effectively meant simultaneous work for both Kumbh and the polls. The border areas of Nepal are generally the first to be alerted under similar sensitive circumstances. The borders were directed to be sealed and in the meetings with the officials of the area, a drive against smuggling of arms and currency, including counterfeit, had to be accentuated.

In a swift action, two terrorists with Jaish-a-Mohammad links were arrested by the ATS from Saharanpur.[72] Both Nawaz and Aquib had been under the watch of the ATS. It was when they had hosted a surprise guest on the intervening night of 22 February that the ATS moved in. Interrogation led to crucial evidence and a plan to strike it big in UP. This sent the entire state into high alert.

In a brief from the chief electoral officer, in the first week of March, the handout for the pre-poll drill was straightforward—all licensed arms were to be deposited with the local police stations, there was to be a complete clampdown on all criminal and communal elements, there should be strict eyes and ears on provocative and hate speech and a comprehensive check to be done on social media. A sudden increase in the incidents of crime in the state before elections was a regular feature. Kanpur, Jaunpur, Ghaziabad, Meerut and Gorakhpur were already showing signs of disturbance. We had to move in quickly. I was determined to conduct a peaceful general election.

Four hundred and eleven interstate barriers and ninety international barriers were set up to prevent the movement of criminals, illegal arms and black money. Interstate border meetings were conducted in Bhopal and Noida for better coordination. Criticality assessment and vulnerability mapping had been done as per guidelines of the Election Commission. The UP Police took qualitative preventive action such as ensuring all convicted and undertrials on bail furnished security bonds. A centralized database, comprising name and telephone numbers, enabled supervisory officers to communicate directly and gather information quickly. A digital volunteer scheme was put in place to keep a check on rumour-mongers.

Ayodhya verdict, 2019

The revocation of Article 370, which provided limited autonomy to the state of Jammu and Kashmir, by Parliament on 5 August 2019 was a decision that was largely welcomed by the nation. Certain sections of the media and vested individuals, however, tried to give it a communal spin. A tense Jammu and Kashmir was silenced, with communication networks shut down, a large number of security forces being stationed across the state and most of the political bigwigs put under house arrest. Consequently, in a high-powered meet on law and order, CM Yogi Adityanath sounded the alarm for the UP Police regarding the Ayodhya verdict, which was still ninety days away.

October saw the launch of an exercise to identify illegal migrants living in the state on the basis of illegal means, including through fake identities. The UP Police was entrusted with the task. The process fuelled media reports and rumours that the National Register for Citizens had been implemented across the state on similar lines as was done by the state of Assam.[73]

On 18 October, Kamlesh Tiwari, the founder of the lesser-known Hindu Samaj Party, had his throat slit by two Muslim zealots in Lucknow.[74] This incident saw acrimonious expressions on social media. Graphic images, speculative comments, provocative language and strong opinions were posted. More than seventy FIRs were registered and some arrests made. But the lesson learnt was that in order to ensure that there was proper monitoring and order on the social media, a well-planned, rehearsed and proactive strategy was needed.

Barely three weeks later, the top court of the country was about to announce the verdict on a case that had been bitterly fought by Hindus and Muslims. A tense state and the nation looked up to the security agencies of the state. My force and my personnel, guided by an efficient infrastructure, set out on the task of doing just that. In forty-eight hours, our Special Task Force arrested the mastermind of Tiwari's murder and his co-planners from Surat (Gujarat) and two more individuals in Bijnor (UP) for providing logistical support to the perpetrators.[75] It was a grave mischief to create terror and we nipped it in its bud.

Boots on the ground, drones in the air, eyes and ears in the digital air waves and intensive deployment became the norm for the Force. The tense situation and the sensitivity of the matter had us literally hanging on tenterhooks. There had not been a single incidence of rioting in my entire tenure so far. The clean slate had to be preserved at all costs. My tours and inspections multiplied and wherever I went, the message was straightforward: not even the slightest of communal mischief would be tolerated. Areas around Ayodhya found my special attention. Hundreds of people were detained in Ayodhya and thousands of police officers were deployed to meet up with the challenge. Social media was closely monitored to pick up unwarranted chatter. About a thousand individuals active on social media creating nuisance were marked and cases registered against them. The state went through some very tense moments right up to the declaration of the verdict. Hotspots were marked, foot patrolling and random checking became a norm. The D-Day was a Saturday, 9 November 2019. Schools and colleges had to be shut right up to Monday. We were even prepared to shut down the Internet if need be. It was difficult to predict the scale and nature of the activity on social media, therefore we had to be prepared for everything. I held a meeting with ADGs Law and Order and Lucknow Zone as well as ADGs of Railways, ATS, Technical Services, UP 112 and other officers to seek their input on the best way to handle social media. This was a critical meeting as it not only sensitized all stakeholders but also emphasized integrated team action. In the meeting two objectives were clearly defined, and these were also to become the basis of the graded response in the coming days. First, get any objectionable post removed and second, register FIRs and make arrests in serious cases. The sub-objectives included countering fake news, ensuring adequate publicity of action taken and community engagements. I also instructed that social media offenders of the last three years should be identified and kept on a close watch. Instructions were issued to all district Social Media Cells (SMCs) to create 'lists' and monitor sensitive social media users and rebut fake news. A short training was also organized on how to archive pages, save evidence, seek information from intermediaries, get posts removed and accounts reported. An ATS social media team was tasked with social media analysis, using specialized tools to aid in social media intelligence. I issued an appeal to all citizens to refrain from spreading rumours and making objectionable comments on social media. At the same time, I assured them that the UP Police was well prepared to ensure law and order. This appeal went viral on WhatsApp. It was also posted on the official the UP Police Twitter handle and was carried prominently in the papers the next day.[76]

The clock was ticking. India's most significant and sensitive case was just away from Supreme Court's final pronouncement. The entire state and the bordering states were on high alert. The security measures were unprecedented, but equally surprising was a call from the office of the Chief Justice of India (CJI), Justice Ranjan Gogoi. It was 7 November. The Chief Secretary and I were directed by the CJI to give a briefing about the law-and-order situation in his court chamber in New Delhi the following day. This was an unprecedented move, never before had the court directed UP DGP for such a briefing. The Ayodhya verdict was surely coming, but what was the verdict, we had no inkling as we both (Chief Secretary and I) boarded the state aircraft to keep the meeting time at New Delhi.

The air in the chamber of the CJI was stiff. Three judges were in attendance when we walked into the room. Terse introductions followed. Justice Ranjan Gogoi, Justice S.A. Bobde and Justice

Ashok Bhushan sat with focused attention as I began the detailed presentation of the security scenario and the sectoral measures. The meeting lasted for more than an hour, and we returned only after each concern of the Justices was addressed.

The judgment was announced on 9 November, 10.30 a.m. onwards. This saw an expected surge in the number of tweets and hashtags. For example, the hashtag #AyodhyaVerdict, saw an unprecedented surge in several lakhs right through the day. Similar was the trend for about twenty other relevant hashtags. These had to be quickly scrutinized for objectionable content both manually and by using tools available with the ATS. Content analysis, searching the same user across other platforms, comment analysis, reverse image search of profile pictures, etc. were some of the techniques used to ascertain location. If these did not work, then based on probability, digital volunteers of specific regions were asked if they recognized the individual or account. In all cases, evidence was first saved before taking any action. By the end of the day, warnings, reporting of posts and FIRs worked well and, to a large extent, the message had been conveyed. The most striking find was that many WhatsApp group admins had blocked posting rights to other members to avoid any controversy or legal action. The district social media cells rose to the occasion and applied themselves in fairly new territory. Social media action became one of the main talking points of the UP Police's strategy.

The leadership played a stellar role in the management and CM Yogi positioned himself in the police headquarters to monitor the situation by the second and ensure immediate decision if an emergent situation was to develop. An emergency desk was established for every zone in the state. It was a massive, calibrated police show, and it goes to the credit of the UP Police, for it yet again displayed its fortitude and efficiency.

As I felt that human touch personalizes the conversation, I directed all my police chiefs of the districts to visit just five static pickets of police personnel of their choice within their jurisdiction with the objective to pat our men on the back individually and express their gratitude for doing such great work in maintaining law and order.

Lieutenant Governor Kiran Bedi, one of the legends of the Indian Police, in her inaugural address at the 47th All India Police Science Congress in Lucknow specifically praised the role of the UP Police in managing Kumbh 2019 and the Ayodhya verdict with great elan.[77] Union Home Minister Amit Shah, in his address, also lauded the role of the UP Police in drastically reducing crime rate and establishing the rule of law. He promised sweeping reforms in the IPC and CrPC, as well as the establishment of a forensic university in every state.[78] National Security Adviser Ajit Doval, in his letter to me, appreciated my role in keeping the state calm and peaceful during the Ayodhya verdict period. Honestly, it was a moment full of pride.

Police Commissionerate, 2020

Barely a couple of months remained for me to hang my boots. Deep inside I felt a nagging void. The Commissioner system or the Commissionerate was close to my heart and intent. I made it a point to revive the idea in a manner that it became a thriving reality. The Commissionerate system was once the foremost agenda in the state more than four decades back, when it was proposed to be first introduced in the city of Kanpur. Vasudev Panjani, a 1954-batch IPS officer, was personally selected to assume the role of the inaugural commissioner of police in Kanpur in 1978. In a bid to prepare for this role, he, alongside the then Home Secretary K.K. Bakshi, embarked on research trips to cities like Mumbai, Pune, and Chennai to study the Commissionerate system. However, during this period, elements within the bureaucracy undertook covert efforts to undermine the project, ultimately leading to its cancellation. Unfortunately, no clear explanations were provided for this decision, and the proposal remained dormant for more than four decades. In the year 2018, police leadership in UP took up the matter with the CM as the new government headed by Yogi Adityanath had dedicated its focus on crime and law and order which forced a rethink on the system.

The successful organization of the 2018 UP Investor's Summit brought for the state MoUs worth Rs 4.28 lakh crore. Indian and global investors had reposed trust in the region and its ability to offer a consummate climate of law and order. The subsequent months of dedicated commitment of the police machinery brought about dramatic improvement in the law-and-order situation in the state. Losing no time, I started talking about the need for police Commissionerate in bigger cities because urban policing challenges were distinctly different from rural. Challenges such as frequent protests, rallies and agitations required constant vigil under the command and control of a senior officer. Besides, frictions in the society due to heterogeneous population mix could lead to sudden eruption of law-and-order disturbances. Additionally, large-scale migration and related problems of anonymity created tough challenges in crime detection. CM Yogi Adityanath understood clearly that urban areas were more prone to terrorist attacks, organized crimes, drug trafficking and cybercrimes, which required higher degree of professionalism to effectively handle them. During an informal discussion, I could sense he was encouraging, but he wanted to know what major difference the Commissionerate would make to the existing system and how exactly people would benefit more. The benefits of the Commissionerate were extensive. The authority to accord permission for any protest or demonstration would rest wholly with the police. Any dispute regarding the passage to be followed by any demonstration or protest would directly be decided or approved by the police. The police would have the direct command to act against any form of encroachment. In short, the magisterial powers would rest with the police.

In a momentous development, Governor Ram Naik gave a public acceptance to the Commissionerate system and advocated its implementation to further improve the law-and-order scenario.[79] That was in December 2018 when he came to inspect the police parade in our annual UP Police Week. Hailing from Mumbai and being in active politics in the Centre as well as in the state of Maharashtra, he was fully aware of the system. In fact, I was taken aback about his curiosity when I went to Raj Bhavan to invite him for police week function as chief guest. He asked me as to why we did not go for this policing system in the big cities of UP. It never occurred to me what he had in mind. Governor Naik, in his address, said that the state government should introduce the pilot project of police commissioner system in Lucknow, Kanpur and Ghaziabad where the population was over 2 million, to get the feedback. He made the suggestion in the presence of CM Yogi Adityanath. However, there was no progress till November 2019.

The precipitous moment for the implementation of the Commissionerate came when the Shaheen Bagh formula of protest was attempted to be replicated in the state. The Citizenship (Amendment) Act, passed by the Indian Parliament, 11 December 2019, ensured citizenship to persecuted minorities who are Hindus, Sikhs, Buddhists, Jains, Parsis and Christians from Afghanistan, Bangladesh and Pakistan, and who entered India on/before 31 December 2014.

I was at the newly inaugurated police headquarters when news came in that a crowd of about 500 people had descended at one of the roundabouts near Hazratganj, Lucknow, and were refusing to budge. The protest against the Act in Delhi had already seen continued occupation of public roads and spaces, throwing into disarray public convenience. I was determined to ensure that no such scenario emerged in UP. Any attempt to occupy public spaces for protest would be thwarted, I assured the CM over the phone. I knew the situation demanded quick and decisive action. In the moments to follow, I donned a bullet-proof vest and a baton in hand. I led my team towards the protest site, which was a very prominent traffic junction of the state capital and connected with the old areas of the city. There were women protestors in the crowd, and they had chosen to squat all around the roundabout and the peripheral area of the place. The lady contingent of the police had already been alerted. Banners and posters were also crowding the area. The crowd was swelling by the minute and the traffic was at their mercy. Before getting in the car, I had directed ADG Traffic to divert the vehicles converging and passing through the roundabout. 'I want that roundabout devoid of any traffic in the next fifteen minutes.'

At the protest site, the police bandobast was visible. Buses to remove the protestors from the site were on the way. The presence of the DGP at the site energized the battery of media persons present there. 'Sir, will there be police action?' The questions were distinct, but this was no time to mull over the obvious; it was time for focused action.

'Start the announcement to the protestors to disperse. And sound the warning in the first call itself. Repeat it thrice.' I directed the seniormost officer present on the site.

I was grimly aware of the world scanning and recording our every move.

Sensing their end game even before the announcement over the public address system could begin, the restless protestors broke their ranks and their sticks, lathis and *dandas* were transformed into weapons. Parked vehicles, hoardings, pickets, motorbikes, police booths, all faced the brunt of the unruly crowd. To our surprise, from nowhere the crowd also began pelting stones and bricks. In minutes, the real intent of the protestors became evident. The police swung into action. In a short span, the area was wrested from the protesters and normalcy restored. The CAA protests saw, for the first time, a state police chief at the protest site, moving about to douse the fires of raked-up discontent.

Post-CAA protests set the tone for a face-to-face exchange with CM Yogi Adityanath. The police had no magisterial powers yet, but they needed the moral-boosting support of being capable of taking timely decisions. A city like Lucknow, with a population of nearly 4 million, needed the Commissionerate. At the first instance of the CM enquiring about the CAA protests and how to prevent them from recurring, I seized the moment and mentioned outright, 'Sir, had the Commissionerate system been in operation, we would have contained the agitation far more effectively and in good time. The lack of it limits the actions of the police. We need a faster mechanism that would allow the police to respond in quick time.'

It was 11 November 2019 and my time to put in my papers was just days away.

'I will give your proposal serious thought. How soon can we get the paperwork done?'

Trust me when I say that was music to my ears. A major hope of ray flashed in my heart.

It was an open secret, since the date of my joining, that bringing in the Commissionerate system held a priority. The CM had given his nod in principle, but everything was in the air, as they say. Personally I took it as a major signal, and the consequence was that I roped in few brilliant officers such as P.V. Ramasashtry, Asim Arun, Sanjay Singhal and Sujeet Pandey to prepare some drafts taking a cue from the states where such systems were in vogue. Ramasashtry's expertise in matters of governance and legal drafting is exemplary. He had served in the CBI and National Investigation Agency (NIA) in the past and was deeply involved with policy formulations. A recipient of several distinguished and meritorious medals from the Government of India, Ramasashtry gave a good account as ADG (Law and Order). I wanted him in my team to draft the provisions of the new system. Arun, another outstanding officer who is now a member of Yogi Adityanath's council of ministers, was a great master of detail. His focus was an articulation of thought process and how operating system could be evolved. Arun looked every inch a man brimming with new ideas and confidence. Singhal had been working as general staff officer to the DGP for a long time and as a thoroughbred field professional, always led his team with immense passion and energy. Pandey was instrumental in bringing an intellectual approach and objective analysis to issues of police concern. Once I had shortlisted the best people, I created ownership. The enormous amount of work and the pains these officers took were beyond me. Back-room operations included seventeen such policy drafts that were slogged and sweated over. States such as Odisha, Rajasthan and Telangana had either urban Police Acts or provisions in the Police Act for metropolitan city policing, while in other states, the Commissionerate were constituted through executive orders. Across cities, there is also wide variation in the powers of the Commissioner of Police. My team of police officers entrusted with the task, after a detailed study, finally drafted a proposal which suited the UP context and recommended executive order approach since legislation was time-taking.

The proposal was then examined by a legal team followed by a series of discussions involving senior administrative officers. Certain crucial decisions were to be made regarding how many Commissionerate will be created in the beginning and what powers will be vested with the commissioners. There was naturally some resistance on the expected lines. Some of the demands from the administration side were conceded and some proposed powers under the Arms Act, Excise Act and Sarai Act were dropped. Initially only Lucknow, the state capital, and Gautam Budh Nagar (Noida), a district forming the part of NCR, were taken up.

For a few days, the Lok Bhawan saw a flurry of hectic draft finalization sessions that stretched into the wee hours of the morning. The draft proposal began to flow to and fro, as the CM took upon himself the task of going through the minutest of detail. Thus went the discussions and the finalization of the hierarchy and related rules. The CM dug in and my team of policy drafters was not found wanting. It was another weekend that I was more than willing to sacrifice at the altar of policing excellence. The CM promised to put the final draft of the proposal to the next cabinet for approval. The cabinet meeting broke out on expected lines. The Commissionerate system in Lucknow and Noida was announced by the Government of UP. The CM personally spoke to the media. My months, if not years, of parley, bore fruit. I was acutely aware of the formidable challenge of implementing the police commissioner system in a state as complex as UP. Yet, I firmly believed that the success of this endeavour hinged on the strength of the relationship and mutual understanding between the CM and the DGP. The DGP's ability to command respect, earn trust and carry himself with dignity played a pivotal role in the realization of such a system. My strong bonding with the CM was rarest for any of the DGPs in the recent past. I used the CM's trust for wresting benefits for the UP Police, system building and strengthening the institution of the DGP. The police commissioner system was welcomed by the police fraternity. Many former DGPs—Prakash Singh, S.V.M Tripathi, Brij Lal, K.L. Gupta and Vikram Singh, to name a few—called the decision a bold step of the state government.

It is such a humbling moment. 'We should treat it as a challenge rather than as a reward,' I told my officers.

I was on cloud nine. A perfect parting gift!

12

The Last Hurrah

Well, every dawn finds its dusk, every beginning its end and so did my service in the Force. By the time the media exchange about the Farrukhabad hostage case ended and all the officials finally retired to their dwellings, it was almost 1.30 a.m. The thought returned to me—my last day in office had begun. Sleep eluded me. It was the dead of the night. An ungodly hour. The slight snoring of my partner and the distinct hoot of a distant rail engine caught my attention. A police patrol siren began to blare; then, as if in consideration of the odd hour, it went silent.

I let the moment hang. Thoughts remained suspended. I bowed to the moment, acknowledging the beauty of the still, dead night. The morning was still far away. A journey of thirty-seven years was about to get its final salute. Post the farewell parade, some hours later, at the Lucknow Police Lines, I was to hang my boots. I checked the watch, it was 3.40 a.m. The new day had broken. I had just enough time to catch a few hours of sleep. The decibel of the snoring had more purpose now. The engine and its rake had moved on. The police patrol guys had possibly found a warm escape. Almost in reflex, I redrew the comforter around me.

The morning newspapers were agog with news about my last day in office. The apex position in the police department of one of the largest states of India was on the verge of being vacated. The successor had not been picked yet. I had scotched all rumours and talks about getting a three-month extension, by clearly indicating my resolution to the CM. There was a precedent where an outgoing DGP attended the ceremonial farewell parade at the Reserve Police Lines on the morning of his last working day, but by the evening, just prior to the traditional tea party at DGP's residence, was handed the letter of extension. I had denied any hope to such speculators. For me, the moment to hang the boots had truly arrived. The newspapers also speculated about my role as Chief Information Commissioner of UP post-retirement. Bemused, I let the news pass. The morning tea was served, and my mind was already on the beverage.

Post the satisfying hot sips, I took to my official Twitter handle. In quick time I had the following characters to float in the digital space: 'Today is my last day in uniform. (Trust me, the first line threatened to open sluice gates of delicate emotions.) For thirty-seven years it was a privilege to serve this country and the state. I thank each and every one of you with whom I had the honour to work with. Gratitude to my fellow citizens who offered their selfless help.'

'Papa, oh Papa!' That was my princess, a budding legal eagle on the verge of starting her independent legal practice. The warm hug came at the perfect time and was followed by the young mind's youthful inquisitiveness.

'You have so many firsts to your name, Papa. The Commissionerate, the 112 story, besides managing the state so well. The post-Ayodhya verdict was a breeze, the baddies are dead or cooling their heels, CAA protests . . . I could go on. C'mon, Papa, you should continue. I'm so proud of you. Everyone has such good things to talk about you.'

'I love you, princess, but your world is small. The state is a huge ocean. It's easy for me to ask for an extension, and I'm sure my request would be considered with respect, but your father has served his time, and did that with pride, diligence and respect. Now is the time to go.'

More hugs followed. It was time to put on the khaki for one last time.

The stiff, rectangular flag in deep crimson and blue held its head and pride. It was held by the small mast at the central pivot on the bonnet of the vintage beauty. It was a 1956-model Kingsway Car. The baby of Chrysler Corporation, it was specifically meant for the export market when the Indian State acquired it. The silver and turquoise blue metallic beauty had me in it, the ceremonial drive to the Reserve Police Parade ground, where I had to take the farewell arms salute. It was an honour ride. A humbling moment. My thoughts rushed to the memory of my mother and father. How I wished that they were there physically in that moment. The crisp feel of the khaki, the firm leather support belt of the holster, the ace insignia and symbols, the proudly crested medals of honour and the click of the boots. I was aware it was the last real thing before everything would fade away into time.

The parade was commanded by a young IPS officer, Pooja Yadav, DCP, South Lucknow. The salutation platform was decked in red, the gossamer white curtains and top set the mood for the huge gazebo that accommodated the battery of the state police officers.

'*Saare jahan se accha, Hindustan hamara,*' the police band set the tune and beat, the cymbals and the drums reverberated and contingent after contingent marched across me. Selected districts, battalions, dog squad, the cavalier contingent, the 112-response team, they were all there.

Finally at the podium, I spilled out the memories of my journey of the last thirty-seven years. The journey had been fulfilling and satisfying, and the leftover work had to be done by all of you, I exhorted. Handshakes, salutes and congratulatory messages poured in.

The farewell protocol concludes on a festive note—a tea party on the lawns of the official residence. My mind was made up about my evening wear for the informal do; a *band galey ka* Nehru jacket with a Mandarin collar. Of course, with the necessary interiors, I didn't want the evening chill to get to me on such an important day in my life. But before I got to welcome the CM, the police brass, the civil and judicial executive and the who's-who of the state, I had another official duty to fulfil—the handing over the charge to the new incumbent. The apex seat had a new DGP, albeit an interim one. Hitesh Chandra Awasthi, posted as director vigilance, was ready for the formality in the afternoon. It's a mini *tilak-abhishek* ceremony, with an apt photo opportunity. The outgoing officer acknowledges the presence of the new incumbent, gets up from his official chair, welcomes and directs the new to the chair and then strikes the perfect pose for the photographers.

The clasped hands, the direct gaze from underneath the peaky cap, the perfect smile and the clicks of the camera. It was all over in a flash.

The evening literally brought the stars to my garden. My partner looked resplendent in her six yards of ivory grace. The clicks of the boots were smothered by the soft greens, instead the light clink of cutlery and joyous laughter took over. The icing of the cake was the indomitable presence of CM Yogi Adityanath. A visitor's book manned by my staff on the occasion had numerous entries and expressions. One entry amongst the many stood out and I shall always relish it.

> *On the occasion of the retirement party of DGP Shri O.P. Singh, I congratulate him on his excellent deliverance. After thirty-seven years of impeccable service for the country and as the head of the biggest police force, his work is exemplary. His achievements are many, and the Investor Summit, Kumbh, NRI Summit in Kashi, Lok Sabha Elections, Youth Festival and their successful*

organization is synonymous with his name. I congratulate him for
his achievements and wish him for the future.

Yogi Adityanath CM, Government of UP

The dusk was upon us, the silhouettes had begun to take shape.
Visitors and well-wishers still filtered in. My mind was far away.
I closed my eyes. Ma and Babuji were there. I could faintly feel
Mira Bigha in the backdrop. I wanted to just be.

The beauty of life is complete and resplendent when you accept
the challenges that come your way with dignity and respect. Life has
its way of surprising you with moments that seem insurmountable.
For me, the rule has been simple: perform or perish. Change, adjust
and innovate or become rustic and redundant.

I can go on to pen scores of initiates, both big and small, but
the idea is not to show myself in glory, not at all. My message is
simple: the only limiting factor in our life is us, the self, no one
else. We are our best friend and our worst enemy. Look within,
believe in you, trust yourself and simply perform. Success will
be yours. Mahatma Gandhi rightly said, 'Satisfaction lies in the
effort, not in the attainment: full effort, full victory.'

Well, I can proudly say, I tried. Always.

Epilogue

In the dark alleys of our cities, behind closed doors, and within the unrelenting chaos of our society, there exists a world that is unknown to many—a world where the thin blue line stands as a shield between order and chaos, where the duty of upholding the law often requires confronting the worst aspects of human nature. This memoir is my attempt to peel back the layers and reveal the complexities of the life I had chosen as a police officer.

As I pen these words, I am reminded of the countless nights spent patrolling the streets, of the adrenaline-pumping moments when life and death hung in the balance, and of the quiet moments when I bore witness to both the best and the worst of humanity. It is largely these experiences that I wish to share, not to glorify or vilify, but to shed light on the multifaceted world of law enforcement.

This memoir is not an exhaustive account of every call, every arrest and every investigation. It is, instead, a collection of reflections that have left an indelible mark on my career and my understanding of the world. I write with the intention of humanizing the badge, of revealing the men and women behind the uniforms, and of showcasing the challenges, triumphs and heartaches that are an intrinsic part of this noble yet demanding profession.

While the narratives within these pages are mine, they are also a tribute to the countless officers and people who have stood beside me, their sacrifices often going unnoticed. Policing is a collective effort, and it is essential to remember that it is not a monolith. The officers and men who serve our communities come from diverse backgrounds and experiences, each bringing a unique perspective to the job.

This memoir is also a personal journey, one that has tested my resilience, empathy and beliefs. It is an exploration of the thin line between justice and vengeance and the constant struggle to balance the scales. I hope that by sharing these experiences, you, the reader, will gain a deeper appreciation for the challenges law enforcement officers face and the sacrifices they make. This memoir is also my attempt to provide a glimpse into the heart and mind of a police officer. As you turn the pages, I invite you to walk in our shoes, see the world through our eyes, and, in the end, reflect on the shared responsibility of ensuring a just and safe society for all.

* * *

The challenge of writing a memoir post-retirement is a complex endeavour deeply rooted in the ephemeral nature of memories. Time, with its relentless march, often erodes the sharp edges of recollection, making the task of chronicling a life in law enforcement a formidable undertaking. The experiences narrated by me in places like Almora, Lakhimpur Kheri and Lucknow happened more than two decades ago. As the years roll on, moments tend to lose their sharpness. The clarity of faces, the nuances of conversations and the raw emotions felt during those critical incidents begin to blur. While the practice of keeping notes and diaries may serve as valuable tools, memory remains the underlying force that breathes life into the written words. I was amazed at how much my ability to recall events, facts and emotions came back to me in rich detail when I started writing. I sincerely wish this book transports the readers into the heart of my police life.

Acknowledgements

Writing a memoir about my police life has been a deeply personal and introspective journey. I am immensely grateful for the support, encouragement and assistance I received throughout this challenging yet rewarding process.

First and foremost, I express my thanks to my family who stood by me through thick and thin. To my wife, Neelam—your patience, understanding and unwavering support sustained me during my long and demanding career in law enforcement. To my children, Avni and Apoorv, who have always been proud of their parents' dedication to protecting our community. Thank you for your love and understanding.

I extend my sincere thanks to my colleagues in the police forces—the UP Police, CISF and NDRF—for their camaraderie and shared experiences.

To my friend Dr Viveik Pandit whose constant prodding and insightful inputs on not just book writing but on how to successfully survive such a long body of work, guided my instincts in this journey. Thank you Viveik for being part of my journey.

Special words to my publisher, Penguin and Milee Ashwarya, who believed in this memoir and helped bring my story to life. To Dipanjali, whose editing was instrumental in turning my words into a published memoir.

I offer my sincere appreciation to Christy Reeba Steephen and Aksa Johnson, whose help I received whenever I needed computer work to be done. Many thanks to them.

I owe Jhanvi a big thanks for helping me in the process.

Notes

1 Natural toothbrush made from the stem of neem plants.

2 The Honorable Society of the Middle Temple, commonly known as Middle Temple, is one of the four Inns of Court exclusively entitled to call their members to the Bar as barristers, the others being the Inner Temple, Gray's Inn and Lincoln's Inn.

3 A *salaam* with a flourish bowing low in a sweeping gesture.

4 Dr Sachchidananda Sinha, *Some Eminent Behar Contemporaries* (Himalaya Publications), pp. 18–23.

5 https://statisticstimes.com/demographics/india/uttarakhand-population.php

6 Harpal Singh, 'Intelligence Sleuths Suspected to be behind Burglary at Arun Singh's Almora Cottage', *India Today*, April 30, 1990, https://www.indiatoday.in/magazine/indiascope/story/19900430-intelligence-sleuths-suspected-to-be-behind-burglary-at-arun-singh-almora-cottage-812536-1990-04-29 (accessed September 16, 2023).

7 The big farmhouses in the region were popularly referred to as jhala.

8 Indigenous knowledge amongst the Tharus of Terai Region of Uttar Pradesh, 2000 Gene Campaign: pp. 9–10; Gentlemen farmers of the Terai, A Report on the struggle for land and state repression in Nanital: People's Union for Democratic Rights, Delhi, June 1989: p. 4; 'Punjabi Farmers Reap a Bountiful Harvest in the Terai Region', *India Today*, 29 February 1984.

9 UPI Archives, 3 August 1992.

10 '47 UP cops convicted for killing 11 Sikh pilgrims in 1991', *Times of India*, 2 April 2016, https://timesofindia.indiatimes.com/

india/47-up-cops-convicted-for-killing-11-sikh-pilgrims-in-1991/
articleshow/51655902.cms; Criminal Appeal No. 549, 513 and 551
of 2016.

11 '4 Ultras killed in Lakhimpur', *Pioneer*, 8 July 1992.

12 'Kheri mein muthbhed ke dauran chaar ugrawadi maare gaye',
Dainik Jagran, 8 July 1992.

13 Ibid.

14 *Rashtriya Sahara*, 9 July 1992.

15 UPI Archives, 3 August 1992; 'Terai is still not free from fear',
Pioneer.

16 'Lucknow jail escape exposes security flaws', *India Today*, 15
September 1992.

17 'K.C.F. ka Jinda pakdada gaya', *Dainik Jagran*, 8 August 1993.

18 'Ek achhi shurwat', *Swatantra Bharat*, 22 December 1992.

19 'Badbolappan aur dilai ka nathija hai megalganj narsanhaar', *Dainik
Jagran*, 13 June 1993, Lucknow.

20 'Dreaded ultra killed in encounter', *Times of India*, 28 July 1993.

21 Brijlal IPS (Retd), *Police ki Baraat: Phoolan Devi aur Chambal Gange*
(Shivank Prakashan, New Delhi), 2022, pp. 9–11.

22 Ajay Singh, 'Beyond Google with Ajay Singh: How encounter
killing of Mahendra Fauji in 1994 shaped Uttar Pradesh politics',
Firstpost, 15 February 2017 https://www.firstpost.com/politics/
beyond-google-with-ajay-singh-how-encounter-killing-of-
mahendra-fauji-in-1984-shaped-uttar-pradesh-politics-3276874.
html; Atul Chandra, 'CM sacrifices Lucknow SSP to placate
Mayawati', *Pioneer*, 1994, Lucknow; 'Mayawati: Fauji killing cost
seat', *Hindustan Times*, 7 June 1994.

23 'Mayawati ab SSP ke pichhe padi', *Dainik Jagran*, 14 June 1994;
'Hastinapur mein haar ki wajah Fauji ki hatya: Mayawati', Rastriya
Sahara, 8 June 1994; 'Puri press conference mein Mahendra Fauji
ki stutigaan karti rahi Mayawati', Dainik Swatantra Chetna, 7 June
1994, Lucknow; 'Rajniti ki bhet chadh gaye Lucknow ke bade
captain', *Aaj*, 27 June 1994.

24 'Land Grabbings Increasing Threat in City', *Pioneer*, 1 November
1987.

25 'Ramghat road par yuva inkaiyo dwara maar-peet', *Amar Ujala*, 26 March 1988; 'SP City ka Tabadla', *Aj*, 26 March 1988, Aligarh.

26 'SP City ka Tabadla Radd Karne ki Maang', *Dainik Jagran*, 2 April 1988.

27 'Guest house "assault": The 1995 infamous incident that had turned SP-BSP bitter foes', *Indian Express*, 14 January 2029, https://indianexpress.com/article/what-is/the-1995-infamous-guest-house-incident-that-had-turned-sp-bsp-bitter-foes-5537680/

28 Statement of DM in Inquiry Report regarding the incidents and related sequence of events at the State Guest House, Meera Bai Marg, Lucknow, 2 June 1995, p. 18.

29 The letter is part of the FIR. This has been mentioned in the order by district judge Lucknow in Criminal case no. 7 of 1995.

30 Criminal Case no. 7 of 95, Order dated 28 June 1997, District Judge, Lucknow.

31 Criminal Case no. 7 of 95, Order dated 28 June 1997, District Judge, Lucknow.

32 Criminal Case no. 7 of 95, Order dated 28 May 1997, District Judge, Lucknow.

33 National Disaster Management Authority, Annual Report 2014–15, p. 44.

34 National Disaster Management Authority, Annual Report 2014–15, p. 44.

35 National Disaster Management Authority, Annual Report 2014–15, p. 44.

36 National Disaster Management Authority, Annual Report, 2015–16.

37 'Uttarakhand forest fire spreads, 6 districts worst- hit', *Times of India*, 2 May 2016.

38 *Times of India*, 22 September 2015; *Indian Express*, 22 September 2015.

39 OCHA/UNDAC Mission Report Nepal Earthquake, 25 April–17 May 2015, https://vosocc.unocha.org/GetFile.aspx?file=59497_Nepal_Mission_Report.pdf

40 Richard Mahapatra, 'How Nepal ignored threat of imminent earthquake', Down to Earth, 26 April 2015.

41 Kekti Angre, 'After Being Trapped under Debris for 50 Hours, Woman Pulled Out Alive by Indian Rescuers in Earthquake-Hit Nepal', NDTV, 29 April 2015, https://www.ndtv.com/india-news/after-being-trapped-under-debris-for-50-hours-woman-pulled-out-alive-by-indian-rescuers-in-earthquak-759138

42 'Special to the Express: How the NDRF raced against time in Nepal', Indian Express, 9 May 2015, https://indianexpress.com/article/india/india-others/nepal-earthquake-special-to-the-express-how-we-raced-against-time-in-nepal/

43 Utpal Parashar, 'Nepal earthquake: Indian media faces complaints about "insensitivity"', Hindustan Times, 4 May 2015, https://www.hindustantimes.com/world/nepal-earthquake-indian-media-faces-complaints-about-insensitivity/story-uiDOyFUnKcxnwRdwFun9GL.html

44 Hridayesh Joshi, Rage of the River: The Untold Story of the Kedarnath Disaster (Penguin, 2016), p. 97.

45 Ibid.

46 International Search and Rescue Advisory Group (INSARAG) was established in 1991 based on lessons learnt from 1988 Armenia earthquake and other disasters prior to that (e.g. the earthquake in Mexico City 1985). The mandate of the INSARAG is to develop global standards on minimum capacity required for international USAR Operations, to develop standardized procedures for international cooperation and coordination in collapsed structure response. Its mandate also includes disaster response preparedness and capacity building promotion in earthquake-prone countries.

47 Leading from the Front: Awareness, Engagement & Intervention for Community Empowerment: A Case Study of NDRF, IIT Delhi 2016.

48 P.K. Mishra, 'India's G20 Presidency Can Show the Way on Disaster Management', Indian Express, 25 May 2023, https://indianexpress.com/article/opinion/columns/indias-g20-presidency-can-show-the-way-on-disaster-management-8627412/

49 Shweta Senger, 'Uttar Pradesh Tops List with Most Crimes Recorded against Women, Delhi Registers Drop as Per Latest NCRB Data',

India Times, 22 October 2019, https://www.indiatimes.com/news/
india/uttar-pradesh-tops-list-with-most-crimes-recorded-against-
women-delhi-registers-drop-as-per-latest-ncrb-data-378322.html

50 'A Strategic Omission of Inquiry', *The Hindu*, 17 November 2021,
    https://www.thehindu.com/opinion/columns/Muzaffarnagar-riots-
    A-strategic-omission-of-inquiry/article56845506.ece

51 'Three years on, poor law and order still haunts Akhilesh', *Deccan
    Herald*, 4 March 2015, https://www.deccanherald.com/opinion/
    three-years-poor-law-order-2115246

52 'Vyapari ko pratadith karne wale panch sipahi barkasth', *Navbharat
    Times*, 6 March 2018; 'Uttar Pradesh police dismisses 5 constables
    who thrashed an innocent shopkeeper', OPIndia, Lucknow,
    6 March 2018; https://www.opindia.com/2018/03/uttar-pradesh-
    police-suspends-5-constables-who-thrashed-an-innocent-shopkeeper/

53 'UP Police constable informed about her [sic] daughter's death
    while on duty, what he did next will restore your faith in humanity',
    Financial Express, 2 March 2018,

54 'DGP ne raaste mein ghayal padee yuvati ko bhijwaya asptal',
    Navbharat Times, 10 September 2019.

55 'UP Govt Has Adopted Zero Tolerance Policy towards Criminals: Yogi
    Adityanath', *Business Standard*, 21 October 2019, https://www.business-
    standard.com/article/pti-stories/up-govt- has-adopted-zero-tolerance-
    policy-towards-criminals-yogi-adityanath-119102100720_1.html

56 'UP Govt. hits back at opposition, says, 16, 415 criminals got
    bail cancelled', *Hindustan Times*, 20 August 2019, https://
    www.hindustantimes.com/lucknow/up-govt-hits-back-at-
    opposition-says-16-415-criminals-got-bail-cancelled/story-
    NybBgbUnz0EzAXDigZwQzI.html

57 'UP Govt Has Adopted Zero Tolerance Policy towards Criminals: Yogi
    Adityanath', *Business Standard*, 21 October 2019, https://www.business-
    standard.com/article/pti-stories/up-govt-has-adopted-zero-tolerance-
    policy-towards-criminals-yogi-adityanath-119102100720_1.html

58 'Apradhiyo mei beh peda', *Aj*, 22 October 2019, 'All criminals of
    organised crime in jail now: CM Yogi', *Indian Express*, 22 October 2019.

59 'POCSO: UP court convicts accused within 9 days of filing
    chargesheet', Live Law, 30 October 2019; 'UP Court passes
    jugdement in record 9 working days', *India Today*, 3 October 2022.

60 *Hindustan Times*, 31 August, 2019; Manish Sahu, 'POCSO case: 29 days after minor's rape, UP man gets life imprisonment', *Indian Express*, 31 August 2019, https://indianexpress.com/article/india/pocso-case-29-days-after-minors-rape-up-man-gets-life-imprisonment-5952748/

61 'Sangadith Aapradho par nakal karne mei sarkar safal', Daily News Activist, 22 October 2019.

62 Criminal Appeal no. 1255 of 1999.

63 'How UP made the big jump to number 2 in EODB ranking', *Economic Times*, 5 September 2020.

64 'UP Board Exam 2019: CCTV Vigilance, STF Mobilization & ESMA', *Times Now*, 7 February 2019, https://www.timesnownews.com/education/article/up-board-exam-2019-cctv-vigilance-stf-mobilization-esma-measures-to-ensure-58-lakh-students-won-t-cheat/361295

65 'At global event, UP Police bags 3rd prize for response to emergency among 500 forces', *Business Standard*, 14 November 2019.

66 '4 saal mein UP ko mile aath DGP, in kamo ke liye rahenge yaad', *Dainik Bhaskar*, https://www.bhaskar.com/news/UP-LUCK-profile-story-about-uttar-pradesh-dgp-in-akhilesh-government-5211494-PHO.html.

67 Kumbh, 2019, A Splendid Saga of Securing over 240 million lives by UP Police, A Times Group presentation, p. 26.

68 Maseeh Rahman, 'Holy man's gift blamed for 39 dead in stampede', *Guardian*, 28 August 2003, https://www.theguardian.com/world/2003/aug/28/india.maseehrahman

69 'PM Modi donates Rs 21 lakh from personal savings for Kumbh Mela sanitation workers', *Times of India*, 6 March 2019, https://timesofindia.indiatimes.com/india/pm-modi-donates-rs-21-lakh-from-personal-savings-for-kumbh-mela-sanitation-workers/articleshow/68283113.cms (accessed 1 October 2023).

70 Anuj Cariappa, 'When UP police donned the role of media during Kumbh Mela', OneIndia.com, 4 March 2019, https://www.oneindia.com/india/when-up-police-donned-the-role-of-media-during-kumbh-mela-2859686.html (accessed 1 October 2023).

71 Kumbh, 2019, A Splendid Saga of Securing over 240 million lives by UP Police, A Times Group presentation, p. 266.

72 Rohit K. Singh, 'JeM suspects, arrested by UP ATS from Deoband, had invited 'special guest' to hostel: Police', *Hindustan Times*, 25 February 2019.

73 'Yogi Adityanath hails NRC, says will implement in Uttar Pradesh if needed', *India Today*, 7 February 2022, https://www.indiatoday.in/india/story/yogi-adityanath-hails-nrc-will-implement-uttarpradesh-if-needed-1599712-2019-09-16.

74 'Hindu Leader Kamlesh Tiwari Killed over Remark against Prophet, 5 Arrested: Police', *Outlook*, 19 October 2019, https://www.outlookindia.com/website/story/india-news-hindu-leader-kamlesh-tiwari-killed-for-remark-against-prophet-3-arrested-police/340751; 'DGP ne 25 baar ki Gujarat ke DG aur ATS Chief se baat', *Amar Ujala*, 20 October 2019. 'Taar jude Gujarat se, Paanch pakde gaye', *Rashtriya Sahara*, 20 October 2019.

75 Ibid.

76 'Ayodhya verdict: 40 more arrested in UP for offensive social media posts', *Hindustan Times*, 10 November 2019; 'UP mein shanti, Kanoon evam vyavastha niyantran mein: OP Singh', Voice of Lucknow, 10 November 2019.

77 'Kiran Bedi praises UP Police for peace after Ayodhya verdict, suggests beat reforms', *Indian Express*, 29 November 2019, https://indianexpress.com/article/cities/lucknow/kiran-bedi-praises-up-police-for-peace-after-ayodhya-verdict-suggests-beat-reforms-6142069/.

78 'IPC, CRPC mein hoga badlaav', *Dainik Jagran*, 30 November 2019.

79 'Guv for police commissioner system in UP', *Hindustan Times*, 28 December 2018.

Scan QR code to access the
Penguin Random House India website